TIVADAR SOROS

MASQUERADE

Dancing around Death
in Nazi-Occupied Hungary

EDITED AND TRANSLATED FROM THE ESPERANTO
BY HUMPHREY TONKIN

FOREWORDS
BY PAUL AND GEORGE SOROS

ARCADE PUBLISHING • NEW YORK

Copyright © 1965 by Tivadar Soros
Forewords copyright © 2000 by Paul and George Soros
Translation, Editor's Afterword, Notes, and Works Cited
copyright © 2000 by Humphrey Tonkin

All rights reserved. No part of this book may be reproduced in any form or
by any electronic or mechanical means, including information storage and
retrieval systems, without permission in writing from the publisher, except
by a reveiwer who may quote brief passages in a review.

FIRST U.S. EDITION 2001

First published in Esperanto in 1965 by J. Régulo
First published in English in 2000 by Canongate Books Ltd.

Library of Congress Cataloging-in-Publication Data

Soros, Tivadar.
[Maskerado.English]
Masquerade: dancing around death in Nazi-occupied Hungary / Tivadar
Soros : translated from the Esperanto by Humphrey Tonkin.
    p. cm.
ISBN 1-55970-581-7
    1. Jews—Persecutions—Hungary. 2. Soros, Tivadar. 3. Holocaust, Jewish
(1939–1945)—Personal narratives. I. Title.

DS135.H9 S599813 2001
943.9'004924—dc21   2001022626

Published in the United States by Arcade Publishing, Inc., New York
Distributed by Time Warner Trade Publishing

Visit our Web site at www.arcadepub.com

10 9 8 7 6 5 4 3 2 1

EB

PRINTED IN THE UNITED STATES OF AMERICA

Contents

Foreword

Paul Soros

T ivadar, my father, was always an unusual and original
person. He had great judgment, based on a deep understanding of the world and of human nature. 'It is amazing
how well people can bear the suffering of others' was one
of his typical comments that stick in my mind.

His set of values, of what is or is not important in life, the ability
to see things as they really were, not as they appeared to be, were
formed not by middle-class beliefs, conventions or ambitions, but
by his experiences of survival during the Russian Revolution as an
escaped prisoner of World War I.

I have observed that it is often when playing bridge or com-
petitive tennis, or when money is involved, that the true nature
and personality of someone reveals itself. The public persona of
high moral standards, generous and gracious, may reveal cracks,
offering a brief glimpse of what the individual is really made of.

The period described in this book was more revealing than a
mere bridge game, because the stakes were truly life and death. I
hope the reader will gain the same impression I had as a participant
– no matter how mad or threatening the world and society, or
how difficult the circumstances, a responsible person must try to
cope, not follow like a sheep, but take control of the direction of
his or her destiny. My father did, managing to remain a civilized

and humane person, without capitulating to fear or hate, keeping his dignity and cool, doing his best for his family and fellow humans in danger.

In 1956, he escaped from Hungary and made his way to the United States. There he decided to write a book about his experiences during the Holocaust period, as he had done with his earlier adventures in Russia. As *Maskerado* this was published in 1965 in Esperanto, a language he had learned in World War I. In 1998, my daughter-in-law, the writer Flora Fraser, came across a family copy of a very rough English translation of *Maskerado*. Enamored with Tivadar's story, she envisioned the appeal of an English publication. Her unstinting editorial efforts led to collaboration with Professor Humphrey Tonkin, of the University of Hartford, Connecticut. He has now produced a more polished translation into English, provided a fascinating commentary on the background to Tivadar's story, and thereby given *Maskerado* a new life and a wider audience.

I was eighteen at the time my father describes, old enough to comprehend, young enough to learn. Having been fortunate to survive, I have no doubt that these were the formative experiences shaping the rest of my life.

Foreword

George Soros

I cannot be objective about this book. It deals with the formative period of my life and it is written by my father who was the most important figure in my life at that time. The book brings back memories which are sharply etched in my mind, more sharply than anything else that happened to me.

The Germans occupied Hungary on March 19, 1944. We were liberated by the Russians on January 12, 1945. During those ten months we lived in mortal danger. More than half the Jews living in Hungary, and perhaps a third of the Jews living in Budapest, perished during that time. I and my family survived. Moreover my father helped a large number of other people in a variety of ways. This was his finest hour. I had never seen him work so hard. As a lawyer he prided himself on working as little as possible. When his most important client, the landowner Okányi Schwartz, considered engaging him, he was advised against it on the grounds that my father spent most of his days in the swimming pool, on the ice rink or in cafés. He used to run his office out of his home and it was a rare occasion when there were people in the waiting-room; during the German occupation, the rented room which four of us shared in Vásár utca could be approached only through the bathroom: the bathroom was often crowded with people waiting to seek his advice.

It is a sacrilegious thing to say, but these ten months were the happiest times of my life. I was fourteen years old. We were in great peril, but my father was seemingly in command of the situation. I was aware of the dangers because my father spent a lot of time explaining them to me but I did not believe in my heart of hearts that I could get hurt. We were pursued by evil forces and we were clearly on the side of the angels because we were unjustly persecuted; moreover, we were trying not only to save ourselves but also to save others. The odds were against us but we seemed to have the upper hand. What more could a fourteen-year-old want? I adored and admired my father. We led an adventurous life and we had fun together. I think some of that feeling comes through in the book but my father was far too modest to brag about how many people he helped.

My father was exceptionally well-prepared to cope with the German occupation because he had lived through a somewhat similar experience earlier in his life. In the First World War he escaped from a prisoner-of-war camp in Siberia and got caught up in the Russian revolution. He learned how to survive in a situation where the normal rules do not apply. The experience transformed him. He had started out as an ambitious young man eager to get ahead in the world. In the prisoner-of-war camp he established a wall newspaper, called *The Plank*, which made him so popular that he was elected the prisoners' representative. When in a neighbouring camp some prisoners-of-war escaped, the camp commander executed the prisoners' representative in retaliation. This made him realize that it is not always so healthy to be prominent. Rather than awaiting his fate placidly, he decided to organize an escape. He chose people with the appropriate skills: cooks, carpenters and so on. His own skill lay in leadership. He did not pride himself on actually doing anything. The plan was to cross the mountains, build a raft and drift down to the ocean. There was only one thing wrong with it. All the rivers of Siberia drain into the Arctic Ocean. They drifted for several weeks before they realized that they were getting further and further north. And it took them several more months to fight their way back through the taiga. In the meantime the Russian revolution had broken out and there was fighting again. The Reds killed those who had aligned themselves with the Whites and vice versa. This was the time when a brigade of escaped Czech prisoners-of-war roamed over the trans-Siberian railroad in an armored train. After many adventures my father managed to get away from Siberia to Moscow. Eventually he found his way back to Hungary. He recounted his adventures in a book similar to this one entitled *Modern Robinsons* (*Crusoes in Siberia*).

My father returned from these adventures a changed man. Gone were the ambitions. He was happy to be alive. His ambition was to enjoy life. He liked to live well but he did not want to amass wealth. He considered material possessions an encumbrance which could drag you down or even on occasion cost you your life. He is the only man I know who systematically decumulated his assets. He balanced the gap between his earnings as a lawyer and our rather comfortable way of living by selling off pieces of real estate. As a result he had little left to lose in the war. 'The only capital I can rely on is in my head,' he used to say, making a pun on the word capital which in Latin also means head.

He loved to spend time with his children. As a little boy I used to visit him in the café in the afternoon and he would treat me to a chocolate cake. Later on we used to go swimming, rowing, skating together practically every day. I would meet him at the pool after school and after swimming we would sit together and he would tell me an installment of his adventures in the First World War. In this way I absorbed his outlook on life. It served me well later on. I learned that art of survival from a grand master.

My mother was very different in character. This comes through quite clearly in the book. I loved them both dearly. I tried to model myself after my father but I was much more intimate with my mother. I internalized them both. Since they were so different the two characters continued to do battle inside me throughout my life – but that is a different story. Here let my father speak for himself.

Chapter 1

Some History and Geography

Life is beautiful – and full of variety and adventure. But luck must be on your side.

It was in September 1939 that Neville Chamberlain, the English prime minister, announced that war had been declared. I listened to his announcement on the radio with some of my friends. 'The human race has just lost twenty-five percent of its value,' remarked one of them; 'but a Jew's life will not be worth a penny.'

We duly noted this gloomy prediction, yet life went on. Men kept working, enjoying themselves; women kept going to beauty parlors, gossiping with their friends, giving birth.

But the handwriting was on the wall, even if we had difficulty deciphering it.

The year before, in 1938, I had been visited by a Jewish lawyer who had fled from Austria following Hitler's annexation of that country. He asked me for help. I felt sorry for him, so I gave him 300 pengős, which was a fairly substantial sum for me (around $30 at the time), especially since my finances seemed constantly teetering on the brink of embarrassment.

The Austrian took the money, but instead of thanking me, he said, 'My dear colleague, you give as though your money will be always yours.'

Only later, when Jews lost not just their wealth but their lives, did I fully realize the bitter truth of his remark.

When Hitler moved into Austria, Hungary became Germany's immediate neighbor and hence the immediate neighbor of Nazism. Her geographical position being what it was, she was really forced to behave as ally and friend, given the German theory of *Lebensraum* – a notion that maintained, in essence, that Germany had the free and open right to occupy territory in Eastern Europe if that would ensure a better life for the German people. The theory of *Lebensraum* made brute force the operating principle in Eastern Europe. Because of its proximity, Hungary became Germany's first satellite.

But the pistol shot that took the life of the then Hungarian prime minister, Count Pál Teleki, made it clear to the world that the tilt towards Germany was no affair of the heart for the Hungarians, but an obligation. Teleki killed himself because he was deeply conflicted. As a politician he had to be friendly to the Germans, but as a person he could not tolerate the twisted and ugly measures such politics required. In 1940 he signed a Pact of Eternal Friendship with Yugoslavia and three weeks later had to sit quietly while Hitler sent his troops marching across Hungary to crush his new ally. Teleki acted, one might say, as the noble aristocrat he was: in his family there were plenty of examples of resolving personal conflicts through suicide.

The proximity of Germany, together with Hitler's anti-Semitism, made the situation of Hungarian Jews close to desperate. As early as 1939 the first 'Jewish law' was promulgated, openly breaking with the democratic principle of equality before the law. Quotas were established in the professions and no businesses could be more than partly owned by Jews. But the law was not limited to economics: it also declared that only those Jews whose families were resident in Hungary before 1914 could claim Hungarian citizenship. Everyone who had acquired citizenship since 1914 would automatically lose it. In other words, such people could be expelled from the country. While only a limited number of people were affected, their families' lives were shattered, even if they had resided in Hungary for centuries. There was a rush to acquire documents, because everyone wanted to prove that they were citizens of long standing. But how could they? Before the passage of this law, nobody had bothered to obtain a certificate of citizenship, since proof of residence was considered satisfactory for most purposes, and anybody who needed further proof could obtain it in a day or two from the appropriate office. But now it suddenly took months, or even years, to receive any kind of document at all. This was step one in what was to become a war of nerves between the government and the Jews.

By 1940 stories were circulating that more than ten thousand people of 'doubtful' citizenship had been arrested and deported to Poland, then under German occupation. The Germans drove the larger part of these people into the river at Kamenec-Podolsk and simply shot them dead. Word of mass shootings, slave labor, and Jewish rebellion in the Warsaw ghetto became more and more frequent, but we preferred not to believe such things. Untouched directly by such calamities, we felt that we were somehow above them. Our final line of defense was not to believe that such barbarisms were happening at all.

1941 . . . 1942 . . . 1943 . . . The war years passed slowly. The German military situation steadily worsened, and every day we expected the Third Reich to collapse. Like the optimist who fell out of the skyscraper window, 'So far so good,' we said, as we passed the second floor . . .

March 19, 1944. A day like any other. Nice weather. It was a little chilly, but there was a touch of spring in the morning air that warmed one's heart. I was sitting in a café, at a table with a pleasant view. Breakfast was neatly laid, as always. But there was one difference: as the waiter gave me the morning newspaper, he whispered, 'Have you heard? During the night, the Germans took over.'

I hadn't heard. For years the threat of occupation had been hanging over our heads – in fact for so long that we had forgotten all about it. The news took me completely by surprise.

Precisely in order to avoid such an outcome, the Hungarian government had fulfilled the Germans' every wish. Miklós Kállay was prime minister at the time, a member of an old Hungarian family that had often figured in Hungarian history. In fact the family was so well known and popular that a dance had been named after them. The Kállay two-step, as it was called, involved two steps to the right, two steps to the left, and a lot of turning round in between. The dance matched the prime minister's politics: on the one hand, dispatching special envoys and diplomats to convince the Allies that he would join their side at the earliest opportunity; on the other hand, trying to persuade Hitler that he was the best of friends and his loyal servant – in fact the best ally Hitler ever had. Political necessity obliged Kállay to give more and more advantage to the Germans to prove his reliability, until eventually he was willing to do almost anything to please them, if only to make it unnecessary for them actually to occupy the country. After all, it was not good policy to turn a friendly country into an occupied one: the Germans understood that piece of wisdom as well as anyone. But their military situation was deteriorating. On March 18, the day before the occupation, the BBC had summarized matters as follows:

The Russians have reached the Romanian border. Ten German divisions have been destroyed. In the Ukraine the encirclement and mopping-up of German troops is proceeding. The American air force has launched bombing attacks on Germany.

But, the report added,

Not only has the military position of Germany been radically weakened on the Eastern front, but the continued allegiance of Germany's eastern satellites is now more and more in question.

It was this problem that precipitated the decision to occupy Hungary. The German general staff saw clearly that if Hungary deserted she would be uniquely situated to destroy the German army in the Balkans, because she could cut off supplies to the troops, not only in Romania but throughout the Balkan peninsula – in Yugoslavia, Bulgaria, and Greece. Hitler had already learned the bitter lesson of Italian betrayal and, at the very least, he wanted to postpone, if not avoid, a similar setback.

On the night of March 18, 1944, he acted.

There was no apparent resistance. Regent Horthy, along with his ministers and the chief of the General Staff, had been summoned to Germany, supposedly for conversations with Hitler, and so were not around to give orders. Many of the high-ranking officers and bureaucrats who stayed behind were German sympathizers.

Hitler generally timed his initiatives for weekends. The Hungarian occupation took place on a Saturday night. The Sunday papers were already printed, and there would be no further editions until Monday. Without newspapers, the city was full of rumors.

'Hitler has had Horthy arrested . . . The rumors of Horthy's arrest are false . . . The Germans have refused to give Horthy a train for the return journey . . . The prime minister has disappeared . . . The post office, radio and police are already in German hands . . . Lots of well-known people have been arrested.'

Such were the rumors, but there were no signs of Germans in the city. The sun shone, seemingly oblivious to the historic nature of the occasion; the city streets slumbered in the peace of a Sunday morning. I had heard that the castle at Buda, on the other side of the Danube, where Horthy had his residence, had been closed to the public, but I went round that way to take a look and found Hungarian soldiers still on guard, as always. It took me a while to notice a tiny German tank, camouflaged in green and yellow. This battered little tank, it seemed, had taken Budapest.

As the morning progressed, people came out to stroll through the streets and the parks, as they usually did on a Sunday, but their faces wore puzzled expressions. Both the Jews and the more progressive of the non-Jews, socialists for example, were full of uncertainty and foreboding. They whispered disconsolately, unable to assess the situation, like fish out of water. Hitler's threats against the Jews were too serious to be taken lightly. How prudent were those who had had the sense to flee long since, while the going was good!

Up to this point I had thought of life as one big adventure.

I was just twenty years old when World War I broke out. I headed for the front immediately, volunteering while still a student, before my studies were completed. I did so not out of patriotic enthusiasm but out of fear that the war would finish too soon. In fact, I was sure that this was the last world war: if I let it go by, I would miss a unique opportunity.

I risked my life not only in the customary wartime ways, but in other ways as well, often quite unnecessarily. As an officer, I received special orders from time to time. On one such occasion I was asked to command what was described to me as a 'crater attack'. I soon learned what this meant. Only about thirty yards separated the two fronts. The technique was to bore a tunnel of sufficient length and depth and fill it with dynamite. Unfortunately, the Russians used the same technique from the other side. Since each side worried that their opponent would blow their tunnel up first, both sides were apt to move too fast. As a consequence, the entire area was full of craters. The fear lent a certain extra excitement to our daily life.

Then there was the occasion when, as commander of a small stretch of the front, I was ordered to send a soldier over the top to find out what the enemy was doing. In my opinion the order was stupid: we were within spitting distance of the Russians and nothing new could be discovered on the ground. But as a soldier I knew that an order was an order. I read my instructions to my men.

'Who wants to volunteer?'

A tall, thin soldier stepped forward. We exchanged a few words.

'You can't go,' I said decisively.

'Why not?' he asked in fearful surprise.

'Because you're afraid. I can see that you're trembling.'

He could hardly deny it.

'But, sir, for God's sake let me go. I'm only a lady's dressmaker, but I want to be an artist. I am good at drawing. I can't stand the roughness and brutality of an ordinary soldier's life. If my mission succeeds, I'm sure to be promoted, right? So give me a chance.'

I have a soft heart. I let him go.

He got down on his belly and crawled forward. He had covered no more than five or six yards when, bam!, he was hit by a bullet and lay still.

'Do I have a volunteer to bring our comrade back?'

An uneasy silence. No one volunteered.

'Do you expect *me* to do it?'

Silly question. No reply. In seconds I would have to decide. It dawned on me rather too late that it's better to give orders to one's men than to ask them questions. But now it was too late for an order: I had to do something. I quickly got down on my belly and crawled towards my wounded comrade. It took me only a few minutes to drag him back to our trenches, but by that time he was dead of a bullet to the head.

A soldier's story doesn't mean much unless the hero lives to tell it: the dead don't tell tales. There were many other occasions in my life when without much thought I accepted some unreasonable risk or embarked on an unlikely adventure, such as my escape from a prisoner-of-war camp in Siberia and my return through a revolution-torn Russia – a trip that took two years and that was one long sequence of incredible scrapes.

But time had passed. I was now fifty years old, with a wife and two sons, and disinclined to risk my life, and especially not theirs. Yet I knew that my peaceful middle-class existence had come to an end. A new adventure was beginning, even if I could not embark on it with the carefree spirit of my youth. I was seized by a fear such as I had never known before. I did not want my family to think me afraid, or a defeatist, but I had to explain to them, as delicately as possible, the nature of the danger we all faced. It was different from anything we had ever known before.

All the usual guests appeared for our regular Sunday bridge game. Perhaps they were there less for the game than to discuss the day's bewildering events – looking for information and for reassurance. There was general indignation at the absence of any army or police resistance, and much criticism of Horthy. People felt he should have resigned rather than accept such humiliation. While we were playing, news came that various prominent politicians, journalists, socialists had been arrested, and that Polish refugees had been imprisoned.

A new arrival excitedly reported a further piece of news. 'Have you heard about Bajcsy-Zsilinszky? The Germans went to arrest him first, and when they knocked on his door he wouldn't open it. The soldiers broke the door down with machine-gun fire, and Zsilinszky shot back. Eventually they killed him.'

We were shocked on hearing the story, because Zsilinszky, a member of parliament, was known as an implacable opponent of Hitler.

Later in the evening, a doctor arrived.

'Is the story about Zsilinszky true?' we asked.

'I'm afraid so. I saw the autopsy report myself.'

In the face of such certainty there could be no denying the news. Only later did we discover that the doctor had lied: Zsilinszky was ultimately executed nine months later in the Sopron-Kőhida prison.

The bridge game broke up earlier than usual. We were all alone now.

When I got home I turned on the radio, as always when I had nothing else pressing. Things were going on as usual, like any normal day. Radio Budapest was broadcasting light music, and there was a Mozart opera. I tuned in to London and listened to the news in several languages. The occupation of Hungary was the lead story – but on the radio it sounded just like any other piece of news. I had the feeling that no radio could convey the real news – the death sentence of a million Jews. Then came a message that brought me face to face with reality. It was President Roosevelt, appealing to the Hungarian people to do what they could to help the Jews who now faced death under German occupation. It was a poignant and human statement, the first touch of humanity I had heard all day. (Sixteen years later I searched in vain for this speech in the *New York Times*, one of the world's most trustworthy newspapers, but was told that transmissions from the Voice of America were never published in the United States.)

I turned the radio off. My wife and I were alone in the stillness of the night. The children were sleeping and the maid had the day off. The silence was disconcerting. In the past, our comfortable apartment had always seemed a refuge from the turmoil of the outside world, but suddenly it felt more like a trap. It was laid out so poorly! There was only one exit, no winding staircase at the back, no secret doors, no underground hiding-place. If they were to come in the middle of the night to take us away, where could we hide? I examined the place carefully, in a way I had never done before. In the process I made a surprising discovery: there was a double ceiling above the dining room, with a space big enough for all four of us to hide. We could put some boxes in front so we wouldn't be noticed. But the beds would be warm, and that would give us away. And what should we do about our maid? Should we take her into our confidence? Or let her go? My wife could hardly imagine life without domestic help. But even if we let the maid go, there was still the problem of the superintendent. No, we really could not hide ourselves in the house. And, as for concealment, if they were going to find us and arrest us anyway, I would prefer not to be hauled ignominiously out of hiding, but to face up to our arresters like a man. After all, we had done nothing wrong. The fact that we were born of Jewish parents could hardly be called a crime. In any case, it wasn't very likely that the Germans would come for us on their first night in the city. What made me think we were so important?

So I dismissed thoughts of concealment and stretched out on the silk quilt so carefully spread on our bed. Close to my head the radio connected me to the world outside. I turned the dial to the major stations: London, Moscow, Paris, Berlin, Tangier. Nothing new. So I went to sleep as though nothing had happened – as though it was a day like any other.

Chapter 2

Meet the Germans

The first day was full of foreboding. Yet the beautiful spring weather belied the gloomy future.

But then came the second day.

In the early morning the telephone rang. My mother-in-law.

'You know I have two girls from the provinces living with me. Yesterday they got worried and decided that they had better go home. So in the evening they went to the station to find out about train times. They've been gone all night and there's no sign of them. Could you please do what you can to find them? I'm really worried.'

I promised I would. What else could I say? A minute later the phone rang again. This time it was my sister-in-law. The Germans had caught my brother Zoltán on the street in the center of town and locked him in the synagogue. He had found a telephone in the building and called his wife for help. He had no idea what they were going to do with him.

'Please get him out!'

'I'll do my best,' I promised. At eleven o'clock a friend of my older son came by. He had decided not to go to school at the regular time. But then he felt guilty, so he walked over later on, only to discover that the school was closed for the day. He also learned that the Germans had rounded up several boys aged sixteen to eighteen. He had come by just to check whether Paul had come home. Not yet.

These Germans were beginning to get on my nerves. What was to be done? What could I do against them? Declare war? My powerlessness made me furious, though I tried hard to hide it. The fact is that I always lose my temper when something happens that I want to change and find I can't. Although nothing bad had actually occurred, my wife was already beginning to look at me reproachfully. In her mind's eye she could see her slender son led off along a dusty road by merciless SS men. She looked at me as though I could change the fate of the world if I just cared enough to do so.

'You don't care about anything. You just sit and listen to the radio. It's your own son's life that we're talking about!'

Without much internal conviction I did what I could, calling four or five people, friends and strangers. I tried everything that could be done by telephone. I called the president of the Jewish community and, among others, a building manager, a member of the Arrow Cross Party, who lived close to the school. (The Hungarian Nazis were known as Arrow-Crossers, and the Hungarian equivalent of the National Socialist Party was the Arrow Cross Party.)

My son's friend silently observed my unsuccessful efforts, then said, brightening, 'Maybe Paul went to play table-tennis. Hang on! I'll go over there on my bicycle.'

A few minutes later the telephone rang. It was our lost sheep. He explained: 'School got out at ten. I'm at our usual table-tennis place.'

I didn't even scold him. In fact there was something symbolic about the table-tennis episode. Perhaps the entire German abomination was nothing more than a kind of nightmare? My newly recovered optimism was bolstered by the news that my captured brother, Zoltán, had come home. Zoltán was a pious, God-fearing fellow, who believed in the strength and power of

God and faithfully observed all the commandments of the Jewish religion. When he was detained he turned to God for help. As an observant Jew he knew the layout of the synagogue pretty well. As soon as he could collect his thoughts, he remembered that the building had a second exit on a side street – something the Germans presumably didn't know – and so he quietly headed for the other door. He heard hammering. He waited anxiously – until he realized that the hammering was simply his own heart. Running down the stairs, he reached the other door, which was unlocked and unguarded. There were no Germans around. He was saved. Without further incident he went home, thanking the Lord for his deliverance.

The pattern of German occupation grew gradually clearer over the next few days. The Germans were discriminating. They didn't actually 'arrest' anybody. Everybody who might participate in any kind of resistance movement was taken into 'protective custody'. Leftist journalists, opposition politicians, trade-union officials, simply disappeared. Newspapers that were not Nazi-oriented ceased publication 'voluntarily'. Those that remained made ardent declarations of their love for the Germans and their hatred of the Jews.

A new pro-German government was formed under the leadership of Döme Sztójay, former Hungarian ambassador in Berlin. Fifteen members of parliament resigned in protest. The Germans, though they were now in complete control, stayed behind the scenes. They had plenty of Hungarian stooges to provide them with information and ideas. A kind of epidemic of calumny swept the country, and thousands of people were denounced to the Germans.

Apart from a few hundred outspoken liberals or socialists, Jews provided the obvious target. They were numerous and continued to control a large part of the nation's wealth. But initially persecution was haphazard and disorganized. The first to be caught were people trying to leave town: the railway stations and highways were patrolled. Those arrested were led off to undisclosed locations. The patrols did not pay too much attention to documents: they just arrested anybody who looked Jewish or otherwise suspicious. In the process a lot of non-Jewish people were rounded up as well. They could be sorted out later. At the final stops on the suburban streetcar lines, everyone who looked Jewish was led off to the local jail, with the result that the jails were jammed with people. German soldiers entered Jewish houses and took whatever caught their fancy. Radios, typewriters, and suitcases were their favorite spoils.

At the house of a friend of mine the Germans were in the process of stealing a carpet when one of them noticed a piano.

'Who plays the piano?'

'The lady of the house.'

A couple of the German soldiers were of a sentimental turn of mind. 'Can you play any songs by Schumann?'

'Yes.'

'So what are you waiting for?'

The terrified woman sat down without a word. The soldier listened enraptured, forgetting about the stolen carpet, still clutched under his arm.

The Germans sometimes played stupid games. A group of soldiers asked a building superintendent which apartments were occupied by Jews. They went into one of these apartments. One of the soldiers, a good-humored fair-haired lad, did the talking.

'I'm sorry to disturb you, but something rather unpleasant has happened. We've found the body of a German soldier outside the building – murdered. There are footprints leading to this apartment. I'm afraid we must escort you to our headquarters.'

The Jews didn't share their sense of humor. In fact they were terrified.

'How could you possibly think we would do such a thing? We haven't been outside our apartment in days.'

'I believe you,' said the blond soldier politely, 'but an order is an order. For us, an order is sacred, and failure to carry it out means death. It's a real shame, because no Jew has yet been released from headquarters, innocent or not. But we're reasonable people, and we're willing to make an exception, if you are willing to compensate us. But the compensation will have to be pretty significant. Remember, we're playing with our lives here.'

After a certain amount of haggling a sum was agreed upon and the soldiers pocketed the money. They apologized for the intrusion and were about to leave when the woman suddenly realized that she didn't have a penny left for food. The German graciously returned to her one of the larger bills he had received.

'*Gnädige Frau,*' he said, bowing, 'how can I refuse a lady?'

Chapter 3

The Jewish Council

When systematic persecution of the Jews began, it was carried out not by the Germans, nor by their Hungarian lackeys, but – most astonishingly – by the Jews themselves. One of the first things the Germans did was to form a so-called Jewish Council, consisting of the leaders of the Jewish community. Council members were made personally responsible for the implementation of the various German measures relating to the Jewish population. As a reward they, their families and those who worked for them were exempted, at least at the beginning, from these restrictions.

The Germans invented this 'brilliant' scheme at the beginning of World War II. It had already been used in other occupied countries with conspicuous success. The Jewish Council carried out German wishes far more conscientiously than the Germans could themselves. There was nothing the Germans could request that they were not ready, without a second's thought, to provide. Of course, their own skins were at risk: if they did not comply they would be the first to be punished; if they did, they would be safe – or so they thought. They appealed to the Jewish community earnestly, almost desperately, to follow orders. As they were respected citizens, their word carried weight. They succeeded in convincing themselves that they were serving the Germans not out of selfish motives but in the interests of the Jewish community: as long as the Jews complied voluntarily their ill-treatment would be kept within bounds. Nothing could have suited the Germans better; they saved themselves the trouble and expense of having to enforce their own orders. It was a master-stroke.

The headquarters of the council, on Síp Street, became a bustling center of activity. Every Jew who had suffered injury ran immediately to Síp Street seeking remedy: there were people who had been evicted from their homes, people who were trying to trace a member of their family who had disappeared, people who had been robbed, people who wanted to travel, people who needed medical care or money, or people who were just hanging around in the hope of finding protection. The council was besieged by people looking for administrative jobs in the hope of entitlement to some kind of exemption as council employees. Within days it became a huge bureaucracy.

As Jews couldn't go to school any more and their teachers couldn't teach, they were ordered to report to council headquarters. The children were enlisted as couriers under the command of their teachers. My younger son, George, also became a courier. On the second day he returned home at seven in the evening.

'What did you do all day?'

'Mostly nothing. But this afternoon I was given some notices to deliver to various addresses.'

'Did you read what they said?'

'I even brought one home.'

He handed me a small slip of paper, with a typewritten message:

SUMMONS

You are requested to report tomorrow morning at 9 o'clock at the Rabbinical Seminary in Rökk Szilárd Street. Please bring with you a blanket, and food for two days.

THE JEWISH COUNCIL

'Do you know what this means?' I asked him.

'I can guess,' he replied with great seriousness. 'They'll be interned.'

Children are often good guessers. I wondered whether he knew what being interned meant. Did this child of mine realize that these people would be deported to Germany and very possibly murdered? I felt too ashamed of the world I had brought him into to enlighten him.

'The Jewish Council has no right to give people orders like that,' I told him. 'You are not to work there any more.'

'I tried to tell the people I called on not to obey,' he said, clearly disappointed that I wouldn't let him work any more. He was beginning to enjoy his career as a courier: it was all a big adventure.

'What kinds of people are on your list?' I asked him.

'They're lawyers, and their names all begin with the letters B and C.'

As a lawyer I found this all most enlightening. Within a few days it transpired that all the more prominent lawyers were being called for internment – in alphabetical order.

Although I forbade my son to work for the Jewish Council, the council continued to operate diligently and with enthusiasm. By the end of the week they had reached the letter G. Since my own name started with an S, I felt I had a little time.

Was I on the list, I wondered? Fortunately I had never considered myself among the highly paid lawyers, so it was likely that, given the principles of selection, they had omitted me. But my wife, driven less by logic than by fear, was convinced that my name was on the list. I had never been too ambitious, and on that account had had to put up with a lot of nagging from my wife, who, perhaps with a touch of vanity, didn't want to be the only person with a high opinion of me. Over the years, I tried to justify my natural laziness with a philosophy that was especially developed for the purpose: it doesn't pay to be prominent. You become identified with the ideas or opinions you hold, and if those ideas are attacked you have to sacrifice either the opinions or yourself. As I had no wish to become a martyr I preferred to stay in the background. I used to tell my wife how, as a prisoner of war in Siberia in World War I, I had led a campaign to improve living conditions in the camp. When our effort was successful, the major who was in charge of the camp offered me an official position as the 'prisoners' representative'. It carried with it various small privileges and represented the highest position a prisoner of war could attain.

I refused, because I felt the offer was a bribe.

Shortly afterwards there was a new wave of agitation which broke into violence and the prisoners' representative was executed as an example to the men.

This story generally satisfied my wife, and me too, because it implied that the only reason I didn't become prominent in civilian life was that I didn't try. If my name was not on the list now, my philosophy would be vindicated for ever.

In any case, I was determined not to answer the summons if I got one. Let them come and get me if they could: I had no intention of making it easy for them.

In conversations with my lawyer friends, I found not a single person who planned to resist. I was reminded of a visit I had paid years ago to Swift and Armour, one of the great Chicago slaughterhouses. In front of the building was a vast area where thousands of cattle were penned. My guide showed me how the sides got gradually narrower towards the entrance to the building, where there was a trapdoor no more than about three feet wide. When the trapdoor was opened, all the cattle started pushing towards it, until one by one the exhausted animals passed through the door and into the slaughterhouse, on to an enormous turntable. The workers chained each animal to the turntable, hit it on the head with a hammer, and dispatched it on a conveyor belt to its death to make room for the next one.

My friends were going to the slaughterhouse, of their own accord. They did not need to be pushed: they took the streetcar. After the war a marble plaque was unveiled in the Bar Association bearing the names of over six hundred Jewish lawyers who perished through Jewish Council summonses in 1944. Many of them could have avoided the glory of martyrdom by refusing to answer the call.

Not for a minute did I waver in my decision not to obey if the call came. I would go into hiding. But what about my family? What would happen if they took my wife instead of me, or my two sons, or all three of them? It was clear that there could be no half-measures: we would all have to arrange to disappear.

That was easier said than done. Middle-class existence holds us by a thousand and one ties. Our homes, our furniture, pictures on the wall – these are all insignificant in themselves, but most people can't break free from them.

It was only now that I fully understood the Latin saying '*Navigare necesse est, vivere non necesse*': navigating is essential, living is not.' Right now, the apartment seemed more necessary than life itself.

And what would happen to our aunt, who ate Sunday dinner with us every week?

But it turned out that four years of soldiering and a long period as prisoner of war had taught me a lesson – to value life more highly than anything else. So for me it was relatively easy to break free of my middle-class material existence.

But then there was the moral problem of breaking the law. Lawyers are trained to act within the framework of the existing legal structure. You try to make the law work to your advantage but you know that if you transgress it you become an enemy of society. None the less, as a lawyer I understood the principles of necessity and self-protection. I felt fully entitled, morally and legally, to disobey the state when it threatened me unjustifiably.

At one time I had played with the idea of writing a book about the moral foundations of international law under the title 'Everybody Is Responsible'. In my view, international life will never be healthy until we change current notions of national sovereignty. Given the extraordinary technological advances now going on all around us, we must recognize that such concepts are out of date and morally indefensible: we must place limits on the absolute power of the individual state. Not only does every state have a right to intervene in the internal affairs of another state if that state violates fundamental human rights, but it has a moral responsibility to do so. If laws are supposed to embody certain moral precepts, there must be some fundamental principles of justice that no state ought to be allowed to break. And if those principles are broken, it is the duty of the other states to enforce them. No state has the right to take away the civil rights of any group of its citizens, to treat them like slaves, to exterminate them. We all of us have an obligation to help the helpless when their human rights are violated and when atrocities are perpetrated against them.

And what is true of states is true of individuals, too. The citizen should not accept injustice or arbitrariness from the state to which he belongs. If his life is endangered by an unjust action of the state, he is morally justified in fighting back. He even has a legal justification in the principle of self-defense in extreme need. The great German poet Friedrich Schiller put it like this:

> There is a limit to the power of a tyrant. If the oppressed cannot find justice elsewhere, he reaches his hands with confidence to heaven and appeals to the eternal rights that dwell there as indestructible and imperishable as the stars.

I never wrote the book, but thinking about it cleared my head.

So I felt no compunction about breaking the law. For me the law ceased to have moral sanction the day the Germans occupied the country. The only thing that mattered was to survive the next few weeks. It never occurred to me that the German occupation might last longer than that.

In times of danger, the biggest problem is getting people to choose among unpleasant options. I saw the matter quite clearly: we would get through the coming months only if we ceased to live as Jews. As I moved around, I tried to get a sense of how other people felt about these ideas, and what obstacles they saw. I particularly remember one such discussion early in April at the home of my good friend the pediatrician Dr Radnóti.

A heavy-set photographer, whom we knew as Tubby, asked, more or less out of the blue, 'Have you ever thought what kind of a person Hitler is, as a human being?'

'What kind of person would anyone be who could get into his head the notion of exterminating a whole race just because he doesn't approve of them?' asked my friend Osi. 'He's crazy. A megalomaniac.'

'Yes,' someone said. 'A megalomaniac, but not a madman.'

My pediatrician friend, who was given to quoting Greek philosophy on such occasions, took over the debate:

'In my view the wisdom of the ancient Greeks applies to Hitler as well: "*Koros, hybris, ate*: pride comes before a fall". Like every dictator he is haughty, cruel and blinded by success, but his ultimate fate will be that of all dictators: catastrophe.'

I didn't entirely agree:

'I think Hitler himself knows that his success can't last long. Even at the time of his greatest victory, when France surrendered, there was a kind of gloomy undertone in his speeches, a dark sense that things would not end well. When the whole continent of Europe lies prostrate at his feet, as he puts it, he talks about his own surrender: "*Ich werde nicht kapitulieren, nur fünf Minuten nach Zwölf*: I won't capitulate until five minutes past twelve." If he himself doesn't really believe in his ultimate victory, why should anyone else, especially those of us who stand to lose our lives in the process?'

'But isn't there a chance that Hitler might change his attitude towards the Jews, or that the Western powers might force him to do so?' Tubby asked, always looking for compromises.

'The great shortcoming of the Western powers is that they cooperate only at the time of ultimate danger: when war breaks out. In peacetime, it's every nation for itself.'

'Perhaps worldwide public opinion will influence him,' persisted the photographer.

'Worldwide public opinion carries no weight any more. Democracies are certainly dependent on public opinion, but their populations are not educated to consider international problems more important than national ones. The Western powers should have intervened to punish Hitler way back in 1934, when the persecution of the Jews started in Germany and when all internal opposition to Hitler was silenced by firing squads, starting with the execution of Generals Schleicher and Röhm. If the rest of the world had been determined enough not to allow such flouting of the elementary principles of justice, Hitler would not be ruling Germany today. But Baldwin, the English prime minister, blithely declared that 'England is not the policeman of Europe.' The democracies refused to lift a finger. All that was needed then was a police action, but they begrudged the minimal costs needed to do the job. As a result, Britain is now in the fourth year of a world war, with huge losses, and fighting for its very survival. The *Leitmotiv* of Hitler is not pride but fury. And fury is a poor teacher. Where can Hitler unloose his fury? On the Americans? The British? First he has to overcome them, and that's no easy task. It's a whole lot easier to pour his fury out on the Jews and the Gypsies and the poor prisoners of war. They can't defend themselves. If you think Hitler will ever change his anti-Jewish policy, you're living in a fool's paradise. Why on earth should he feel concern for the Jews, when he feels no concern for his own people? He's sacrificing the flower of German manhood in the pursuit of his nightmarish vision. If Hitler can't find it in his heart to pity the *Deutsche Jugend*, the youth of Germany, what makes you think he'll find pity for the Jews? Exterminating the Jews is the one point in his political program that he can carry out through the principle of least resistance.

'So,' I concluded, 'we have nothing to protect us against Hitler's threats; there is nobody we can turn to; we are on our own. We must fight for ourselves. And since we can't stand up to Hitler's fury, we must hide from it.'

I don't know whether I convinced the fat photographer, but I certainly convinced myself.

Such conversations had their use: they raised new perspectives and gave me ideas on how to start crystallizing my plans. But mostly they were only words, words and more words.

What matters is not the decision but the implementation.

Chapter 4

In Search of an Identity

We could stay alive in the coming months if we lived as Christians. So I had my guiding principle, but the next problem was carrying it out. We would have to give up our current identity and, in effect, crawl into a new skin. But how? Where should we begin?

Somehow we would have to obtain new identity papers, move to a new apartment, start a new life with a new name.

For the moment, as I thought about our survival, I limited my horizons to just five people: myself, my two sons, my wife, and my mother-in-law, for whom I felt a special responsibility. But what about brothers and sisters? Friends? Clients? My sons' friends? At what point can a person say that he's done everything he can do? The slightest omission can bring deadly consequences.

My plan was to obtain documents from Christians whose identity more or less fitted ours. My first move, as a lawyer, was to search the files in my office for any personal documents I could use. They were full of such papers, since our Hungarian bureaucracy always required the fullest documentation whether it was relevant or not. One reason behind such unreasonable requirements was to make sure that an applicant was not tainted with Jewish blood. Just the sort of foolproof documentation I needed.

I studied the files with much excitement. But of many particulars that these documents contained there were always some – age, height, weight, color of eyes, or heaven knows what else – that did not fit. People are more individual than we suppose.

I made no attempt to keep my plans secret from my friends, not least because I felt I had to share my conviction that living under a false identity was the only way out. But I also hoped to make contact with people of the same persuasion. Nobody opened up to me. Being outspoken is natural to me, like breathing: I dislike lying, not on moral grounds but because it requires such concentration. As a young student I learned the Latin proverb: '*mendacem oportet esse memorem*: A liar must have a good memory.' I preferred to use my memory for other purposes, not to cover up lies. Yet in this case my frankness in sharing my plans with others failed to bring the results I had hoped for. Instead of countering with frankness, people stayed lukewarm, probably not from a lack of sincerity but out of a natural desire for self-preservation. Still, here and there I managed to gather quite a lot of valuable information, which helped me to keep my feet firmly planted on the ground and to abandon any romantic ideas.

Knowing the Germans' blind respect for uniforms, I had played with the romantic notion of obtaining a German officer's uniform and exploiting its magical powers. But my friends told me that my knowledge of the German military would not be enough to carry it off, and, anyway, it would not have solved the problem of my family's survival.

My other romantic plan was to escape to Soviet Russia. I toyed with the idea for quite some time and considered it at least feasible. Why? Around this time Hungary had a common frontier with the Soviet Union, and these two giants, Germany and the Soviet Union, were engaged in a struggle to the death. Furthermore, Hitler was busily carrying out his extermination campaign against the Jews, so it was no wonder the Jews hated Hitler. Logically, it followed that the Russians ought to receive Jewish refugees with open arms. I had the added advantage of fluency in Russian. But the news I was able to gather about the unhappy fate of German and Spanish communists who made it to Russia convinced me that one could not make judgments about the Russians on the basis of logic.

The Russians never really understood the political zigzagging that took place right before their eyes between 1939 and 1941. Until 1939 Russian propaganda represented Hitler as a fascist executioner, who murdered communists and whose hands were drenched in blood. Then in 1939 the Soviet Union became Germany's ally. When, two years later, Hitler attacked his new allies, it was like a bolt out of the blue to the Russians. Russian films, *The Fall of Berlin* for instance, depicted the war as coming on with no warning or explanation.

Later, after war had broken out between the two, I often listened to Russian radio programs. I heard not a word about Hitler's anti-Semitism. I have no idea why this information was never shared with the Russian people. Perhaps it was because Stalin was an anti-Semite as well.

So, even if a Jew managed to get through the barbed wire to Russian territory, the soldiers would be unlikely to believe that he was trying to escape from Hitler. They would be more likely to assume that, given that all Jews were cowards and obviously lacked the courage to cross the German lines, this one must be a spy. Spies are never treated very gently: they tend to get arrested and beaten up. Furthermore, people who had traveled and lived in Russia told me that women were particularly at risk of molestation and rape. So, all things considered, setting out with the family to Russia hardly seemed like a good idea.

In addition to arranging new identities for my family, I was increasingly preoccupied with another, completely different plan: going into hiding until the dark times were over. These two problems seemed to contradict each other: if we had the necessary papers, why hide? Maybe my fear addled my brain? Anyway, I thought a lot about ways of hiding out, and about whether I should use false documents at all, or at least only as a last resort. Deep in my heart I was convinced that the Hitler regime was in its last months and would soon collapse. So we might not have to hide for long.

Little by little my various grand plans proved unworkable and there was only one way left – to live with false documents. But a number of issues remained unresolved. Could I pull it off? Weren't there unavoidable external signs that would reveal a person's Jewishness – something characteristic in a Jewish face, the sad glint of the eyes, a typical gesture or intonation?

In Hungarian literature Jews were often presented as hook-nosed, with crooked backs and guttural speech. Some writers described them as sly, self-ingratiating, and given to much gesticulation. The Jewish personality obviously underwent great changes over the years, though the literary stereotype persisted. Many Jews, perhaps in response to the stereotype, chose to get involved with sports, cultivating their muscles and coming across as tough. Hungarians were often Olympic champions, and among the champions were numbers of Jews, even in that most characteristic Hungarian sport, fencing. Of course, people of a progressive turn of mind, socialists and the like, made no distinction between people of Jewish or Christian background.

Plastic surgery made the correction of crooked noses possible; as for Jewish intonation, the Hungarian actors best known for the purity of their speech, Kálmán Rózsahegyi and Irén Varsányi, both happened to be Jewish. Judged against the Jewish stereotype, none of our family 'looked' Jewish. So on that score we had no need to worry. The truth of the matter was, that, except for Orthodox Jews, whose unusual clothing and hairstyle proclaimed their religion, it was hard to tell a Jew just by appearance. That was why the authorities ultimately prescribed the wearing of a yellow star, to show to all the world who was a Jew and who was not. The star simply declared: this person is a Jew, so it's okay to beat and persecute him.

Looking back now, it seems to me that my decision to try to survive with a new identity was a natural one for my character and personality.

Two incidents will illustrate why I feel as I do. I remember an incident from my early childhood when I lay low, playing the innocent to escape punishment. I was four or five years old. My mother had left the pantry door open, so I sneaked in. What an amazing sight! There on the shelves glistened row upon row of freshly preserved jars of fruit. It was like a treasure house. They all looked so tempting, so mouth-watering. But my mother might appear at any minute and there was no time to think. Each jar looked more attractive than the last. So, one by one, I bit through the parchment tops of the jars, just to get a taste of each.

It didn't take long for this act of vandalism to be discovered, and the family launched a thorough search for the culprit. I meanwhile feigned complete innocence. Although my stomach was in knots with fear, I knew how to put on a good face and show a complete lack of interest in the whole matter. My worst fear was that they would somehow match my teeth with the tooth-marks on the jars. But fortunately my parents had other matters to attend to.

My first successful play-acting as an adult took place under rather different circumstances, when I was twenty-seven or twenty-eight years old. In the summer of 1919 the communist regime of Béla Kun collapsed in Hungary. The four months of his 'Red terror' were followed by Horthy's 'White terror'. About this time I was in a Russian prisoner-of-war camp. The Russians refused to allow the return of Hungarian officers who had been prisoners of war. Their plan was to use them as hostages to curb the excesses of the Hungarian authorities against their communist captives.

Austrians, on the other hand, were leaving for home at the rate of five hundred a week. I watched them sadly. Seven years of war and prison camp made me very anxious to get back home. By chance, I got hold of a Baedeker guide for the Austrian city of Linz. The book was full of maps and pictures. I studied it with care and then presented myself to the repatriation committee as an Austrian, born in Linz. It worked: I answered all their questions correctly and they scheduled me to leave, as an Austrian officer, on August 14, 1921.

Later I became a lawyer and often had to play a part to

convince a judge. My life so far gave me hope that I would perform my new role well. The decision was made: now on to the implementation.

Chapter 5

A Little Jewish Philosophy

Before going further, I should say a word about my Jewish background – the kind of education I had and the surroundings I grew up in.

Jews come in different sorts and sizes. Most actively religious are the Hasids, who even wear different clothing from other Jews and tend to regard everybody else as insufficiently observant, even the Orthodox. Orthodox Jews are not all the same: there is a difference between those of the East, called Ashkenazi, and those of the West, the Sephardic Jews. Then of course there are the Reform Jews, and freethinkers, and converts. In any community where the principal uniting factor is religion, there are also various other distinctions among groups, such as comparative wealth, profession, education, family background, and so on.

I must have been no more than four or five years old, when neighbors invited me to a pig roast. I accepted the invitation, though I was not sure what the words actually meant. Along with the other village children, I took part in the ceremony of butchering the pig. Everyone laughed a lot and had a good time. In fact, I had the impression that my presence added to the level of hilarity, though I didn't understand why. I didn't realize that observant Jews are forbidden to eat pork.

There was a Catholic church in our neighborhood. Some six or seven steps led up to the main door. I liked to jump off these steps and was very proud when I was at last brave enough to jump off the top step. The Christian children seemed envious of this feat, because I heard them shouting, 'Hep! Hep!' as they ran by. I had no idea what this word meant; in fact, I had no idea it meant anything in particular. It was only many years later that I learned its meaning. The letters HEP stand for '*Hierosolyma est perdita*', Latin for 'Jerusalem is lost'. The Romans occupied Jerusalem seventy years after the birth of Christ. Some 1,800 years later these initials were still being used in a little Hungarian village, to make fun of the Jews.

In addition to this word, I remember a mocking song from my childhood. A notorious trial held the people of Hungary in suspense towards the end of the nineteenth century, the so-called blood libel of Tiszaeszlár. The Jews of that town were accused of murdering a Christian girl and using her blood for religious rituals. This song stemmed from those days:

> Hundred Jews in a row
> March on to Hell below,
> Nathan is the leader,
> A sack on his shoulder,
> Hundred Jews in a row . . .

I understood every word of the song, but not why were they marching to Hell. What was the point of the song?

I remember my grandfather, a village shopkeeper, very clearly. One day – I couldn't have been more than about nine years old – he showed me his accounts. He kept a special set of books, not because he cheated on his taxes but so that he could calculate his exact income and reserve 10 percent for charity as prescribed by Jewish law.

Every Friday at synagogue, he looked around for unfamiliar faces in the congregation and invited two poor Jews back to his house as guests. He was especially pleased if it turned out that the guests could sing. They would sing Jewish melodies together at lunch or dinner and tell one another fantastic stories.

There were seven daughters in my grandfather's family and there seemed to be a wedding every year. Grandfather took out one high-interest loan after another to pay for the dowries and wedding expenses. He hired the best entertainers to enchant the guests with their songs and their witty interpretations of the Talmud. Guests came from far and wide and sometimes stayed for weeks.

I sinned against my grandfather, and my conscience has bothered me ever since. We used to play chess. Sometimes I stole one of the chess pieces from him to increase my chances of winning.

My father was not a particularly religious man, but, preferring to avoid conflicts in the village, he followed the religious formalities. He insisted that I learn the Hebrew prayers, but pretended not to notice if I failed to recite them.

In 1919, as I have already mentioned, a communist regime took over in Hungary for a period of four months. Quite a number of its leaders were Jewish, with the result that a wave of anti-Semitism swept the country when the regime fell. Then the following year the government put legal provisions in place to limit the number of Jews entering the university. The law, named *numerus clausus*, permitted only six Jews in every hundred students.

I returned from military captivity in 1921, by which time this wave of hatred had died down, but savage anti-Jewish posters were still very much in evidence.

On various occasions in my life, I have found myself in a group of people in which someone has suddenly started vilifying Jews. How does one respond? When I was young, I often dealt with such situations by reminding people that there was really no need to use terms like 'dirty Jew'. As a result, I sometimes ended up in a fight, in which I was not always the winner. On the other hand, if I pretended not to hear the remark, or to assume that it didn't relate to me, I always felt bad about it afterwards and reproached myself for my unwillingness to stand up and be counted.

I took solace from a Jewish story that helped me deal with these internal conflicts. The story goes like this.

A poor Jew goes to a rabbi. 'I have a complaint. I was going along the road with a loaded wagon. A nobleman was coming from the other direction in a coach-and-four. "Get out of the way, Jew!" he cried from some distance away. "Go round me, excellency. You can see that my wagon is loaded." So he went round me, but as he went past he suddenly cracked his whip in my face. Was I right when I asked him to go round me?'

'You were right,' replies the rabbi, 'but it's not enough for a Jew to be right: he has to be smart, too.'

I am very fond of Jewish humor. There's a lot of truth in such jokes: they are often witty, circumspect, profound. Sometimes they make fun of human shortcomings, but they always give pleasure. Consider the following.

A Jew stands in court. The judge asks, 'Do you have any final words?'

'Yes, I want an old-fashioned judge.'

'I don't understand. What's an old-fashioned judge?'

'In the old days, when the judges got together they used to say, "He's a Jew, but he's right." Now they say, "He's right, but he's a Jew."'

Then there's the story about the rumor that Jews who converted would receive special treatment. Two brothers decide to get baptized. The older brother goes in first. The younger brother stays outside. After a long time the older brother reappears.

'How was it?' asks the younger brother.

The older brother eyes him from head to foot and says with disgust, 'None of your business. I don't talk to dirty Jews.'

Hitler has conquered the world. He comes to Tokyo, the capital of Japan. All across the world Jews have been exterminated. There are only two left, disguised as Japanese and taking part in the celebration. There's a big party. Fireworks. A beautiful little girl presents a bouquet to the Führer. One Jew says to the other, 'Just you wait. This is where he'll finally fall and break his neck.'

Literature was a big influence on me in my youth. Naturally, those heroes appealed to me most who clung to their ideals to the very end – heroes like Jules Verne's Keraban the Inflexible, who crosses continents to avoid having to pay an unjust toll on the Bosphorus, or Kleist's Michael Kohlhaas who causes all Germany to rebel and takes over the government, all because he was treated unfairly by a court in a relatively minor matter, or like Tolstoy's Prince Nekhlyudov in *Resurrection*, who sacrifices his title and his fortune to atone for a sin committed in his youth, the seduction of a peasant girl.

Such were my ideal heroes. Like them, I reacted vehemently to the smallest injustice, or to the slightest bureaucratic arrogance. By rights, I should have spent half my life in jail – if I hadn't learned the lesson that it isn't enough for a Jew to be right, he has to be smart, too.

As a young lawyer, I ran into a situation in which the Finance Ministry refused to return to a client a sum of money that the finance officials had collected without authority. All my efforts were in vain: they promised to return the money but did nothing. I got angrier and angrier. Eventually I sent them a registered letter requesting, politely but firmly, that they settle the matter immediately, otherwise I would have to take the necessary legal steps. Of course I knew perfectly well that there were no 'legal steps', since there was no redress against the upper reaches of the Hungarian bureaucracy. All I could do was go to the Salt Office, as we Hungarians laughingly recommend to constant complainers.

But my letter brought results. It stirred the bureaucracy into action, but not exactly in the direction I intended. The ministry reported me to the Bar Association for 'using threats' in an attempt to force them to settle the matter. They asked for disciplinary action. The chairman of the disciplinary committee saw immediately that I had threatened no one, but he tried to persuade me to express 'regret' that I had written the letter. Good relations between the Bar Association and the ministry required it, he said. (Lawyers had special tax advantages.) I refused to budge, because I felt that my client had suffered real damage and I was disinclined to pander to the hurt feelings of a collection of bureaucrats.

An incident of a different kind took place in 1939. A group of Jewish merchants from my home town called on me to complain that their taxes had been raised without explanation and that they had been hit with all kinds of penalties. If they appealed, the higher authority in question, instead of giving them relief, would simply double the penalties. They begged me to go to the Ministry of Finance to try to solve the problem.

The young government clerk I was referred to was a desiccated, fair-haired fellow, with a rather bigger Adam's apple than most. He received me with great courtesy. This didn't surprise me: politeness was a requirement at the ministry.

After listening to my story, the young man suggested that I approach a certain Mr Tóth, head of the finance office in Nyíregyháza.

'Finance Director Tóth?' I repeated, 'But he's the conveyor belt that delivers these injustices against the Jews.'

To my surprise, my response had a stunning effect. The young man made an effort to reply: his mouth moved but no sound came out. Finally, he was reduced to stuttering. I must confess that I always get embarrassed when someone stutters: I feel almost apologetic for the other person's handicap. This was my response on this occasion: I kept going as though I had not noticed his stuttering, in an attempt to save him from an awkward situation. I changed the subject, saying something non-controversial about his work. After a while he began to talk normally again, and I couldn't believe my ears at what he said.

'Counsel, I plan to put your last remark on the official record.'

So this miserable stutterer, whose embarrassment I had attempted to ease, was about to make an official complaint about me!

'Hold on a minute,' I said. 'Right now I'm too busy for reports.'

Without waiting for a reply, I grabbed my briefcase and headed for the door.

'Goodbye,' I cried as I left, with a friendly wave of the hand.

In those days such a report could easily result in a year or two in prison.

So occasionally I was forced to use unconventional methods to avoid the consequences of my behavior and conform to what was an increasingly reactionary atmosphere. In short, my philosophy of life was formed in the households of my father and grandfather, with the suggestive influence of an occasional teacher, and most of all by the books I read.

There were periods in my youth, when the problems of God and religion, and of mankind and the universe, were foremost in my mind. This preoccupation was strongest around the age of thirteen, but returned periodically later in life. I was interested not only in the supernatural, but also in ordinary everyday phenomena: the changing of seasons, the coming of spring, the strength of a growing seed, the dew on the grass, the mystery of the human body. I tried to understand the strange forces that keep the earth and other planets in balance. I was particularly interested in the problem of death and the afterlife. It was only later, after I had read the Bible and the Koran, the Bhagavad Gita, and other books, like Papini's *Life of Jesus* and Martin Buber's *Jewish Legends*, that I formed any definite opinion on religion.

I came to the conclusion that not only did God make man in his own image, but also man imagines God in his own human way. The anthropomorphic nature of the deity frightened me away from organized religion. Instead of going to services, I was happier worrying about human lives. Understanding, a love of people, tolerance – these were the virtues I cultivated. Such tolerance came in handy quite early: my wife was an enthusiast for all kinds of religious mysticism.

Chapter 6

Initial Experiments

irst I had to find the documents I needed. I reviewed my
list of Christian friends, my Esperanto acquaintances, and
so on, to think of people who might give me suitable
documentation. I had one Esperantist friend who was in
constant need of money. I called him, since that was easier than
making the long trip to his distant home. I was a great believer
in cost/benefit principles – getting the best result for the least
expenditure of energy.

'Here's a chance for some easy money. One of my rich clients
is trying to obtain personal identity papers. I immediately thought
of you. There's no risk involved, because you can always tell the
police that you lost yours. It's good for a few thousand pengős.
Think about it.'

He said he would think it over, but he didn't call back. I don't
believe he lacked sympathy towards the plight of the Jews, because
he was very much a humanitarian. Perhaps he didn't care for this
manner of making money, or he was a little upset at me because,
as editor of the Esperanto literary magazine *Literatura Mondo*, I
sometimes shortened his articles.

I had more luck with a left-wing journalist friend of mine.
He hated the Germans and everything they stood for. Without a moment's hesitation he promised to give me his own

and his wife's identity papers. Early next morning the phone rang.

'I apologize for calling so early: I have been up all night. I just don't dare do it. You see, they're observing my every move. If they find you with my papers, no one will believe that it's an accident.'

I realized at once that I couldn't count on him. Even if he gave me his papers now, he might get so worried that he would ask for them back at any time. Courage is an intangible quality that you either have or don't have. If a coward tries to act like a hero, something is bound to go wrong. So I told him that under the circumstances he should definitely keep his papers, and thanked him for his good intentions. Since I admire people who have the courage to say they lack it, I accepted his decision without complaint. But he kept on apologizing and regretting his inability to help people who needed help until in the end it was I who had to comfort him.

I wrote off my failures and tried some acquaintances who were less close to me. I remembered a smiling chimney-sweep who used to come to my office once a month with the bill for sweeping the chimneys of the houses I administered. He was such a cheerful, ruddy-cheeked fellow that I always liked to chat with him when he came. Once he had vaguely mentioned that he had been in prison for several months for some kind of political activity. Perhaps he had no love for the current government and would be willing to help. I looked for a way of meeting him. After much searching, I found his address and wandered around in the vicinity of his home in the early morning, in the hope of running into him – by chance, as it were. Eventually, one morning I succeeded. We were delighted to see one another.

After we got through the formalities, I asked him, 'Would you be willing to help me in a Jewish matter?'

'How can I be helpful?' he asked, in some surprise.

'Would you be willing to give me your identity papers?'

I explained again, as I had to my Esperantist friend, that there was no risk involved.

'Dr Soros, please don't ask me. I've burned my fingers once.'

We parted as friends. He was a decent, good-hearted man, I could see that. But the incident left a bitter taste in my mouth.

The days passed and I made no progress. Each evening, as I reported to my wife on the day's activities, her expression grew increasingly reproachful. The trouble was that she and the children had too much confidence in me, and believed that it was only my laziness and negligence that got in the way of success. They didn't say so in so many words, but I could feel it.

The atmosphere in the country was becoming more stifling by the day. Stories of theft, persecution and disappearances multiplied. My hopes that Regent Horthy would try to salvage at least the appearance of Hungarian sovereignty went unrealized. In my opinion, given what was happening in Romania and Finland, the Jewish problem was really a secondary issue, and they would yield if they had to. If Horthy had made it a condition of his continuing in office that Hungarian Jews not be deported from the country, the Germans might have complied in order to secure his continued collaboration. But he made no such demand. National sovereignty was no longer an issue for him. Horthy was one of those punctilious people who do their duty, within certain limits, during the good times and lack the courage to take a stand when things get difficult. Others expressed their disapproval of his leadership rather more concisely.

For Horthy, we Jews had become *vogelfrei*, free as birds. I had never realized the full significance of this beautiful expression. To be free as a bird is also to be fair game. Anyone can shoot a bird, knock it out of the sky. We had no laws to defend us. I have never heard of birds lodging formal complaints. The same was true of us – only we had no wings.

On April 5, 1944, two weeks after the German 'arrival', a regulation was put in place obliging every Jew to wear a yellow star of David on his or her coat. Jews were forbidden to visit public places, such as parks, restaurants, swimming pools. Jews were allowed to employ no Christians, nor could they have servants. They were not even allowed to use a public telephone. Jews who broke the rules would be deported. 'Deportation' was a new word to us: no one knew precisely what it meant. But our imagination could conjure up some pretty dark possibilities.

It was risky to go out on the streets without a star. But during the working day it was also dangerous to wear one, because identity papers might be checked at any time and anyone who was unemployed could be deported immediately. If the streets were safe at any time, that time was in the early morning, between six, when factory workers set off to work, and nine, when offices opened. During those hours, people on the street with yellow stars would presumably be on their way to work. As for me, I had already been forced to hand over my attorney's papers, my seal, and the keys to my office to the Gentile lawyer appointed to handle my practice, so in fact I was unemployed.

On the day when the yellow star decree came into effect, I suggested to my younger son that we do a little field trip on the streetcar to see how people were taking it. He agreed, and so we set out to sample public opinion on this brutal attack on human rights. People seemed a little grimmer than usual, but that may have been because it was so early. They pretended not to notice that some people were wearing yellow stars on their coats. I heard only one offensive remark, when someone whispered, 'I would never have guessed that that blond piglet-faced kid was Jewish.'

In a way, this remark was good to hear, given my plans for the family.

Later, however, my son accidentally blocked the way of somebody who was trying to get on to the crowded streetcar.

'Stop hogging all the space, son of a pig,' the stranger cried.

I hastened to reassure my son: 'Pay no attention. People who have no manners ought not to offend you.'

But my son insisted that the remark was intended primarily for me, not for him. 'Who's the pig I'm supposed to be the son of?' he asked me.

We had a little discussion, he and I, about whether the remark said more about him as a son or me as his father. We were generally pleased at how people were taking matters and we went home in good humor.

On one of my subsequent early morning walks I met my old friend Sold. In the good old days we used to meet in the cafés at the Ritz or the Hungaria for tea at five o'clock. He used to be a passionate dancer and I a devoted spectator. When I told him about my problems and plans, I saw immediately that I had finally found a true hero.

'No problem,' he told me breezily. 'Child's play. I have several Christian girl friends among my dancing partners who will do anything for me.'

I jumped at the offer, and immediately asked him for a set consisting of five documents: birth, marriage, parents' birth and marriage certificates, all for the insignificant sum of 600 pengős, some $20 at the time. We arranged to meet next day at my home. He came as arranged and handed over the documents. In age and every other particular they fitted quite well. The only snag was that the occupation was given as 'teacher and choirmaster'. I spent my youth in a village so I knew that the combined function of teacher and choirmaster involves not only teaching but also leading the singing in church. This was a bit of a problem: I could not decide whether to learn some hymns or pretend to be a choirmaster who had been struck dumb. Neither idea seemed very attractive.

As our contacts continued, it became clear that my friend Sold might turn out to be a real treasure. He could provide blank but ready-stamped residence forms. The Hungarian system required that all changes of address had to be registered with the police, who then provided a certificate of residence. You could register a new address only if you already had in hand a stamped form indicating that you had left the old one. So the route to a false certificate of residence lay through a forged residence form.

'Get me a hundred of these.'

'A hundred is too many. I can't get you a hundred.'

'I don't understand. If your policeman friend can hide the stamp, there's not much effort involved in stamping a hundred forms.' I made a stamp with my fist and banged it up and down on the table. 'I have a lot of friends: I need a lot of forms. So bring me eighty.'

He shook his head.

'Sixty.'

The same shake of the head.

'So bring forty – as many as you can.'

In the end he brought me only four. He charged me 5 pengős each, which was as good as giving them away. I begged him to get me more but he refused. Instead he came up with a new proposition. Through a printer friend of his he could get a certificate of membership in the Order of Heroes.

The Order of Heroes was established following the collapse of Béla Kun's communist regime after World War I. Horthy created it as an anti-communist organization to honor those right-wingers who had helped him into power. With the assistance of right-wing elements in parliament, he set it up as an imitation of a medieval knightly order, the only one in existence at the time. Induction into the order involved an elaborate medieval ceremony and membership carried with it many privileges, including country estates. Naturally no Jew could belong to this privileged caste.

'The membership certificate is printed on special paper,' said my friend. 'It's a lot of work to get the paper and to set the type. I should point out that for technical reasons I can't get you an embossed seal such as they have on the originals. In this case it will have to be printed.'

I had never seen a certificate of membership in the Order of Heroes, either with or without an embossed seal, and I had no intention of using such a certificate. I had had a bad experience with such documents.

At the time of the fall of the communist regime in Hungary

in 1920 I was living in Irkutsk as an escaped prisoner of war. The city had recently been in the hands of the Whites. Kolchak, their leader, ordered a general mobilization to confront the Red Army, which was advancing on the city. Several members of the Irkutsk Jewish community wanted to do everything they could to avoid serving with the anti-Semitic Whites. They had no wish to become soldiers and, in any case, between the Whites and the Reds, they regarded the Reds as the lesser of the two evils. They paid a lot of money to get their names on to a list that stated that they were members of Kolchak's counter-espionage operation and were exempt from military service. But what happened? The Red Army defeated the Whites. They got hold of the counter-espionage list. On it were the names of the Jews. Naturally the Bolsheviks regarded double agents as the worst kind of enemies. The unfortunate Jews vainly declared that although their names were on the list they had played no part as spies. No mercy was shown. Every one of them was executed, or, as the Russians put it, 'liquidated' (the Bolsheviks were squeamish about the word 'executed').

My wife, unencumbered by such memories, recommended that I speak to the Barabás brothers about the certificates. These brothers, relatives of hers, were wealthy manufacturers who had converted to Christianity long since and lived the lives of aristocrats. Such a certificate would surely appeal to them greatly.

She was right. I explained to the younger brother that the certificates were less than perfect, because they would not have the proper seal.

'That's a detail. It's simply important that we have in our hands, or rather our pockets, some kind of weapon.'

He instructed me to obtain certificates for him and his brother and proposed 10,000 pengős. I was amazed. I knew the brothers: they were hardworking, competent people, but very tight with their money, and they thought very hard before they spent anything. Only extreme concern about their future would cause them to offer such a huge sum for a document of such doubtful value, if any. I was even more surprised when Sold declared that he wanted

1,000 pengős for the documents. I ordered them at once and could hardly contain myself until the moment came when I could inform my clients that the documents were ready. Barabás himself came to my apartment to take the documents. Now I was really taken aback. He put on the table two wads of banknotes, 20,000 pengős in all. I was so surprised that I gave one of them back. He explained that he was under the impression that the certificates cost 10,000 pengős each. So I earned 9,000 pengős instead of 19,000, but the money kept me going for a long time. In fact, this unexpected windfall took care of our living expenses for the following months; I had no other income.

Although I was no longer practicing as a lawyer because all Jews had had their licenses suspended, the government forgot to ban Jews from administering real estate. So I continued in that function for a few weeks. One of the houses that I looked after was a six-story building, the top three stories of which were rented by the Csepel Free Port. One day I received a call from the firm's general counsel, who was not only a lawyer but also a member of parliament.

'My dear colleague, why aren't the offices properly heated?'

'They're heated according to the regulations. According to the regulations, we're supposed to provide only moderate heat because of the shortage of fuel. Sixteen degrees Celsius is the maximum allowed.'

'Please see to it that they are heated better.'

'I'm not going to break the law for anyone.'

'You talk as though the Brits had already arrived.'

I had no reason to treat the caller rudely, but I felt a certain suppressed fury against everybody in high positions, feeling that they were all implicated in what was happening to our country. A single promise that I would do what I could to satisfy his wishes would have been enough to end matters. It was almost the end of the heating season, but I refused outright and I didn't mince words. In fact my sharpness so annoyed Dr Téli that he reported me to the police. In normal times such things were not police matters, but these were hardly normal times.

A few days later my building manager and I received a summons from the police. My wife was extremely upset. She urged me not to go in person but to send a non-Jewish lawyer to represent me. It was widely believed that any Jew who visited the police station was deported. With such beliefs circulating, Jews didn't go voluntarily to police stations, so there was no way of testing the theory. I tried to calm my wife's fears by explaining to her that these stories related to police headquarters, while I had been summoned simply to a precinct station, where there was no danger. They wouldn't have room to keep me there even if they wanted to. In reality I felt a certain obligation to what was left of my self-respect: I would defy the danger and go in person.

The building manager came with me. I was invited in first, while the manager waited in the outer office. In spite of my internal agitation, I did my best to show a calm exterior. Dr Téli was already there. No doubt he and the police captain had discussed in advance how to handle the matter. The captain, senior in both age and rank, opened the conversation, in carefully neutral tones.

'I am convinced that our lawyer friend is not responsible for the heating. The error clearly lies with the witless building manager, who is not providing heat in the right way at the right time.'

Despite his neutral and conciliatory tone, I felt obliged not to allow the responsibility to get shunted in the wrong direction.

'I have to tell you that the building manager is perfectly conscientious. The order to economize came from me.'

I explained that there were forty people living in the building, in addition to those working there, and the regulations did not allow enough fuel for adequate heating both during the day and at night.

Now the building manager was called in. The captain's demeanor changed. He used the tone of voice he had used for years to intimidate people.

'I warn you: if you don't do your duty properly I will have you jailed.'

'But, sir, I do do my job properly. As my boss has certainly explained, we have to provide heat round the clock and there's not enough coal to do so.'

'Shut up. I'm not looking for excuses. You have been warned. Now you may go.'

The captain turned to me politely and thanked me for taking the trouble of coming along.

The manager and I left the police station together. I was relieved that I hadn't been detained. He was upset because he felt that he had been unjustly threatened. We walked in the sunshine along the edge of the Danube.

I was the first to break the silence.

'You know, it's amazing. Although I'm a Jew, the police officer and the member of parliament treated me as an equal. But you, a Gentile, get treated badly because you're "only" a building manager.'

I studied his face to see the effect of my words.

'It was very kind of you, sir, to defend me.'

'I am sorry I couldn't do it more effectively, but I have to be careful, being a Jew.'

'It's a shame what they are doing to the Jews. If there's anything I can do for you, you can always count on me.'

I looked at him and I saw that he really meant it. He had made the offer on the spur of the moment, but it evidently occurred to him that he really could help me. I felt that it was a genuine offer and it was up to me to accept it.

'If you really want to, you can help me. You can help me quite a lot.'

His face remained impassive, but he replied without a moment's hesitation, 'Both my wife and I will do anything you want. You have done enough for us in the past.'

I knew what he was referring to. In Budapest at the time it was common for building administrators to sell caretaking positions in their buildings. I never liked this way of proceeding because it made me too dependent on superintendents who felt I was somehow indebted to them. It seemed like a bribe. So when Balázs applied for the job I took him on because I liked him. When he told me he would have difficulty raising money, I told him I would give him the job anyway.

Balázs was a few years younger than I, but his wife was about the same age as mine and his only son was born on almost the same day as my elder son. In fact, the two of them were friends. I told him about my plan to start living under a false name and asked him whether he would be willing to give me his family's documents. He took me straight away to his apartment and handed me all the documents he could find. He also gave me details that would allow me to order the missing documents. I ordered two copies of each. I was overjoyed. At last I had what I needed to put my plan into operation. Among other things, I now had a complete set of documents for one of my sons and my wife. To replace the documents I had taken, I ordered copies for Balázs.

On the same day I had another stroke of good fortune. A young man came to my home from Nyíregyháza, sent by my younger brother. He presented me with a folder full of papers. My brother had obtained the documents from an old employee of my father, who was about the same age and build as I. In fact I remembered him well: we had been in the same class at school. The papers were fairly complete. There was even a military discharge among them. My brother wanted me to move to Nyíregyháza with these papers because he felt that I would be less exposed in a provincial town. Little did he know that within a few days the Jews of Nyíregyháza would be herded together in a ghetto, himself included, and shortly afterwards deported to Auschwitz.

As I talked to the young man who brought me the documents, he struck me as very enterprising. He was evidently a commercial traveler, a salesman, who spent most of his time traveling in the provinces. He was willing to try anything that brought him some money. When I mentioned to him that I might be in need of some assistance and hinted at the rich rewards awaiting those who would help me, he appeared more than willing to be of service. He suggested that, as he was away most of the week, his wife would be glad to have my wife stay with her.

He was a complete stranger, but I took his name and address and arranged to contact him one weekend when he was in town.

After he had gone, I inspected the documents and the military papers thoroughly. They were just what I needed. So I became Elek Szabó. I decided to grow a moustache.

Having secured most of our personal documents, we had to consider who should disappear, when and how. In my view it was not a good idea for the family to stay together. It would be better if we each lived separately, independently. If we stayed together, the risk of betrayal or discovery was far higher. We had a better chance of survival if we lived apart.

It was most urgent to take care of my son Paul, who was already approaching his eighteenth birthday. He might be drafted for 'labor service' at any time. Jews were not considered good enough to be soldiers, but were put into labor battalions under military command. It was generally believed that the army was the only organization that did not permit the deportation of its members, not even the Jews on labor service.

So we had to decide whether to let our son be drafted or not.

His Christian papers were by now in order. If he did not report for labor service he could continue living as a Christian student. He could spend most of his time in libraries: such activity attracted little attention and in the mornings relatively few people visited libraries.

As for myself, I would have preferred to live in a hotel, with a swimming pool and other facilities, so that I would not have to go out much. I thought about the Lukács Spa or the Hotel Gellért, where they have everything under one roof, including athletic facilities. My wife, who, though I hardly merited it, seemed more concerned about my fate than I was, strongly protested against my plan. Many people meant many eyes, and the risk of recognition and betrayal in such a public place was accordingly much higher. One must disappear from sight.

A new plan began to take shape.

As the administrator of the building on Eskü Square, I knew its layout pretty well. The building manager and his family could be trusted: they had, after all, given me their documents. On the ground floor of the house, in the courtyard next to the entrance to the air-raid shelter, there was a tiny windowless room, generally used to store furniture. If I could adapt this room to my purposes, I could stay there for the short time needed for the Nazis to fall. The building was well located on the bank of the Danube, just a step away from the Rudas Baths, where I could swim in the mornings. So I would get my daily exercise. At night, when it was dark, I could walk along the river.

But it seemed a boring proposition to live alone in such a hole. If I were a bachelor I could have invited a member of the opposite sex to share my solitude, but for a married man with two children this was hardly a possibility.

Finally I decided on Lajos Ozma as a possible partner. He was one of the most successful architects and interior decorators in Budapest. He and his family were friends of ours and I was especially fond of his rather temperamental younger daughter, Zsuzsi. The elder daughter was also very attractive. Lajos was an artist with wide interests and a great deal of knowledge, somewhat older than myself, balding, but with a thick black moustache. He looked more like a Chinese mandarin than a Budapest Jew. Even his skin had a yellowish tinge and his eyes were a little slanted. At least, that's how I saw him. Maybe in the company of such a man and some good books it wouldn't be too hard to wait for the collapse of Nazism.

The building manager and his wife could get us our meals from a restaurant. There were three famous restaurants in the vicinity: the old Kriszt Restaurant and the modern restaurants in the Carlton and Bristol hotels. We could have our dinner brought every day from a different restaurant, giving us more variety and causing less suspicion.

I discussed the plan with Lajos and he enthusiastically agreed.

So I commissioned him as architect to make our hiding-place as safe and comfortable as possible. He had to take proper care of ventilation, electricity, sink, toilet, and so on, and also make sure that no sign of life could be seen from outside. For added safety a buzzer was installed, with a push-button in the building manager's office. Signals could be of varying length, depending on the nature of the danger. In an emergency we could run down to the air-raid shelter in a matter of seconds, where by pressing a button we could close a huge iron door behind us or, by crossing the full length of the shelter, walk through another door into a different street. The entrance to the courtyard was locked, which would give us time for these maneuvers. To use military terms, you could say that the arrangements seemed to be both strategically and tactically satisfactory. We had time to consider all eventualities in great detail, and the money involved was not a problem. In fact, the arrangements showed that we had both been avid readers of Jules Verne in our youth.

Only my poor mother-in-law, who lived in the house, could not understand why we were renovating the building in such uncertain times. Meanwhile I tried to make arrangements for her safety, too. I explained the danger that was threatening us. She did not believe me.

'They can't go around murdering innocent people,' she insisted; she was quite stubborn about it.

'Look, Mama, two beautiful young girls, relatives, who were living with you, simply disappeared, as you well know. We searched high and low and we still haven't found them. In fact, there's been no sign of life from them at all.'

'They've been taken away to work; that's why they don't write. Your brother Zoltán came back. Murdering innocent people isn't possible. It says so in the Bible.'

In an odd way she was right: it simply wasn't possible. Such things were happening around me, and I knew the facts, yet I continued to have this odd sense that somehow it wasn't true. In fact, the feeling has never left me.

Early in April the first air raid hit the southern part of Budapest. From then on, day and night, British or American planes flew over to bombard industrial targets. Many people attributed the raids to the persecution of the Jews, some suggesting that they confirmed all the stories of an international Jewish conspiracy and some assuming that they would continue until the murders and politicians stopped the torture.

The air raids created a new situation. Normal life disintegrated. The hospitals filled with the wounded, and places had to be found for those made homeless. As a result, there were so many changes of address reported to the police that not much attention was paid to Jews registering under false names. Oddly, I and my fellow-sufferers had little fear of the raids, though the bombing was certainly no picnic. I was visiting someone when the first raid occurred. My host had other guests, and, to avoid drawing attention to the size of the group, I said I would stay in the apartment and not go to the air-raid shelter. It was hardly pleasant to hear the explosions getting closer and closer: with every explosion I was afraid that the building was going to collapse. But, in spite of my fear, I was pleased – as I was whenever a raid took place. Of course, it helped to have a decent air-raid shelter and pleasant company while the raids were going on.

Our lives and those of the almost one million Hungarian Jews depended not on the bombing raids but on the military contest between Russia and Germany. It was a race against time. Would the Russians succeed in driving the Germans from the Carpathian basin before the Germans had time to complete their extermination program? I followed every move of the Russian army on the Eastern Front with rapt attention, listening to the BBC several times a day. Just one breakthrough, and hundreds of thousands of lives might be saved.

Chapter 7

Among Forgers

M y frantic search for documents kept me fully occupied. I looked everywhere. My circle of relatives and friends was so extensive that even the huge collection I had already amassed was not enough to take care of them. And the more documents I obtained, the more I seemed to need: no longer willing to limit my efforts to births, marriages and deaths, I felt that I needed to back these basic certificates up with additional confirming documents relating to personal identity, occupation, and other relevant matters.

It may seem strange, but I even used chance meetings on the street to continue the search. I noticed that a middle-aged woman of forty or so, with suntanned features, came regularly to the park across the street from our building. She was accompanied by two children, whom she brought there to play. She always spoke German with the children, and her accent indicated that she came from somewhere in northern Germany. One day I spoke to her.

'Aren't you from Berlin?'

'Yes.'

She explained that she had lived in Berlin and married a Hungarian. Her husband had died and so she was now a widow. Fine. We met on several occasions.

One day I was clearly in a bad mood, because she asked: 'What's the matter? Something bad has happened.'

On an impulse I decided to reveal my identity. 'I have plenty to be worried about. I'm Jewish.'

When she didn't reply I continued: 'I ought not to tell you this, but I trust you. I'm living in hiding under an assumed identity. I've obtained papers for most of my family but I still need some more and I'm stuck. Perhaps you could help me.'

I looked at her. I couldn't decide how she was taking my words.

'There's a seventeen-year-old girl I need papers for.'

I had in mind my elder son's girlfriend, a charming, dark-eyed, shy girl who had nobody to look after her. Her mother had died a year earlier and her father and brother were away on wartime service

'I wish you could meet her. I am sure you would want to help.'

The woman had tears in her eyes. She whispered, 'I also have a confession to make. I'm Jewish too. I escaped from Germany. If you knew what I've been through!'

I was startled. She began telling me all her troubles. Suddenly our roles were reversed: I had hoped for her sympathy, but now it was my turn to console her. I had taken a big risk in revealing my Jewishness to a stranger, but without risks we gain nothing. Without risks, there's no life.

And her confession was even more dramatic than mine. I realized that I had found yet another person whose well-being I could hardly ignore. We agreed that I would visit her home the next day and discuss what we could do. She lived in Buda, in a poorly furnished, or rather unfurnished, maid's room. I went to the meeting well prepared.

First I showed her the residence certificates from Sold.

'*Nicht anrühren!* Don't touch them. This is amateur work. The circle on the stamp has been drawn with a compass. Look!'

She held the little slips up to the light. I could see the pinpoint in the center of the circle where the compass had gone through the paper. I was embarrassed. I felt like a naughty child caught in the act. You had to be blind not to see the hole in the middle of the stamp. I suddenly realized why my friend Sold had been acting so strangely lately and why he wouldn't accept larger orders and made only partial deliveries: when we first started working together he had failed to mention the fact that the papers were not originals but forgeries, and later on he didn't have the courage to confess it. Wishing to minimize the potential damage, he provided me with only a few blank forms, despite my requests for more. Even so, his deceit could have been disastrous. The danger lay not in the fact that the documents were forged, but in that they were such primitive forgeries and that their users would not be aware of it. Such documents should clearly only be presented in extreme necessity, as a last resort. I was very upset at his irresponsible behavior. At the very least he should get rid of the hole in the middle of the stamp. Was he perhaps as inattentive as I was and simply hadn't noticed the hole?

I told my friend Ozma about my meeting with the German woman and the discovery of the problems with the forms. He didn't seem unduly distressed, and there was a mocking twinkle in his eye.

'This is no laughing matter,' I said.

'Look,' he replied, reassuringly, 'I've got this terrific address for you – an authentic peacetime forger. But first I have to get his permission, because when he did my documents for me he made me swear not to give his address away without his permission.'

The permission was forthcoming, and next day I set off, with a good deal of curiosity, to visit the 'maestro' at his fourth-floor apartment across from the Western Station. An elderly woman opened the door on Berlini Square and ushered me in. There were several tall bookcases in the living room, but the apartment looked much like any other three-room apartment. A tall, thin man, aged about fifty and quite bald, greeted me. He was not alone, so I simply mentioned Ozma and asked him when I might visit him to discuss my business.

'Early in the morning.'

'How early? I'm an early riser.'

'As early as seven, if you like. You may find me still in bed.'

Exactly at seven the following morning I was there. The maestro was in bed, clad in rather splendid pajamas. At first the conversation was strictly business. He stated his terms.

'One document costs 600 pengős. I need to have all the details when you place the order. It's best if you type them rather than writing them out by hand. The documents will be ready for you to pick up in twenty-four hours. I must have payment in advance, because you never know what might happen. Special orders cost more.'

'What do you mean by special orders?'

My question revealed that I was an amateur in these matters. It brought an immediate reaction.

'Do you think I enjoy doing this kind of mass production?' he asked angrily. 'I don't deny that it pays well compared to the kind of really challenging and complicated work that I used to do. But the quality! The quality of the work is nothing to what it used to be. Imagine how it was, back in the old days, when someone wanted, say, the title of royal chamberlain. You had to prove that eight patrilineal and matrilineal relatives were members of the nobility. Think of the effort, the study, the heraldic research that had to be done! Getting all the details and then painting the coats of arms could take months, years even. But today . . .' His voice trailed off and was replaced by a gesture of despair. 'Today all the work and care and study that I devoted my life to is worth nothing. Today all they want is stamped forms. Quality means nothing. You should know that when I copy a signature it's indistinguishable from the real thing. Even the writer can't tell the difference.'

I expressed my incredulity with a slight movement of the head and muttered something under my newly grown moustache. He took it as a challenge to his veracity.

He jumped out of bed and said excitedly, 'Let's do a little test, sir. Sign your name on this piece of paper.'

He gave me a piece of paper and pushed his pen into my hand. I signed my name. Holding the paper with his right hand and writing backwards with the left, he copied my name three times in a row. Each signature was exactly like the other. One might almost say that the copies were better than the original. I felt that I should express my admiration for his artistic skill. I searched for the right word.

'Remarkable,' I said.

My recognition of his talents visibly pleased him.

'When I have time, dear Doctor, I will show you my collection of signatures. There isn't a public figure in the country whose signature I don't have in my collection. I've got the original signature of every priest and every registrar in Hungary, down to the smallest of villages.

'Amazing,' I said, still incredulous. 'How did you manage that?'

'Quite simple. I sent each of them a printed letter asking them for a short sketch of their lives and a signed photo. I told them it would be published free of charge in the projected volume *Who's Who in Hungary*. The book never came out, but I got all the signatures.'

After that, I used to call on my friend the forger quite frequently, always in the early morning. I had good reason for choosing that time for my visits. As a lawyer I was familiar with the usual working hours of the police. Early-morning arrests were rare, because 'the authorities' tended to make their arrests during normal working hours, or in the nighttime hours after midnight if they needed to take someone by surprise.

I had to be circumspect in every way. So I told the elevator operator that I wanted the fifth floor, where there was a dental laboratory, rather than the fourth. After a while, she let me operate the lift myself. I just had to be sure to send it back down to the ground floor, since otherwise she would have to climb up to the top of the building to get it.

My friendship with the forger grew steadily deeper. More precisely, he grew increasingly fond of me and was glad to have somebody around to whom he could pour out his artist's heart.

'You know, Doctor I can't go on like this for long. True, I earn quite a lot, but it's very dangerous. Soon I'll give it up.'

This had me worried. I didn't want this comfortable and reliable source to dry up.

'When?'

'I haven't decided. Obviously, first I have to complete the orders I have in hand. But, as far as I'm concerned, the sooner the better.'

He took my orders and added, 'I don't really understand why I didn't give it up long ago. Maybe I'm greedy. It's hard to turn down a good income. Do you know how much I make a day? Three thousand pengős! As much as the prime minister makes in a month. But I would like to think that the real reason why I keep going is because I don't want to leave my clients in the lurch. They really need me, some of them.'

'I understand your dilemma,' I said sympathetically.

The course of events brought me into contact with a lot of other people, including other forgers. But I never found anyone quite as proud of his profession as my friend Miksa.

Chapter 8

Provincial Ghettos

n May 1944 a secret decree was issued ordering the establishment of ghettos in various parts of the country. The newspapers said nothing about the decree, but rumors and stories soon reached us.

The first time our circle of friends became aware of this latest horror was when the tragic news reached us about the suicide of a couple who were good friends of many of us. Dr Heller was a well-known Budapest physician who spent the war years working in a provincial town. His wife was famous for her beauty and charm. The two of them decided that they would rather die than enter a ghetto.

Here in the city, the situation seemed less perilous, but stories of suicides increased. On one occasion, during a visit with friends, I tried to convince them that the best solution was to get hold of forged papers and simply disappear, but they were not convinced that the future of the Jews was as black as I made it appear. None the less, a couple of days later, I learned that the wife had tried to commit suicide. It was only later that I found out why. It seems that her family lived in the provinces and when word reached her that they had all been locked up in ghettos, she slit her wrists. At about that same time Uncle Elemér, president of my ski club, killed himself. This old man was a great lover of life. His parents had been elevated to the nobility by Emperor Franz Josef, and he himself was a high-ranking judge, now retired, but as he contemplated the approaching storm clouds he chose instead eternal peace. The wave of suicides went on, all across the country.

In a few days I had occasion to get direct information about the horrors of the ghetto in Nyíregyháza. One morning a woman appeared, looking for me. She was a blonde, energetic-looking woman, dressed in the uniform of the Red Cross. She asked me, in not very good Hungarian, whether I could give protection to my brother's daughter Eva and her fiancé's family, whom she had succeeded in rescuing from the Nyíregyháza ghetto.

I was surprised that they felt they needed to ask. Within minutes the little company arrived, exhausted from the overnight trip and especially from the horrors preceding it. Their report revealed the extent of the hell on earth the Jews were being pushed into. The miserable people, exhausted and in fear for their lives, were herded together in their own filth, with insufficient food and with no opportunity even to wash themselves.

Most unfortunate of all were those whom their jailers believed to have buried treasure – gold or banknotes. In fact, a kind of ghoulish gold rush had apparently set in among the police and their accomplices, who tried every means to get these poor people to tell them where they had hidden their valuables. Their methods were simple: they kept beating their victims until they ran out of strength. There were still some people who refused to say a word. These 'stubborn' people were simply beaten and tortured to death. Others, unable to withstand the torturer, confessed. But many of these people in fact had no hidden gold and simply confessed to avoid the beating. The urgency and brutality of these attacks surely meant that transportation to Germany was not far off.

These stories touched me more deeply than I can say, but I felt that I could not surrender to despair: if I lost my head, I would lose everything else. I suffered not only for my brothers and my sister in the ghetto, but for everyone imprisoned there. I determined there and then to stay fit and in good humor so that I might do everything I could to help.

I entertained the five new arrivals in the Hungarian fashion. Every delicacy that the pantry contained was put on the table. Our guests, along with the Red Cross nurse, were treated to an ample breakfast. Eva, my niece, at the first available opportunity, whispered in my ear that the nurse had rescued them from the ghetto for a considerable sum of money and that she was in fact a Polish Jew. My enthusiasm for her was somewhat dampened, but I didn't let it show.

As we ate, I asked her, 'How do you get to travel freely around the country?'

'I'm certified by the Red Cross to accompany the sick.' She showed me her certificate.

Here was further proof of the power of the printed word. Despite the fact that I knew she was a Polish Jew, it did not even occur to me that the certificate might be false. That piece of information came out only later. After my exhausted relatives had retired and she and I were alone, the subject of forged documents came up. She was quite charming, and it may be that the hearty breakfast helped. She immediately proposed that we work together, and gave me an address and a password.

Early next morning, I went to the address she had given me. The place was in the suburbs. I looked around very carefully and, seeing nothing suspicious, went in. A soft-spoken, mild-mannered Slovak youth greeted me. Mentioning the name of the nurse, I said, without further explanation, 'I need papers.'

My friend Miksa dealt only in certificates of birth, marriage, and death, but I needed lots of other documents – labor permits, military papers, identification cards with photographs, ration cards, and so on. The boys also needed Levente cards.

'Let me show you my samples,' he said, opening a large book containing sample documents all neatly alphabetized. I always admire other people's orderliness, and in this case I was also impressed by the sheer quantity of material before me.

'I deliver orders within forty-eight hours,' he declared.

For a start, I ordered three identification cards and provided him with photographs. He charged 800 pengős for the three, which was very reasonable. Delivery was right on time. While I was paying for the order, he and I struck up a conversation. He spoke Hungarian with a strong accent.

'How long have you been living in Hungary?' I asked.

'I escaped from Slovakia two years ago, when the Jewish persecutions started.'

'How are things here?'

'I speak Hungarian pretty well, and so far everything is going fine. I've been in this business since April.'

'You've not had any trouble?'

'Only once. I was visiting the office of one of the big companies in town when the place was raided. The police asked everybody for identification papers. I had what I needed, but the police wanted to know what I was doing there. I told them I was a bookkeeper and had come for some figures, and I waved what looked like a ledger at them. Thank God, they didn't ask to see it, but just let me go. I could hardly catch my breath when I got to the street. If I'd been religious, I would have recited the prayer for deliverance from special danger, or whatever it's called. The ledger, needless to say, was my document collection.'

You had to have luck on your side during these perilous times – and it seems that my new friend lost it rather quickly. When I went looking for him a few days later, he was nowhere to be seen. I was told that the police had arrested him. He was never seen again.

In the meantime I discovered the simplest way to obtain a genuine identification card. It was as easy as taking candy from a baby. All you had to do was obtain a monthly streetcar pass. You could buy these commuter passes on the spot, complete with photograph, just by putting down your money and giving them a name. They didn't ask to see any identification.

Another inexpensive way to get identification documents, which I discovered only later, was through the parish offices or the city registry, where you could obtain certified copies of original certificates. The anti-Jewish laws limited the lives and the movements of Jews in all kinds of ways, but the officials forgot to instruct the registries not to give out copies of papers to anyone who wanted them. I was constantly surprised at how quickly and efficiently requests were filled by the registries: clearly 'they' didn't yet realize how many Jews were trying to start a new life, with new papers. It's also possible that only lawyers knew about such means of obtaining documents.

But I was careful not to recommend this way of proceeding for general purposes. There was always the danger that an eagle-eyed inspector would notice the recent date of issue on a document and become suspicious.

The requirement to wear the yellow star made it impossible to appear in public. The only place where we met people was the air-raid shelter. And of course for the moment the apartment was still ours. The early afternoons found us already assembled for a game of bridge, which took place each week either at our place or at the Avases', our neighbors across the street, the game continuing until dinner time. The customary friendly ribbing that accompanied the game – 'Come on, hurry up and make your mistake!' or 'You could use my brains now!' – sounded a little hollow to me, knowing that there were Jews in the next room newly smuggled out of the horrors of Nyíregyháza and trying, so quietly, to survive in their new exiled circumstances.

The Red Cross 'nurse' directed two more groups to my place, since she had confidence in me. I didn't have the heart to refuse. Fear alone would have been justification for refusal, but I was really not worried that any of the tenants would take notice of my numerous new visitors and go to the police: I did not have enemies. Not only did I not have enemies, but people sensed that they could depend on me perhaps rather more than on many others.

Just one example: in those days nobody liked to go out at night, on unlighted streets. On more than one occasion, in an emergency, someone rang my bell in the middle of the night and asked permission to use the telephone. People preferred to wake me rather than venture out into the street to the public phone. They were sure I wouldn't make a scene, or throw them out. There were fifty apartments in the building, and I doubt if any of our neighbors would have let anyone in come into their apartments in the middle of the night.

If anyone asked for my help, one of my principles in life was never to say no – if only to avoid diminishing their faith in human beings. I felt that I was just a little responsible for everyone. My willingness to help was sincere, but my prudence dictated certain limits. I never refused a loan, not even when my funds were low, though sometimes, as a sign of good intentions, I had to give only part of the money requested. I tried always to exercise common sense and to stay within realistic boundaries.

I wanted my sons to understand this principle, too. I explained it to them like this: 'Whenever the anticipated results exceed the energy or sacrifice involved, you've got to help. Don't shrink from sacrifice if it means more to the recipient than the effort you have to put into it.'

Thus I applied Ostwald's 'energetic imperative' to human relations.

To apply such principles you need a measure of financial independence. I tended to present rather larger bills to my wealthy clients to help me finance my philanthropic tendencies towards others. As a result, in small matters or for people who had very little, Gentiles and Jews alike, I did not have to ask for payment.

It is remarkable how powerful instinct is, in people as in animals. In general, people knew when to turn to me for a loan. In earlier days aspiring young artists used to seek me out, when I had money, and managed to unload their paintings on me, the good and the bad. Somehow, during the lean periods, when I had very little money, they knew enough to stay away.

Next to the apartment, the air-raid shelter became the chief center of social life. The air-raid sirens sounded frequently, and, when we heard them go off, we all ran down the back stairs into the basement, which had been converted to a shelter. Little by little the family and I got to know everyone in the building. Because I never lost my good humor and kept an optimistic view of life, people tended to seek me out, especially Jews and converts, listening very happily to my oft-repeated prophecies that Hitler would surely come to grief sooner or later. I firmly believed it.

I provided advice to several of them on obtaining documents inexpensively. In so doing, I made the acquaintance of two very attractive young women, who were not only Jewish but Orthodox Jews. Emi was the sister, and Piri the wife, of a wealthy textile manufacturer. Piri explained that her husband was so devout that she had had to shave her head for their wedding ceremony. She was so elegant and beautiful that I had difficulty believing her story -- at which she removed her wig and revealed a head as bald as a baby's. I joked around with the two of them: they were both of them young and attractive and I found their conversation provocative. But I noticed that – unconsciously, but perhaps out of female jealousy – each was careful that the other did not spend too much time with me. But I had other things on my mind than sexual adventures. In fact the sexual urge seemed less and less important: just staying alive, the most important instinct of all, absorbed all my energies.

It was from these two young Orthodox Jewish women that I heard the first details about the German death camps. What they told me meant that the postcard from Waldsee that I had received from my sister after she was deported from Nyíregyháza was her last greeting and merely veiled the truth about Auschwitz.

My new acquaintances also enjoyed good relations with several members of the Jewish Council, or their sons, and from them they received up-to-date information. They explained to me, in confidence, that someone had succeeded in getting out of the death camp at Auschwitz and had told the whole story. There was a copy of his statement at the Council office with details of the German atrocities. We talked a lot about how we might escape, though they saw the escape route in a quite different direction from mine: their goal was to buy their freedom with cash and gold.

Through them I met a number of refugees from the ghetto in the city of Győr, including the president of the Orthodox religious community. He was a paunchy, balding fellow of fifty or fifty-five. In one of our numerous conversations I mentioned to him that I totally disapproved of the policies of the Jewish Council.

'So what would you suggest?' he asked, narrowing his eyes. It was clear from his expression that he had little confidence in the views of a 'secular' Jew. I, on the other hand, was only too happy to give a religious leader the benefit of my ideas.

'There are two possibilities. One: Hitler wins. In that case they'll wipe the Jews out, or, as the Nazis delicately put it, there will be no *Lebensraum* for Jews. Two: despite the stories about wonder weapons, the Germans lose the war. In my view, there are plenty of clear signs that things are going in this direction – air raids in the west, the steady retreat of the Germans in the east. So we need to be ready for the second possibility. The goal for the Jews ought to be simply to survive the next few months until the fall of Hitler finally occurs. How can we survive? You'll probably be surprised at my answer. Survival will be possible only if the Jews don't allow themselves to be herded into ghettos or other convenient collection points, and if they pay no attention to their leaders and do their best to get out on their own.

'The Jewish Council should resign and disappear. In fact, the leaders of the Jewish congregations should have gone underground long since. If they had, there would have been no responsible people on whom the Germans could rely to tyrannize over the Jews. But there's one thing the council should do before it resigns: it should sell off all its real estate as quickly as possible. Right now, that would actually be possible: with inflation at the present rate, there would be no shortage of Christian buyers willing to make a quick decision to buy. This would give the council members several million pengős, which they could give to needy Jews, who would need money to survive. A few weeks from now, the Jewish community will lose the real estate anyway, because the Germans will simply confiscate it, just as they've confiscated our gold and jewelry.'

Even as I was talking, I knew that I was simply beating my head against a wall. People prefer to stay on the well-trodden road. People with power don't easily give it up. But it was evident from his expression that my words got through to him.

Finally he said, 'The shepherd cannot abandon his flock.'

He promised to convey my ideas to the leaders of the council, but of course nothing happened: everything continued to go just as the Germans ordained it. The inertia that prevents people from accepting new ideas worked much as it usually does.

Meanwhile, terrified Jews whispered the news to one another. People began to disappear from the streets. Boxcars packed with miserable Jews rolled out of the country on a daily basis – at a time when there was a desperate need for the cars for other purposes. As many as eighty or eighty-five men, women and children were jammed into a single car. They locked the doors on them without bothering to give them anything to drink or any access to toilets. The guards acted with extraordinary brutality when they closed the doors: they simply broke the arms and legs that got in the way. Occasionally the railroad workers took pity on the captives, but if they tried to help they were beaten, or in some cases shoved into the cars themselves.

Rumors were everywhere. Following an interment at the Jewish cemetery, the mourning relatives were dragged into a truck and taken away to an unknown destination. Five men on labor service, who were simply passing through Nagyvárad, were pulled off the train and dumped in the ghetto, and then in due course shipped off to an extermination camp. The Nagyvárad story was especially worrying because my son Paul had reached conscription age and his draft papers for labor service might come at any moment. In fact, on May 31 the papers arrived.

Chapter 9

Exodus

P aul was raised from a very early age to be independent. He did well at sports – swimming, skiing, rowing, boxing, tennis. As an accomplished athlete he was used to sizing things up rapidly and making split-second decisions. I thought it best to let him decide what course to follow regarding his draft papers.

Another young man, Tom, who lived in the same building, received his draft papers at the same time as Paul. He also had his false documents ready. That evening I sat down with the two of them. Rather like a judge summing up the facts of the case, I did my best to lay out the situation for them as objectively as I could.

'Consider your options. The simplest and easiest thing to do would be simply to obey the order and report for duty. But once you're in, the whole situation changes. If later on you want to get out, you'll be classified as deserters. Not only that: you'll put everyone else at risk, because they may punish the other people in your unit as an example. If you choose not to go, you won't be considered deserters, because only those who have actually been sworn in under military law can be labeled deserters. Failure to answer your draft papers is a small crime by comparison. Of course, no one can predict how they will apply this law to Jews.

But one thing is certain: if you don't go, you'll put only yourselves at risk and no one else. If you do go, and then choose to desert, you will cause problems for your fellow-workers whether you mean to or not.'

The boys listened attentively and in silence, their faces somber.

'Sleep on it. You have until tomorrow morning to make a decision.'

In the morning Paul told me that he was not going to answer the draft order. I never asked him how he slept that night.

Tom, on the other hand, decided to go.

How fateful that decision turned out to be. Tom never came back.

My son rapidly took leave of his old life. Within minutes he gathered up his new identity papers and his new Levente card, which had previously belonged to a Christian. He put a huge backpack on his back, with a blanket strapped to the top, and over his left shoulder a canteen and a mess-kit. All of this was his mother's idea – despite my resistance – because it would make him look like everyone else reporting for wartime service. She was all for following the formalities, and she was eager to give the neighbors the impression that Paul was answering the draft call. And so he left the house.

Our lanky and overloaded boy set out to begin a new life under the name of József Balázs. The family drama was beginning. He also took with him a little fatherly advice: I suggested that he go straight to the washroom at the train station and cut off his yellow star. If it left a mark on his jacket, he should simply forget the jacket as well. Then he could leave his backpack and the rest of his junk at the left-luggage office and head out to find a room to rent. He also had his false identity papers with him.

All that day I kept wondering how he was doing. Next morning, around six o'clock, the doorbell rang. I jumped out of bed and ran to the door. There stood my much loved elder son, as weighed down as when he left. I let him in.

'What happened?'

He shook his clothes as though he was trying to brush something off.

'I did what you told me to do. I found a room to rent in Rákóczi Street. But there were so many bedbugs in the bed that I couldn't get any sleep at all. I woke up the landlady, but she said there was nothing she could do, because the house backed on to a department store and there was no way of exterminating them. She admitted that the place was uninhabitable and gave me my money back. So I simply sat up and waited for the morning.'

Meanwhile my wife was awake. Concerned that we might end up with an infestation too, she immediately moved into action.

'Into the bathroom, and don't drop any samples along the way! And check your clothes really carefully.'

The poor boy obeyed without a murmur. So again there was a family breakfast, again a mother's kiss, and again Paul sneaked out down the staircase, but now, given his recent experience, he was determined to check his room carefully before renting it. After much searching, he eventually found a small but clean room in Verpeléti Street, originally a maid's room.

With Paul's departure, it was now fourteen-year-old George's turn to slip away. George was the special favorite of my Christian barber, who had been cutting his hair for the past ten years and was a great admirer of his wit. His *bons mots*, even as a little fellow, were a source of amusement for all of us.

Once, when he was about five years old, someone asked him, 'What kind of man is your father?'

'He's a married bachelor,' George announced.

Another time, when he could not have been much older, I noticed he had become unusually polite to everybody in the elevator, greeting people, pressing the button, holding the door open, wishing them good day as they left.

I asked him, 'What's got into you, George? You're never as polite as that at home.'

'But, Daddy, on the elevator I have to stay polite only for a minute or so, and I can have a lot of effect on a lot of people.'

The barber promised to work something out for George. First he did a thorough review of his various clients, and, after much softening up, he broached the subject with a Mr Baufluss, who was an official at the Ministry of Agriculture. Mr Baufluss was of German origin, a jovial, pink fellow, who couldn't be all bad, as the saying goes, since he was extremely fond of strong drink and fast women. We said nothing about money, but that night, when we drank a toast to our friendship, I slipped him a few thousand.

Baufluss was charged by the ministry with inventorying confiscated Jewish estates. He was home only at weekends; the rest of his time he spent taking inventory in the provinces. During the week George passed his time alone in Baufluss's apartment. Lacking anything else to do, he caught the attention of some of his schoolmates, who lived in the building across the way. Communicating by hand signals, they seemed surprised to see him holed up in somebody else's house. The following week the kind-hearted Baufluss, in an effort to cheer the unhappy lad up, took him off with him to the provinces. At the time he was working in Transdanubia, west of Budapest, on the model estate of a Jewish aristocrat, Baron Móric Kornfeld. There they were wined and dined by what was left of the staff. George also met several other ministry officials, who immediately took a liking to the young man, the alleged godson of Mr Baufluss. He even helped with the inventory. Surrounded by good company, he quickly regained his spirits. On Saturday he returned to Budapest.

Next day, Baufluss gave him permission to go out to the Budapest hills. George enjoyed his freedom and independence like a young colt let out to pasture. Budapest is beautifully situated: from the hilltops surrounding the city there is a lovely view of the Danube. He headed out to Gugger Hill, which he knew pretty well, but in the bright sunlight he lost his way in the woods. He had gone no more than a few kilometers when he came upon a guard, who asked for his identity card. He showed him his Levente card, with the name Sándor Kiss on it.

'Okay. You can continue.'

As soon as he was out of sight of the guard George realized that he must have crossed the Budapest city limits. Within the city, the police were responsible for law and order, but guards patrolled the area beyond and in effect surrounded the city. Their only purpose was to catch Jews trying to get out. The boundary was a good seven miles from the city center, so there was plenty of room for long walks or family excursions. Going beyond it was taking an unnecessary risk.

One of my son's friends, Jeremias, was not so lucky. He was a handsome, dark-skinned boy with flashing dark eyes. He was headed for Lupa Island, where our family also had a summer place. At the railroad station he was asked for his documents. He didn't have his identity card with him, so they arrested him and deported him to Germany. At the camp the commandant took a shine to the handsome young man and sent him to the Sonderkommandos as a courier. In June he showed up in Hungary in his fine new uniform. He visited his parents. In fact, he was extremely proud of his position and showed no inclination to leave it. Neither we nor he then knew that after a time (generally around three months) everyone who worked for the Sonderkommandos was shipped off to the gas ovens – even those whose work was exemplary.

The fate of the Sonderkommandos is reminiscent of an ancient barbarous custom. Legend tells us that all the soldiers who buried Attila the Hun were cut down, every last one, so that his burial place would remain forever a secret. And Solomon, King of Judah, known for his wisdom, had three hundred builders of the temple in Jerusalem killed, or so the legend goes. People responsible for building amazing buildings, or people with special secrets, tended to get murdered for reasons of security. In effect, Hitler revived this ancient custom with the Sonderkommandos. It's hard even to imagine the kind of world we lived in at that time.

It was even harder to introduce my two female family members to Gentile society.

My mother-in-law was a sensitive person, but stubborn. She simply couldn't imagine the dangers surrounding her and she rejected out of hand all my suggestions about taking on a false identity and disappearing.

'No, no,' she replied, every time I mentioned the idea . . .

It was only when I located a former governess of the children, who lived on the outskirts of Budapest and was married to a railroad clerk, that she agreed to give up her six-room luxury apartment, where she lived alone, and move into a simple two-room apartment in Alag, where she would live with the entire family of the governess and her husband.

As for my wife, she and I agreed on only one thing – that we agreed on nothing. Needless to say, we were in complete disagreement on how to organize our new life. My goal was to arrange matters in such a way that we could maintain our comfortable standard of living, and our lives could move forward under the most agreeable circumstances possible. I refused a job in a brickworks because I knew that the further down the social scale you go, the harder you have to work, because it gets easier to check on your actual output. If they had offered me the job of manager, I might have taken it. For intellectuals, physical labor is doubly difficult: their heads are always somewhere else and their hearts are not in their work.

My wife was so worried and flustered that it was clear I had to take immediate action. The order that we all wear yellow stars had been particularly upsetting to her. Anyone watching her bitter expression as she sewed the yellow star on to our various garments could see that here was a woman whose very individuality had been wounded, in ways that were perhaps irreparable. She sewed as though she were sewing her winding sheet. After the boys left, the worry and uncertainty increased. She got sick. The doctor diagnosed an ulcer, known at the time as 'the Jewish disease'. I suggested that she move to the Lukács baths, where she could swim, sunbathe, rest. She was dead set against the idea.

But then she remembered Zavics, who had invited us to share his home. In my heart of hearts I was against this plan, but I was too tired to resist. That weekend we went to see Zavics, who promised everything, even the stars in the sky; he had just received his call-up papers and his biggest concern was not leaving his wife alone with two children. He accompanied my wife to the housing office, with a forged change-of-address form.

I used the time until she could move in to coach her in all the details of her new identity. Even the smallest matters were backed up with documents. Her name as of now was Julia Bessenyei, the name on the birth certificate of Mrs Balázs, the wife of my building manager. She was the forty-year-old daughter of a noble Hungarian family, unmarried, who had worked as a typist in a large firm in Berlin before and during the war. She had suffered a nervous breakdown during the bombings, lost her job and returned home for additional medical treatment.

I constructed the German part of her history for several reasons. First, I had been director of two German companies, and their stationery and seals were in my desk drawer; secondly, the Germans impressed people so much with their success that I figured German documents would be more readily believed. But the main reason was the fact that Hungarian papers could be checked easily enough, but, given the growing wartime chaos, it was almost impossible to verify German ones. I wanted my wife to answer any and all questions calmly, and so I made up all kinds of difficult questions, which she learned to answer pretty well. The object of the exercise was to prevent her from stumbling if the police questioned her. Since the documents said she was Catholic, I had a friend coach her in the catechism

And so all members of my family went their various ways. No one asked for money in return for providing lodgings, but I thought that I should give a few thousand pengős to each of our collaborators, to cover their costs; I also of course provided money to my family members. So my supply of cash was seriously diminished.

Help came from two sources.

A decree was issued requiring reports on all Jewish property. These reports were supposed to be extremely detailed, and such items as gold, jewelry and radios had to be handed over right away. Many people found it hard to catalogue their valuables, furniture, and so on, and came to me for advice as a lawyer. As I listened I realized that many of them were much wealthier than I had thought. Without my asking, they paid me generously for my services: I recommended only a formal report and a symbolic transfer of property, taking advantage of the increasing wartime confusion. In essence, I proposed sabotaging the regulations. The advice pleased them because it offered the best chance of defending their material interests. It had the added advantage of creating less work for me. The declarations were duly sent to the finance office, where four rooms were set aside for them, and there they sat. No one visited the rooms, and the reports were not so much as touched for the rest of the time Hitler was in power.

Further help came from the sale of an additional membership certificate in the Order of Heroes. For this certificate I received not 5,000 but 10,000 pengős. The Gentile partner of the famous lawyer-politician Paál bought it, as I discovered, for his brother-in-law. Paál was one of ten former students of the Piarist School in Budapest who had married girls from families of Jewish extraction. His wife was the granddaughter of the patriarch of the Schlesinger family, who played an important role in Hungarian economic and social life in the early years of the century. Schlesinger also became a member of parliament. When another member uttered an offensive remark about his Jewishness, Schlesinger, as the times required, challenged him to a duel. Such a challenge had to be accepted, even if the challenger was a Jew. Schlesinger had never fenced in his life, and his seconds urged him on with shouts of 'Don't give up, Schlesinger!' He didn't, and he ended up wounding his opponent. The occasion became legendary, and 'Don't give up, Schlesinger!' became a standard expression. After the old man died, the family abandoned Judaism and became good, some might say too good, Catholics. In fact, his daughter became so devout that she had an altar built on the lawn of her summer house.

The grandson, for whom my friend bought the certificate, was something of a playboy who simply disregarded all the Jewish laws. Every day he continued to visit the fashionable restaurants and dance halls, right up to the time of the siege, when they were all closed down.

I bumped into him after the war and asked the then usual question: 'How did you get through the hard times?'

'Dead easy,' he said, snapping his fingers. 'Only once did I run into trouble. Some shit-head denounced me as a Jew. Detectives came looking for me at my apartment and, when they didn't find me at home, left a summons to appear at their headquarters at nine o'clock the following morning.'

'So I guess you moved out right away, so they couldn't find you.'

'Not at all. I had this terrific document, and wherever I showed it all doors were opened for me. Next morning I duly appeared at headquarters waving the document and shouting indignantly, "How dare you molest a Hero!" The head detective was so upset by my tone of voice and the certificate that he kept apologizing over and over and let me go. For the rest of the war I was never bothered again.'

I did not reveal how well I knew this remarkable document with its inadequate seal. I took note of the fact that self-assurance is more important than any document. If I had been in that situation, I would not have had the nerve to try to get out of it by waving a forged document in the faces of a collection of detectives.

My connection with Paál turned out to be not only a source of income, but also a means of making contact with the so-called 'English resistance' in Budapest. I had been trying for some time to make contact with the underground movement, where I thought I could perhaps be of some use. I was aware of the fact that several anglophile Hungarians had got together 'underground' under the leadership of an English major, who had remained in the country, by accident or design, during the war. Through Paál's influence I met some of them, but, except for one occasion, all I got to do was practice my English. It was not the kind of underground movement I had in mind, or else they were not willing to let me in on it.

Paál asked for my help in another confidential matter: finding a place for a young Jewish friend of theirs, now hiding out in their villa in the Buda Hills. Since I intended to leave my apartment as soon as possible, I suggested that he register him at my address, without giving much thought to the fact that maybe the new formal tenants would not find the presence of a Jewish boy exactly agreeable. Paál accepted my offer. We did not meet again for the rest of the war. Paál himself was called up and went to the front, though by the time we said goodbye to one another we were certain that the Germans were going to lose the war. Something else also increased my confidence: Paál told me that the family planned to give up their villa and move into the Ritz, at the time the most elegant and expensive hotel in Budapest. Knowing that I spoke Russian well, he asked me, if the Russians occupied Budapest, to go to the hotel and take an interest in the family. I was flattered that a Gentile was willing to entrust his family to me.

And so we took our leave.

So my friend Paál and I had taken care of the outcome of the war. Unfortunately, reality was different: things did not move quite as fast as we expected. By June it was certainly clear that the German star was in decline. The British and Americans were not only victorious in Africa but had also advanced through Italy as far as Rome. The Russians launched an offensive that took them almost to Iaşi, in Romania. It goes without saying that the progress of the Allied advance was altogether too slow for me. The heaviest burden in all of this fell on the Russians. They had plenty of reason for feeling that progress was too slow and that there was a need to open a second European front. A story circulating at the time says it all.

A British and American military delegation arrives in Russia. At the airport they are received by a Russian military delegation. They are ushered into a large carriage and set out across the steppes.

After a while, the driver shouts, '*Volki!*' (Wolves!)

A Russian officer at once jumps up. 'Allow me!'

He climbs down from the carriage and fights the wolves with his bare hands until they finally kill him. Meanwhile the carriage continues on its way. After a while, another shout: '*Volki*!'

A second Russian officer heads out and fights to his death with the wolves. And so it continues. Finally, once again the driver shouts: '*Volki!*'

Dead silence; no one steps forward. The British field marshal looks around. There are no Russian officers left in the carriage.

At this point he declares, 'Gentlemen, there's nothing for it: we'll have to use our rifles.'

Chapter 10

June 6, 1944: D-Day

Finally, the Allies invaded Europe, on the Normandy beaches. Exciting times! We were able to catch our first broadcast on June 8th. Eisenhower said that his confidence in his troops was fully justified: the invasion was a success! Hurrah! If the diabolical German troops were destroyed fast enough, the Jews would be saved. Our hopes rose.

But instead of easing up, rules and regulations against the Jews grew stricter. Hordes of police and officials made sure that the regulations were enforced. A further problem was the fact that liberal and progressive newspapers had ceased publication: only pro-Nazi, anti-Jew publications continued to appear.

'Jews have to be treated like bedbugs' was our tormenters' motto.

Remarkably, the majority of the population refused to be incited by such things, but individual excesses increased, and there was growing brutality.

The right to persecute Jews, promulgated by the newspapers, began to have a negative effect on the entire moral climate. Illegal actions, if they were committed against Jews, went unpunished. In some cases it transpired that entrepreneurs promised to smuggle Jews out of the country (mainly to Romania), then killed them along the way to acquire their possessions and their money.

Because attacks on the life and property of Jews went unpunished, criminals were encouraged in their feeling that this was open season. I recall one case in which someone murdered a Gentile. 'I thought he was a Jew, and that it was all right to murder Jews,' was his defense.

I know of only one case in which a Jew had his revenge.

I was alone in the house one afternoon when the doorbell rang. It was Jancsi Danyi, a young boxing champion and a good friend of my elder son. He practically fell into the hall when I opened the door.

'Help, Uncle Tivadar,' he panted. His face was bathed in perspiration, his clothes filthy.

'Is there anyone else here?' he whispered, looking around.

'No one. Calm down. Have a glass of water. You're all right.'

I knew that something extraordinary must have happened. It was several minutes before my young friend regained his composure sufficiently to tell me his story:

'I was taking a girl home over the Margaret Bridge on the Number 2 streetcar. You know, that sweet little blonde I was with at your summer place on Lupa Island. We were standing there waiting for the streetcar to start, when suddenly someone yelled at me, "Jew, get out!" and hit me in the face twice. I didn't mind the punches so much as the embarrassment in front of my girl. As I got off, he pointed to a house in front of me: "Get in there!" I did what I was told, but I felt the anger rising inside me, and my larynx was jiggling up and down as though it would jump out of its place. The moment we were inside I turned on him and, without thinking twice, punched him in the belly with one hand and bashed his chin with the other. He must have bitten his tongue, because he started bleeding all over me and collapsed in a heap. I got scared. I couldn't see straight: all I could see was red. I don't remember what I did afterwards, whether I hit him again, or whether I simply ran away. What shall I do, Uncle Tiv?'

'First, go into the bathroom and wash. And get those bloodstains out of your clothes.'

I thought it best to go down myself to check on the situation and find out what had happened to the would-be persecutor.

'I'll be back in a moment,' I said, and ran out.

I went by foot, since the place was not far away. There were a few people hanging around, so I started up a conversation and discovered that the young man was conscious when the ambulance took him away. I hastened to take this good news back to Jancsi.

Although his action certainly fitted my belief that attacking Jews should be made as costly as possible, I warned him that next time he should be more careful. He should act on judgment, not impulse. Jancsi was not only a good friend of my son but also flattered me by telling me that he considered me his foster-father – his 'educational father', as he put it. He tended to share with me things he would not dare tell his parents, to get my advice. Amazing things were always happening to him because he reacted to all events differently from the way most of the rest of us do.

To please him, I offered him a cookie of a kind no longer available in the city. He ate it with much pleasure and, when he was completely relaxed, confided in me.

'You should know, Uncle Tiv, but don't repeat it to anyone, that my Christian boxer friends, among them the three Torma brothers, have sewn yellow stars on their chests, and if anyone makes an offensive remark they beat him up.'

As he was talking, I remembered having seen someone recently who was wearing a yellow star, but one not properly sewn on and not made of the prescribed material. This was the explanation of the mystery. It was good to know that there were people out there who, out of a sense of humanity, even if only to satisfy their fighting instincts, were willing to make common cause with the Jews.

But one other mystery I never did solve. People had stuck yellow stars on several statues and pictures of Christ in various parts of town. I never discovered whether it was Jews or Gentiles who did it.

That evening Paál's protégé, the young Jewish college student, moved in. He was twenty-one, the spoiled son of a bank director, who could hold a brilliant discourse on quantum theory or Einstein's theory of relativity, but was totally ignorant of the practical matters of everyday living. In fact, a typical theoretical scientist. I myself enjoyed daydreaming and avoiding routine responsibilities, but his nonchalance toward the necessities of life was simply amazing; I could only admire and envy him. The very first night he left all the lights burning in his room; next morning when I showed him how to prepare his breakfast, he took the tea kettle off, but left the gas on. He would rather not eat than bother with plates, utensils, food. Here was a scientific schlemiel, who none the less somehow managed to survive the Nazis.

The person who was to take over the apartment after our departure had been carefully chosen. She was a former secretary, a serious blonde girl, naturally Gentile, a typical career girl. She had started out as a maid, but her ambition was to become a secretary. So she learned to type, to do shorthand, and so on. Now, as a 'Jewish mercenary', she found herself tenant of a four-room apartment in the best section of town. She had the further advantage that I had paid a year's rent in advance.

Those Gentiles who helped to save Jewish property, either out of friendship or for reasons of gain, were tagged 'Jewish mercenaries' by the newspapers. A wealthy Jew needed five or six such mercenaries to spread his possessions around: he could not leave everything with one person, not only because of the laws against Jews but also because of the normal wartime risks. We gave our things to so many people that in the end we were hard put to remember who had what.

Margit, the secretary, was very happy with the apartment. She was hopeful that it would help her advance an affair of the heart: she was in love with a Slovak confectioner, who kept putting the wedding off. First, his documents hadn't arrived from Slovakia, then they didn't have anywhere to live. Now at least they had a place to live. But unfortunately this proved fatal. Her fiancé moved in, but spent his spare time with the building manager's sixteen-year-old daughter. The daughter was looking for adventure and certainly found it: she got pregnant. The building manager, who saw it as no joking matter, insisted that the confectioner marry his daughter. So Margit lost her fiancé.

But another incident also touched me. In the early days of their occupancy, my so-called tenants made the acquaintance of a leading Arrow-Crosser – a member of the Hungarian fascist party – who also lived in the building and who was a secretary of state. Imagine! A secretary of state! They were much impressed by his position and, willy-nilly, they were influenced by his anti-Semitic views. They asked me to move my young theoretical physicist out. I knew the secretary of the building manager and she was prepared to help rescue the young man, so fortunately I was able to arrange the move.

However, my own situation, as I had anticipated, was growing daily more difficult. So were my attempts to obtain documents, though I continued to do all I could to sabotage the rules of the Nazi regime. Miksa, the forger, continued his work, but how he had changed! The pressure and worry of his work unhinged him completely and he no longer knew what he was doing. He produced birth certificates of grandfather and grandchild written with the same ink and signed by the same registrar, although there were sixty years between them. Where the certificate asked 'Name of person declaring the birth', he wrote the name of the baby, and so on. Occasionally he mixed up the sexes, too. True, when his attention was called to the mistakes, he made out a new document without a murmur, and without charge, but often the new document had a new error. Sometimes I had to go back three or four times. Our morning conversations got shorter and shorter. We were like two disillusioned lovers who had nothing left to say and wanted to end the relationship. He became more and more morose and scarcely spoke at all.

The other forgers were no longer at their old addresses.

Later a new, brilliant technical development eased the situation, though at first people didn't trust it. Secret 'paper laundries' started to operate, where the written text of documents could be removed chemically without damaging the seal and signature of the registrar's office. Documents were returned as blank forms with seals attached. It was then possible to add suitable entries on the old documents. These paper laundries had the added advantage that they were cheap and that they eliminated the need for blank forms.

Experience revealed that people who went into the mass production of forged documents or opened paper laundries sooner or later fell into the hands of the police. This was generally as good as a death warrant. But unfortunately the lure of easy money made people lose all common sense: they were simply unable to stop their clandestine (though lifesaving) activities. I was careful not to get involved in the forging business as a steady occupation. I felt it my duty to get documents for my family and some close friends, but these people were carefully chosen and I made them all swear not to mention my name to anyone anywhere. Everyone promised and gave me their word of honor.

But it seems that the human need to communicate is stronger than the requirement to keep one's word. One morning, returning from some errands, I was dismayed to find six or eight strangers in front of the door. They moved aside to let me through.

'What do you want?' I asked the person closest to me, an elderly lady.

'Doctor, don't you know me? I'm Henrik Trenk's mother (Henrik was a dear colleague, now off doing labor service). In God's name, help me! I need documents.'

I knew immediately what to do.

'Calm yourself, my dear Mrs Trenk. I will be with you in a moment. I just have to check something.'

And with that I ran off as fast as I could. I sensed that only a radical step could save me. If that many people knew about my activities, I could not stay in my apartment any longer. In fact, I decided not so much as to cross the threshold from then on. I had already transferred the essentials from the apartment to my hiding-place. In the meantime, I moved over to my friend and bridge partner Avas on the next street, whose affairs I still had to arrange. He and his wife greeted me warmly. I decided to obtain documents for them as quickly as possible, and also for my friend Sugár, and then retire to my comfortable abode on Eskü Square.

That night the phone rang. They had already disconnected the telephones of the Jews, but Avas still had one, listed under the name of his 'Jewish mercenary' Felsőbati Kiss. Avas went to the phone.

'It's for you.' He handed me the receiver.

I had no idea who might be calling. I had told nobody where I was, and yet somehow someone knew enough to call me! A woman's voice. Mrs Henrik Trenk (I had spoken to her mother-in-law that morning).

'Doctor S! I have left my house. I've taken my father and my two children, but I can't stay here. My husband is off doing labor service and I know you're a good friend of his. I have no one else to turn to. In the name of God, help me!'

Despite my decision to abandon dangerous activities, I simply could not refuse such a heartfelt request. I told her I would help her. She came to see me right away and I arranged for her to receive the necessary documents at cost.

I should explain, by the way, that I had three different price categories for documents. First, I gave the documents completely free to people who were very close to me or in desperate straits. Second, from those people to whom I felt a moral obligation not to make a profit at their expense, I simply asked for my actual expenses, without consideration for the trouble or risk involved. Third, from my wealthy clients I asked for whatever the market would bear. In fact I had no particular limits for this category, or, as they say, there was no ceiling on the prices. Sometimes I received as much as twenty times the actual cost.

I wondered how Mrs Trenk had found out my new address. The answer was simple. Her mother-in-law knew of my friendship with Avas. After waiting around for a long while in front of my apartment, she finally went home, very disappointed, and decided to try their number, which she got from directory information without difficulty.

Such is human nature. Following Socrates' advice, I always tried to know myself. I was alarmed at how easily I changed my mind about things. Yet here I was, believing that I was persistent, obstinate, hard-nosed. I suppose these kinds of internal contrasts give people individuality. Since I am basically a moral person, I had to overcome my internal disinclination to make money by selling false documents. I knew then that you can't live by abstract principles, and that sometimes opportunism is a requirement of success. And people are right when they say that life is really the art of compromise. In other words, life involves balancing internal feelings and instincts against external requirements and needs. Keeping this balance is a necessary characteristic of people of talent.

Most people do not achieve success in proportion to their capabilities. Favorable circumstances play a vital role. The successful man is usually considered a clever man, because success is its own guarantee. The tendency to admire the success of mediocre people is of no great consequence, but it's unfortunate when a person who is merely lucky mistakes his success for wisdom.

I stayed with the Avas family for several days. Speaking of success, Avas himself was a good example of a successful man. He was over six feet tall, quiet, dignified. His appearance was impeccable: his suits came from the best tailors. During World War I, when the Crown Prince came to visit the front, they appointed him his adjutant, despite the fact that he was merely a member of the reserves, and a Jew to boot. He had hundreds of photographs showing him in the prince's company.

His wife was a veritable Rose of Sharon, with flashing black eyes, a beautiful complexion, flawless teeth and figure. I have never met a woman who could blush as prettily as she did. This may have been due to nothing more than vasometric disturbances, but to me it was extremely charming.

The truth is that I have always enjoyed the company of attractive people, regardless of their sex, and so I used to go out with the Avases frequently. Wherever the couple went, all eyes turned in their direction. If we went to dinner at the Ritz on a Saturday night, you could be sure that the prize of the evening would go to Mrs Avas, not entirely without the influence of the hotel manager, who also found her attractive. When we first met, they lived on Rumbach Street, which would have been the center of the ghetto, had there been a ghetto in those days. Our acquaintance slowly ripened into friendship, and this friendship changed their way of life completely: they took up rowing and swimming, learned to ski, and even started playing bridge on our trips abroad together.

Avas came to Budapest when I became a lawyer. He was practically my first client, and we frequently helped each other out. If he needed money to cover losses on the stock market, he turned to me, but more frequently it was I who benefited from him and his contacts. Avas was in arbitrage, but he didn't know the rules of the business terribly well. It was not unusual for him to come to me after closing a deal, to find out exactly what he had committed himself to. Except for his impeccable manners, he was really no better than average. It was remarkable how many people trusted him and asked for and followed his advice. Something emanated from his being and inspired other people with confidence. After carefully listening to his friends' problems, he would say 'Yes' or 'We need to think about that' or 'Possibly' – and his friends would go off convinced that they had received the best counsel possible. Paul brought me a lot of clients. In fact I owe the best client I ever had to him – the one who paid me the most money.

The name of Okányi Schwartz means as much in Hungary as Rothschild in the rest of Europe. On several occasions I heard my client protest at being called Okányi, claiming that his landed title, Fegyverneki, was more appropriate, the Fegyverneki branch of his family being richer at the time than the Okányi.

Schwartz asked Avas to recommend a lawyer, because his own had been drafted. He suggested me. Schwartz was not a man who made his mind up right away. He showed the list of recommended lawyers to the famous jurist Szala B., who happened to be his opponent's lawyer.

'Which lawyer would you choose from this list?'

'If the decision were left to me, I'd go for Tivadar, because he's pleasant to deal with.'

And so I became Schwartz's lawyer – and this alone provided a modest living.

Paul Avas's impressive appearance had such appeal that, besides the Jewish merchants from the provinces, his clients included wealthy members of the aristocracy from beyond the Danube. One of these, Felsőbati Kiss, who was related to Admiral Horthy, lent him his name during the Nazi regime, so he could continue his business in spite of the restrictions on Jews. He offered Paul and his wife the hospitality of his castle in the country, if the situation in Budapest became intolerable. Even in those days, when circumstances worsened, Paul's personality had such magic that many Jews entrusted their jewels and gold to him for safekeeping.

Avas had another unusual characteristic: you never saw him tense or nervous. He knew how to lose quietly, on the stock market or at cards. It seemed that this tranquillity was a part of his nature: there was nothing artificial or unnatural about it. He even kept his calm when he learned that, because of the opposition of Felsőbati Kiss's wife and son, he and his wife could not retreat to the castle after all. He turned to me for help.

My first thought was Alus, whom I had met recently through my barber, when I was looking for a way of hiding my son George in a Christian family. We could not come to an understanding, because of the rather severe conditions that he wished to impose on me. He regarded the matter not as a chance to help a charming and polite young man but as a business transaction. He even wanted to be paid if George failed to survive.

Alus was a tall, impressive-looking man, whose bearing showed he was used to giving orders. His wife was a well-turned-out elderly lady, with silver hair. They owned a sawmill and large tracts of forest in northern Hungary, in the area known as Felvidék. After tense negotiations that lasted for several days, we arrived at a complicated contract for the Avases, backed up with money and securities. It included the price he would get for hiding them, how much he would receive as collateral, and what premium he would receive in case of complete or partial success. The Avases were to help with forest work, and the Alus couple would also move down with them. The deal was made.

For safety's sake, Avas rented a three-room apartment under his new name in a brand-new building in Buda, at the end of town. He furnished it completely, down to a splendid phonograph and a good radio. The rent, in comparison to the old, rent-controlled apartments, was sky-high: one had to be a war-profiteer, a call-girl or a Jew in hiding to be able to afford it. But Avas was never one to haggle, and the officials handling the Jewish situation were not always as sharp-eyed as they needed to be. This apartment was temporarily at my disposal, since its purpose was simply to provide a place for the Avases if, for some reason connected with the war, they had to return to the city.

I was happy that the Avases were settled, but I had one more friend, named Sugár, whom I had promised to help. Since I did not want to participate actively in obtaining any more false papers, I carefully explained to him all the details and walked him as far as the door on Berlini Square, just in case he was not admitted; and I could use what was left of my charm by interceding personally. My intervention was not needed. All went well according to my instructions. We met again next morning at seven, when it was time for him to pick up the order. My friend went upstairs alone, but soon reappeared, greatly agitated.

'What happened?' I asked in alarm. At first he was at a loss for words.

'The old woman opened the door.'

'What did she say?'

'I'm not quite sure, but she muttered something about the police.'

'Wait here. Let me check.'

I ran into the building and rang the bell for the elevator. The superintendent's wife appeared. I gave her the customary pengö (three times the required payment) and got into the lift.

But she got in with me. 'I'm going up too.'

If my head had been working properly, I would have realized that something was wrong, because up to now my generous tips had bought me the privilege of running the lift myself. But I suspected nothing.

'Where to?' she asked.

Miksa the forger lived on the fourth floor, so I said, 'To the dental laboratory, on the fifth floor.'

I got out. The lift descended. I crept down the stairs from the fifth floor to the fourth, where Miksa lived.

His old sister, much agitated, answered the door. 'Haven't you heard? The police took Miksa.'

Without answering, I rushed downstairs, three steps at a time. The superintendent's wife was just leaving the elevator.

It was horrible to contemplate what might have happened if a guard had been posted after the arrest to catch anyone looking for Miksa. Clearly, the corrupt police had found so much money in the apartment that they were more interested in dividing the spoils than in apprehending the forger's customers.

After this fiasco, I could do nothing but take leave of my friend Sugár and head for the nearest streetcar stop. After a few minutes I was once again safe in my new hiding-place.

It was around eight o'clock in the morning when I arrived back at my new lodgings on Eskü Square. It promised to become a pleasant hiding-place. I was welcomed by my faithful Friday, the building manager, and his wife. The room was well equipped with summer and winter clothing, canned goods, jars of fruit and other non-perishable foodstuffs, such as coffee, tea, chocolate, rice. The goal was to make sure that any member of the family could find what was needed among these provisions.

The great moment arrived: I removed the yellow star from my clothing, and thereby broke with my former 'legal' identity. I looked carefully to see whether the star had left any marks. If a Jew was caught without a star, he was immediately deported, thereby reaching his destination, the death camp, even faster. It seemed to me that to be caught without a star one would have to be particularly unlucky, because if people saw a Jew they knew who was not wearing a star, they were surprised but they did not immediately run to the police. It would take a firm belief in National Socialism or a pretty deep personal hatred to cause somebody to take the trouble to go to the Party police and make a report.

I kept my new address a secret. Instead of giving people an address, I designated the nearby Belvárosi church, on Eskü Square, as a place where I could be found every Monday and Friday morning between eight and nine. I was certainly no church-goer, nor did I wish to profane the church with my worldly affairs, but I did not want to cut myself off completely from my friends and it was the closest public place to my hideaway.

Around nine o'clock my new room-mate, Ozma, arrived. We checked the technical equipment. We tried the emergency bell, which buzzed satisfactorily. The bathroom worked, and so did the house phone. The huge air-raid-shelter doors opened and closed easily. The shelves were filled with excellent books, which I had been planning to read for years but had never had the time.

In the street in front of the house, I came upon three beautifully bound German books – Stefan Zweig's *The World of Yesterday*, Freud's *Psychopathology of Everyday Life*, and Trotsky's *Russian Revolution*. Evidently their owner had chosen this unorthodox means of getting rid of them. I added them to the collection of books to be read, and resolved to read them all, now that fate had provided me with the time to do so.

The house was beautifully situated, in one of the quiet spots along the shore of the Danube. I loved the Danube and never tired of gazing at it. The water was always changing, yet always constant: it flowed on untiringly, but it changed color a thousand times. Strauss's waltz got it wrong: the Danube is not blue.

My earlier adventures of that morning were still vividly in my mind and I could hardly wait to tell it all to Ozma, who had originally made the contact between me and the forger.

He listened to my story silently, but with a certain sparkle in his eyes, then asked, 'And what would you have done if, when you rang the bell, a cop had opened the door?'

'I would have been so frightened I wouldn't have known what to say.'

'Well, that's exactly what happened to me: the police opened the door.'

'You must be joking,' I said incredulously.

'Not at all. It's God's truth. The guy asked for my identity papers.'

'And what did you show him?'

'My lieutenant's papers, the ones I got from Miksa.'

'And did he ask you what you were doing visiting a forger?'

'Of course. It so happened that some weeks ago, when I was passing through their kitchen, I noticed a beautiful piece of beef on their table. I hadn't seen beef in ages, and so I couldn't resist: I asked the old girl if I might have a little piece and I promised to replace it. She said yes. Yesterday I noticed a line in the street and when I heard that they were selling veal, I joined it. So I arrived at Miksa's place just when the police were there. It was easy enough to tell the truth: I was there to replace the meat I had taken. I even had it in my hand to prove it.'

'Poor Miksa's fate is sealed,' said Lajos. 'His worries are at an end.' And those two sentences were our obituary for Miksa.

The new hideaway on Eskü Square provided all the comforts, and we felt safe. Such a feeling of security is more important than the reality: one can be in mortal danger and not be afraid, as long as one is not fully aware of the situation. By the same token, one can be scared out of one's mind without any real reason.

The routine of our daily life soon began to take shape. At seven each morning we crossed the Danube to visit the swimming pool at the Rudas Baths. Coming home from our exercise, we tackled breakfast with a good appetite. For the rest of the day we read, rested, argued; and then in the evening we ventured out again for a long walk along the Danube, through the darkened city. But after a while we discovered that our hiding-place had one serious shortcoming that compromised our splendid isolation. Right next to the wall of our room was the toilet. I had not realized that a city ordinance allowed anyone to enter any apartment building to use the facilities in case of necessity, and required each apartment house to provide one toilet for the use of the public. Our toilet fitted the requirement of public toilet. The building manager was inclined simply to refuse entry to intruders, but I thought that inadvisable, because someone could always complain to the police. And we could ill afford to have dealings with the police. There was nothing for it but to wait calmly and quietly while people did their business, since any movement or sound on either side of the wall could be clearly heard. Our involuntary eavesdropping told us that the policeman assigned to our street often made use of the facility.

I vividly remember the day I first ventured out from my hideaway to the pool at the Rudas Baths. I had arranged to meet my younger son, George, at the streetcar stop in front of the building. There I was, waiting for him; as I scanned the approaching streetcar, I saw him near the exit. He got off, but instead of coming toward me, he bent down to look underneath, as if searching for something. As soon as the streetcar left, he picked something up from the rail, and then came over to greet me.

'What were you looking for down there?' I asked.

'My wrist watch. As I was getting off, it came off my wrist and fell on to the rail. Look.' And he pointed triumphantly to the flat metal disc that used to be his Swiss watch.

My son's movements were never too well coordinated, or, more simply put, he was all over the place. So I was not surprised that he had dropped his watch, with great precision, exactly on the rails.

I remember several examples of his carelessness. When he was six years old, the doctor prescribed temporary eye-glasses for him, to correct a small disorder. We bought glasses three times in a row, and three times in a row he lost them. The fourth time I refused to buy new ones and left the rest to nature. And he still doesn't wear glasses.

He got into trouble with his school report book, too. In this little book everything related to a pupil's conduct was duly noted. If he didn't turn up to school, or failed to do his homework, or received a disciplinary warning, these things were all duly written down. Two days after receiving it, George lost the book. His teacher asked the principal for another one, but unfortunately he lost that as well. At this point the principal gave him yet another book but warned him that if he lost this third one he wouldn't receive a replacement and would be thrown out of school. I will not try my reader's patience, and so I come straight to the point: he was clearly under some kind of curse because he managed to lose this one as well. He duly reported this tragic event to his teacher, and informed his parents that the teacher said that in a few days they would learn what action the school proposed to take. In a family conference we established, somewhat late in the day, that he did not have to carry the little book around with him, but was supposed to pin it to the inside of his school desk with a thumb tack, so that he wouldn't lose it. I prepared my son gently for the worst: if he was expelled, his academic career would be over and he would have to move in another direction. I suggested the traditional career of shoemaker's apprentice. The situation was such that only a miracle could save him – and of course the miracle happened.

Next day the teacher pressed a new book into George's hand and explained: 'I went into the principal's office yesterday and, seeing that he was busy, I kind of appropriated another booklet from his cabinet. Do you realize what this means? For you I've broken the ten commandments. From here on, don't count on me.'

That's the kind of kid George was. I didn't reproach him for the business about the watch; he could settle it with his own conscience.

We entered the swimming pool. Nothing had changed. The blue tiles on the bottom gave the water the same shade of blue that it had had ten years ago, when I lived in the neighborhood and spent a lot of time at the pool. The locker-room attendant was the same person. He recognized me immediately.

'Years ago, heaven knows how long ago now, you were a regular guest here. You always came with your little boy.' (He was referring to Paul.) 'You haven't changed a bit. What's the boy doing now?'

I had to be pretty creative in my response, to hide the reality. 'He's at military academy.' Jews never sent their sons there.

The fact that the attendant knew me as a lawyer turned out to be very useful later. Everybody has legal problems, even those at the bottom of the social ladder, but not everyone has a free lawyer. At first, just a few of the employees of the pool came to me for help, but my fame spread, like that of good wine, and soon the waiter in the restaurant, the chambermaid in the hotel, and even the assistant manager, began to seek my advice.

This friendly atmosphere was disturbed by one small incident – like a pebble tossed into a pond. On the roof of the building was a sundeck, with a splendid view of the city. Here I used to meet my two sons. To hide the fact that we belonged together, I made them change in separate cabins and tip the attendant individually.

Paul and I were in the pool one day when George appeared from the locker room. 'Dad, guess what happened. When I tipped the attendant he thanked me in the name of the religious community!'

Needless to say, the boy was alarmed at this odd remark. But, like the good researcher he later proved to be, he wanted to get to the bottom of the matter. So he asked, 'What religious community?'

'The Jewish religious community.'

And there it was. I knew my Budapest humor pretty well, but I wanted to establish whether the statement was meant as a joke or an insinuation. Our antennae were pretty sensitive in those days to anything that might threaten our lives. Hidden tensions accompanied our every move. So I immediately set about trying to discover the meaning of the episode.

I strolled around the building watching the behavior of the
attendants and the other employees, to see whether they were
acting differently in any way. First I spoke to the locker-room
attendant who had made the remark. He was the same as ever.
In fact, there were friendly faces and respectful greetings on all
sides – the kind of thing you would expect for a good customer
(to say nothing of one's unpaid lawyer). Outside, in front of
the building, we held a brief family conference and came to the
conclusion that the remark had been meant as a joke. When I
asked Ozma, he didn't disagree, but he did come to one important
conclusion: he would never so much as set foot in the place again.
At the time, to give up swimming was to give up one of the few
pleasures of life.

Chapter 11

Julia's Adventures

In the meantime, I resumed contact with the ladies of the family. In Alag I visited my mother-in-law, who was not too pleased with the general situation. I tried to calm her down by pointing out that Hitler and his people were bound to fall before very long.

I met my wife every third day in the Városliget, the City Park, which was close to her new home. Our first meeting convinced me that I had acted hastily in placing her with the Zavics family. There were four people in the one-room apartment: Mrs Zavics, her two children (twelve-year-old Annus and five-year-old Imi), and my wife.

'The dirt in the apartment is unimaginable! At night I can't sleep for the bedbugs. And if I put my mattress on the floor, cockroaches as thick as your finger crawl all over me. The walls are covered with spots from the bugs, the bed linen is dirty, and I won't even mention the toilet. I've been in the place for forty-eight hours now, but I still can't bring myself to use it.'

I was filled with heartache when I heard these complaints, as always when I find myself in a situation I can do nothing about. But it occurred to me that there were numbers of elegant restaurants and cafés in the neighborhood.

'Why don't you go to a decent café?' I asked.

The answer was touchingly simple: 'I'm afraid.'

I tried to convince her otherwise, but she kept repeating, 'I'm afraid.'

We finally decided that it would be best if she talked to the landlady and offered to pay for cleaning and painting the apartment, and also for exterminating the bugs. The cleaning operations began; most of the work was done by my wife, who tended to seek relief from worry and depression through physical activity and the tiredness that came from it. But, in spite of all the work involved, she still couldn't settle down. I had the impression that something else was worrying her that she not told me. After much prodding, she finally sighed, 'I think somebody's watching me.'

This piece of information didn't please me at all. I was afraid that it was a figment of her imagination, the first step on the way to a breakdown.

'What makes you think so?'

'That's the problem: there's nothing specific, just that people look at me in a peculiar way. I don't know what's so odd about me – my clothes, my behavior, my unhappy face?

As my wife was explaining her anxieties and her constant state of fear, I kept thinking that, once again, she had not taken my advice. Instead of buying cheap, ready-to-wear clothing in a department store, she had packed her own 'simple' dresses. It could well be that in this new setting their very simplicity was conspicuous – that the women in this neighborhood dressed more elaborately. Furthermore, she went around like someone on death row whose last appeal had just been turned down. I didn't have the heart to tell her all this, because even without my reproaches she was already in despair.

There was no point in tormenting her still further, so I said, 'Observe everything very carefully. If you see anything that confirms your fears, let me know right away. Then we can decide what to do next.'

We said goodbye. But I couldn't decide whether her fears were real or imaginary.

At our second or third meeting she reported that the apartment was beautifully clean, but that she now had proof that someone was spying on her.

'There was an air raid again last night, and as usual we all went down to the shelter. When the all-clear sounded, and people went back to their apartments, I was the last to leave, because I didn't want a lot of people noticing me. Right outside the exit there were a couple of teenage boys. As I went by, one of them whispered to the other, "Look, that's her." I recognized the boy because he comes to the apartment to visit Mrs Zavics's daughter. When I got back upstairs, I told Mrs Zavics what had happened. She was even more frightened at my story than I was. Apparently one of the boys has told her that the other is sympathetic to the Arrow-Crossers. She felt it would be best if I moved out right away. She suggested that I take Imi, her little boy, with me, for company, and go to the family's cottage outside town, at Érd. Her brother-in-law lives in Érd too. An additional advantage is the fact that he's the head of the local Arrow Cross Party, so he has lots of influence.'

'Sounds like a good idea. Go ahead. Today is Saturday, so, even if someone decides to report you, nothing much will happen until the offices open on Monday. Even if you left on Monday morning, you'd be all right. But I suggest you don't make friends with the fascist brother-in-law.'

My wife duly set out for the country much reassured, taking the child with her. The cottage was very primitive, but more agreeable than the apartment in town. There was a garden full of raspberry bushes and cherry trees, and the ripe juicy fruit was just for them. Never had fruit tasted better. Her simple clothes suited the simple life, and she went barefoot, as was customary in the village, in the same dress, or in a bathing suit, much like a summer resort. She soon developed a splendid tan, and her blue eyes looked even bluer.

So the days went by peacefully, and she and the boy observed the busy life of the ants, and followed the flight of the butterflies. But on the fifth day the tranquility was suddenly interrupted. Two policemen, on bicycles, stopped by the garden gate.

'We are looking for Julia Bessenyei,' said the older one, wiping the sweat from his face. He hardly needed to say so: my wife knew the two of them were there for her. But she also noted that they had come a long way, because the bicycles were very dusty and their riders extremely sweaty. So they could not be the local police; it was not the Arrow-Cross brother-in-law who had sent them. With this cool, logical reasoning a change came over her. At the moment when what she had always dreaded was actually happening, she felt an icy calm descending on her, of a kind she had never experienced before. There was nothing left to be afraid of. She felt that she had become two people, one looking over the shoulder of the other, to see how it behaves, and the other, under such observation, walking with sure steps toward the policemen and inviting them into the garden.

They sat on a wooden bench in front of the cottage. No sign of the usual Jewish uneasiness. There and then, Julia Beseny was born – and she calmly and quietly, more out of surprise than anxiety, waited for the two men to speak.

'First I want to check your identity papers. Then I want to know what you're doing here.'

One by one she took out her papers, waiting for them to ask for each one before she gave it to them.

'What kind of work did you do in Germany?'

She showed them the statement about her employment in Germany. They were visibly impressed. They looked at it, but since neither of them spoke German they had no idea what it said.

'Translate it.'

When she translated the statement that she was a typist, one of the policemen interrupted: 'Show us your typewriter.'

'I don't have it with me here.'

The translation went on. 'She was discharged because of illness.'

'Give us that typewriter,' one of them cut in.

Julia Beseny protested with a smile, 'I've already told you I haven't got one. If you don't believe me, come in and look through my things.'

The policemen turned everything upside down in the cottage, but found no typewriter. What they did find was a large box containing all sorts of medicines, which seemed to prove that she had come home from Germany for medical reasons. There were more questions about how she came to stay with the Zavics family and she had to explain why she had brought the boy out to the country to escape the air raids, but with this the interrogation came to an end.

The two men drew aside, exchanged a few words and proceeded to take down a written statement. Beads of sweat appeared on their foreheads: they were unaccustomed to desk work. The statement took them an hour.

'Julia Beseny,' said one of them, 'there was an anonymous report against you. You can read it if you like.'

They handed her a paper. 'The Zavicses are hiding a Jewess in their house,' it said, 'who types and distributes communist pamphlets.'

This explained why they were so intent on finding a typewriter. The anonymous denouncer had added an accusation of communism, as if being a Jew were not enough to get her deported. This excess of zeal may actually have made it easier for the police to believe that the whole accusation was without merit.

My wife happily signed the statement, which finished with the words 'The accusations proved to be unfounded.'

They then said a friendly goodbye to Julia, advising her to register as a resident of the village as well as a resident of the apartment in the city. That way, she wouldn't be bothered any more. With that, they got on their bicycles and pedaled away.

So my wife stood up beautifully to this ordeal by fire – and one would have thought it would help her to regain her assurance and feeling of security. But just the opposite happened. It was as if she had exhausted all her strength during those two concentrated hours of the interrogation. Alone with the child again, instead of triumph she felt only despair. Her confidence simply disintegrated and she was consumed by fear.

For one who is anxious even in daylight, the evening with its lengthening shadows, merging into complete darkness, holds indefinable terrors. Julia listened, terrified of the various noises that night outside the cottage, the soft rustlings and scrapings. When she ventured outside in the pale light of dawn, she of course found the source of the noises: a stray cat had evidently jumped on to the roof, the worn tarpaper making little cracking noises beneath its feet.

After the tortures of the night Julia felt that she could stay no longer.

'If they were to come back, I would be lost,' she thought.

Once again, she was racked in torment. Get out of here – that's the only thing to do. But what about the boy? She took Imi to his Arrow-Cross uncle and muttered something about being sick and needing to see a doctor. She was afraid to go to the train station because there was a police guard there. With her small suitcase she stood next to the road and waited for a good opportunity. A truck full of women factory workers was headed to Budapest. She raised her thumb and the truck stopped. A moment later she was on board and making a space to sit down. She was not alone now, but surrounded by other women, and she relaxed a little. Without incident she reached our central hiding-place at Eskü Square. Over a cup of tea the building manager told her that during the morning the family was at the Rudas Baths.

When I came out of the baths with the boys, there she was.

Slowly she told us the story. We were horrified to hear of her ordeal, but now the family was together again. She needed rest: she was a bundle of nerves. I could find no better solution than the Hotel Rudas itself. Like the baths, this modern hotel was the property of the city. In front of it was a little park resplendent with all manner of flowers. At the hotel, where people were really very friendly, she could even meet me and the boys each morning. She was delighted with this suggestion and moved into a quiet room right away. The room was comfortable, and the price was reasonable.

My wife stayed for a few days, enjoying the delights of the bathroom, and the gypsy music in the restaurant at night. During the day she took walks with the boys, drank in the fragrance of the flowers and listened to the birds. She had a chance to distinguish between the scent of violets and that of petunias. She became a mother and a lady again.

The days at the hotel were the happiest of our life in hiding. We lived like a carefree family on a summer vacation. My wife's will to live returned rapidly and she began to make plans for the future. As a young girl she had sometimes spent her summers at Lake Balaton. She decided she wanted to live there. She knew that all travelers had to show their identity papers, but she quite realistically concluded that if her papers were enough for the police they would be enough for the railroad officials. Evidently Julia had decided to live. She was back on her feet.

She chose Balatonalmádi as her destination because she knew Paul's girlfriend lived there in hiding, under the protection of her teacher. She felt that if she could occasionally get together with this young girl even for a few hours, that would make life much easier. She was very fond of Jutka with her soft-spoken, peaceful way of being. She also felt she would be safer in a country village where she knew no one. In the country she would feel better and her sense of security would return.

Chapter 12

Swimming Free

The Germans planned to solve the Jewish problem in Hungary along the usual National Socialist lines – but they differentiated between the capital and the country. In the country, the Jews were herded into ghettos and from there transported to extermination camps on German territory. We should note that this deportation was done with astonishing speed and efficiency, thanks to the cooperation of interior secretaries László Endre and László Baky – and this at a time when the fascists were already experiencing transportation difficulties, even for the most important and urgent of matters. In fact, Germany was suffering from an acute shortage of rolling-stock.

In Budapest the tactics were different from those in the provinces: in the capital lived foreign correspondents and members of the diplomatic corps, and the Germans were always eager to hide the extermination of the Jews from the world. It was this passion for secrecy that had led them to issue secret instructions that extermination sites should be made to look like labor camps, with '*Arbeit macht frei*' written over their gates. Even in front of the gas chambers they planted flowerbeds, and they made the installations look like disinfecting stations. So in Budapest, to keep the truth hidden, they chose not to create a ghetto. Instead, they first gave the Jewish Council five weeks to prepare a complete inventory of

Jewish homes. In fact, the council was so overzealous that it hired additional personnel and was finished with the job in three. This list formed the basis for the next step, consolidating the Jewish population. Instead of ghettos, the 150,000 Jews of Budapest had to move into so-called 'Jewish Houses' marked with the yellow Star of David. Buildings owned by Jews were chosen for this purpose. It was reckoned that three or four people could each be given one room.

The new regulations appeared on June 22 and five days were given to carry them out. In practice, things turned out very differently from the original plan. Whole families occupied every room in the apartments, even if the family consisted of eight or ten members. Theoretically the Gentile tenants were supposed to move out of the Jewish Houses, but many of them simply failed to do so. Either they did not trust the new regime or they were unable to move because they had no means of transporting their possessions. As for the Jews, they did their moving themselves, with handcarts.

Unfortunately the house on Eskü Square where we had our secret hiding-place was designated as a Jewish House. Although most of the building was occupied by the offices of the state-affiliated Csepel Free Port Authority, which immediately protested against this classification and refused to move out, the change upset our living arrangements. If they moved other Jews into the house, we could hardly use it as a place to hide. Furthermore, I was not sure that I could stand living there without making contact with the other Jews. So we had to make a decision: there were only a few days until moving day.

But even as we were trying to decide what to do, the building manager appeared with other news: 'The old lady has come home.'

Thus fate, a *deus ex machina*, intervened: my mother-in-law had left the village of Alag where she had been hiding and returned to her apartment. She had read in the newspaper that the building of which she was half-owner was to become a

Jewish House and so she thought it would be nice to come back.

'Mother, why in God's name have you done this? Don't you understand the danger? You're playing with fire. You had a nice place in Alag, with people you knew and trusted. Why didn't you stay?'

'I don't see any danger. They're not doing anything more than simply moving the Jews from one place to another. There's no ghetto, no deportation. And if my fellow-sufferers can stand it, I'll be happier here in my own home. Besides, I was bored in Alag.'

Such was her explanation. Even if she didn't say it, the truth was that she didn't want to leave her furniture unprotected if strangers were going to move in. We now saw no answer but to leave our hiding-place and find somewhere else to live, but without trying to create a new hideaway. Ozma never talked much, but when it came to action he always had secret connections. He immediately got in touch with an aunt of his who had escaped from Slovakia to Budapest and so, he presumed, would be familiar with the challenge of renting an apartment, since she had done so recently.

The aunt got us an apartment within twenty-four hours and gave us the address.

Vásár utca 2: 2 Vásár Street.

Chapter 13

Vásár utca 2

The house stood in the center of town, but in a tiny street away from the traffic, not far from the market place in Rákóczi Square. Before moving in, I scouted out the area. On the corner was a tavern, and across the street another. They were frequented primarily by workers from the market-hall and were open round the clock.

I went in and ordered a glass of beer. I had been there for no more than a few minutes when a man came over to my table.

'Want to buy a ration book? It's completely unused.'

Evidently I was sitting in the middle of a black-market operation in ration coupons. The price was low. I'm an easygoing type, but sometimes I like to know what's going on.

'If you sell your ration book, how will you buy food for yourself?'

'Listen, mate, don't worry about me. Look, we're porters here in the market-hall. Did you ever hear of a market porter without food? There's never been one, and there won't ever be, from now to doomsday.'

The new apartment, on the ground floor, consisted of two large rooms, kitchen, bathroom, maid's room. Ours was a large room with double windows giving on to the street and its own access to the apartment door. There were two beds, a sofa, and some additional pieces of furniture. It was neither better nor worse than the average sublet, but at least it was roomier.

Although I could have used a fake registration form and thereby avoided personal contact with the police, I decided to go and register in person. I wanted to see if I could do it. There was a long line of people at the registration office. The air raids had destroyed a large number of homes and the people who had been bombed out needed to move into new places. As I stood in the line I overheard numerous bitter remarks about the war: clearly the Gentiles weren't having a very easy life either. The police were glad enough to stamp the registration forms of these unhappy folk as fast as they could. They had neither the time nor the inclination to explore their faces to see whether any of them looked like Jews.

I took my lawful registration card, duly stamped, with me when Ozma and I called on our new landlady, who gave us a friendly welcome. In her youth she must have been very attractive. Now she was about fifty years old, round-faced and tending towards plumpness, but her eyes retained some of their youthful sparkle. Our general appearance, and our suitcases and clothes, evidently made a good impression. The introductions over, I tried to relax and get into some small talk. Remembering Paul's experience with bedbugs, as well as my wife's, I added 20 percent to the rent in return for a thorough cleaning and frequent changes of bedlinen. The landlady seemed pleased at this generous gesture.

Ozma introduced himself as an architect, and with his real name, but I had to say that I came from the provinces because my identification papers bore the stamp of the village of Tállya, a place famous for its vineyards. To keep things simple, I said I was a vineyard owner.

The landlady's face immediately brightened. 'Then we'll drink well for the rest of our lives,' she said.

'We have the wine; now all we need is the pork to go with it,' I replied, trying to hide my discomfort behind a common Hungarian saying. In the meantime the master of the house, the captain, had appeared, and we went into his room.

The landlord had been an army officer, but was pensioned off as a captain and assigned to work as an inspector in the ministry of agriculture. Though he no longer wore a uniform, everyone continued to call him captain. He was middle-aged, around fifty-five, blond, with regular features. He immediately addressed us in the second person singular, a sign that he regarded us as equals. He said relatively little in the course of our conversation, but it was clear that he was both impressed by the Germans and doubtful about their success. He admitted that he spoke not a word of German.

'*Aber die gnädige Frau spricht sicher Deutsch?* But your good wife certainly speaks some German?' I asked, to see whether either of them understood.

'I don't understand a single word you are saying,' she said.

Her negative reply was the most important outcome of our meeting. Next day, as the first order of business, I went out and bought a short-wave radio, one of the little German Tefag sets that had just come on to the market. I had long felt the lack of a radio in our living quarters. As a passionate listener in the old days, I felt I could now put my hand on the pulse of the world again.

It was dangerous to listen to programs in English, French or Russian, given that we were supposedly at war with them, but now I could happily listen to the German language service of the BBC. I need only take care that no one heard the BBC's call signal. To explain my interest in listening to the radio, I discreetly revealed that I was currently engaged in buying wine under contract for German firms, and for the German army. The letterhead and official stamps on my desk confirmed this. I arranged for the ten barrels of wine recently shipped to me from my vineyard in Pincehely and stored in the state warehouse at Budafok, to be transferred to my new name, Elek Szabó. Now I really had a few barrels of wine at my disposal, and this proved to be very useful later on. It was getting increasingly difficult to obtain any wine at all, and it was completely impossible to buy good wines. Wine is, of course, a national drink in Hungary, even if we also have our share of teetotalers.

So, right off the bat, I charmed my landlord by giving him twenty liters of good wine, without even asking the official price (as opposed to the much higher black-market price) for it.

'My dear Lexi, [the familiar form of Elek, my new name] you can't do that. I can't possibly accept such a gift!' protested the captain, who was afraid that if he accepted it as a gift, it would be awkward to ask for more next time. We agreed that in future I would charge the official price. The captain asked the same favor for some of his friends, and so from time to time I made out withdrawal slips for the wine.

Since the building manager in a Budapest apartment house knew everything that was going on, the building manager soon found out about this wine business too, and so he also had to receive his quota. It was true that the wine was good and the price low – because I was selling it at a tenth of what it would fetch on the open market – but to obtain it you had to take the streetcar, or, if the streetcars were not running, walk, to the outskirts of the city at Budafok. And if the air-raid sirens went off, it could take half the day to get back. But in a good cause a serious drinker does not mind the effort involved. Wine was, after all, a holy matter. I am bold enough to confess that through the charm of good wine I made myself the most popular person in the building. Everyone regarded me with a kind of pious veneration, and even people I had never seen before in my life greeted me as they passed

So things seemed to be running smoothly, in fact more smoothly than I had hoped. But one small episode made my blood run cold. I had been there for about a week when the landlady came rushing into my room.

'Now they're deporting the Jews from Újpest,' she cried. (Újpest was actually part of Budapest, but was a separate administrative unit.)

I made no move to rush out and see this spectacle, but asked with polite detachment, 'And what will happen to them?'

She made a clicking sound with her tongue as she drew her finger across her neck, as though she were cutting a chicken's throat. The gesture seemed to epitomize the poison at the heart of humanity. For days I could not get the sound or the gesture out of my head.

A couple of days later, I happened to overhear a conversation between Ozma and the landlady. Ozma had inquired about the former tenants of our room.

'Two young men, who moved in not long ago. I concluded they were probably Jews. When they refused to leave, I said I would report them to the police as Jews in hiding. That pulled them up short; they moved out immediately.'

So there was a dark drama behind our sublet. At this point the conversation took an unexpected turn. The landlady was speaking: 'You should take a good look at that Lexi, you know, Lajos. It looks to me as though there's something a bit Jewish about him.'

'We'd better tell him that to his face,' said Lajos, opening the door wide and smilingly repeating what the landlady had said. I was not entirely prepared for the question, but instinctively felt that I could best defend myself by laughing it off.

'It could be,' I replied good-humoredly. 'The Latin proverb says, "*Mater semper certa est*: the mother is always certain." But the father never. It could be that some adventurous great-great-grandmother committed an indiscretion.'

We all laughed, and the matter was not brought up again.

In those days I walked around the city a lot. Every morning I went to the swimming pool, where I met the boys. When I was through, I didn't return home immediately because I wanted to give the impression that I was a busy executive. The pool was a perfect place during air raids, because it had no shelter, so we could sit up on the sunroof and talk. If I was caught in an air raid later, in the middle of the day, I went to one of the public shelters in Buda, which turned out to be ideal places to conduct a kind of personal public opinion poll, since the alerts generally went on for two or three hours. On such occasions I did my best to channel general conversation toward the war or the Jewish problem. I found that people were motivated not so much by enthusiasm or hatred as by inertia and their desire for an easy life.

'The heck with it all; it's time we got it over with,' seemed to be the general mood.

Huge numbers of people continued to be fascinated with Hitler's personality and his career. On one of these occasions in the shelter I told the people around me the story of 'my meeting with Hitler.'

In 1936 the Winter Olympics were held in Garmisch-Partenkirchen. Hitler opened the festivities. It was snowing heavily. He spoke from a platform, clad in a raincoat. I was maybe 150 meters from him. As he was speaking, I moved steadily in his direction, looking neither left nor right. I was curious to find out how close I could get to him. The platform was high, so I kept him firmly in view. After a while, I fetched up against a human wall.

Someone yelled at me, 'Where are you going?'

In front of me stood a line of black-clad SS men, all extremely tall, their arms linked.

I muttered, somewhat uncertainly, '*Ich habe mich verirrt* (I've wandered in the wrong direction)' and I turned back.

Nobody touched me, I was not even searched. That was my story.

Hardly fifteen minutes had passed after my tale when there was suddenly a great commotion. They were looking for somebody . . . The somebody turned out to be me. The shelter commander appeared, surrounded by several officers. He clicked his heels and introduced the officers; I in turn introduced myself. It transpired that the air-defense commander, in great excitement that there was someone present who had seen Hitler, had radioed headquarters and a group had come over right away to see this privileged person. I had to tell my meager story again; they thanked me and left.

Besides conducting surveys, I had plenty of time to replenish my supplies of food, tobacco and fuel. Since I did not smoke, I passed my cigarettes on to people wearing the yellow star. They were allowed to leave their homes for only a few hours each day, to do their shopping. At the store, they had to stand in line. Those merchants who showed any sympathy for them were pilloried in the newspapers. The little time allotted for shopping was not enough to buy even the basic necessities, and so there was no time to purchase tobacco. And even if there was time, there was not always merchandise in the shops, sometimes only two or three times a week. One of my protégés was a watchmaker, who had special permission to work for a few hours a day. I regularly left a few packs of cigarettes at his shop for people with yellow stars.

Once I broke the glass on my watch and went to him to have it repaired. He fixed it.

'How much?' I asked.

'How can you ask such a thing? It's on the house.'

'This is the Christian gentleman who brings us cigarettes, you know,' he whispered to the woman working beside him.

At least the Jews got to see that there were still a few decent Christians . . .

Ozma spent most of his time at home. He was happy whenever I left the house and he could work in peace. He was working on a book, *Moderne Baukunst* (Modern Architecture), for a publisher in Zurich, and at the same time busily cultivating his friendship with our landlady. Ozma liked order: there was something of the pedant about him. His belongings were always neatly arranged and put away. I, on the other hand, left everything lying about. The landlady was completely captivated by Ozma's generosity, since he plied her with my various delicacies – chocolates and cigarettes, left around for all to see. Like all women, she had a certain natural curiosity and wanted Ozma to tell her everything about my personal life. Ozma was very careful to pass on to me the essence of these conversations, so that we could keep our stories straight. At one point he informed her that we were both separated from our wives, and that I would like eventually to remarry. I must be pretty well off, he said, given that I had vineyards in the best-known wine region in the country.

Armed with this information, our diplomatic landlady invited a female relative of hers, from the country, to come and meet me. She entertained me daily with anticipatory descriptions of the girl's beauty and charm. She turned out to be an attractive blonde of about thirty-five, with good teeth, but she hardly lived up to the advance billing. She had a charming singing voice, and since we did not have much to talk about, we sat around singing Hungarian folk songs. My repertoire of folk songs expanded considerably.

Ozma frequently asked, with a knowing smile, 'When do you plan to announce the engagement?'

The girl's visit to the city eventually drew to an end; needless to say I didn't declare my intentions. On her last visit she sang a song which always helped to boost my self-confidence, since she always directed it at me: it claimed that when I walked down the village street all the windows opened and a hundred girls turned to look at me. Her voice was more charming than ever that night. I wanted to be nice to her, so as not to hurt her pride.

'Allow me to thank you, Erzsike, for your kindness. I am so very sorry that our nightingale is leaving.'

'You really are a nice man, Lexi, but a mystery to me. You are not what people think you are.'

As if searching for words, she paused. I waited tensely to hear what her delicate female intuition had discovered.

'You don't act quite as one would expect. I just can't make you out. Maybe you don't have a wife at all.'

('All is well,' I reassured myself.)

'Believe me,' I said, 'I am as transparent as glass. But it bothers me that my divorce is not yet final. When it is, you will hear from me.'

Since I never carried a notebook, I wrote her address on a slip of paper and sealed our farewell with a kiss of her hand.

Chapter 14

Life in the Country

eanwhile, my wife continued to live in the village of Almádi. She rented a room at the house of a retired school principal, whose greatest ambition was to write fascist newspaper articles. As soon as she arrived, she set out to visit Jutka, who was staying at the house of her dancing teacher, named Brandeisz.

The Brandeisz family was of German origin. In winter they lived close to the city, in summer in a little one-room house at the end of the street in Almádi. Four of them shared the only room: old man Brandeisz himself, retired long since and now blind and deaf; his wife, Aunt Zsuzsi, a lovely lady, whose spiritualist inclinations helped her deal with the burdens of life; and their two daughters, both around forty. Erna was a remarkable gardener, whose talent was borne out by the marvelous grapes growing in their garden, and Elza was a dancing teacher. The room was hardly big enough for four, but this did not keep them from accommodating Jutka, too.

Jutka had a rather exciting trip down to Almádi. We had just finished getting her false documents together when a boy of about nineteen arrived, sent by Elza to accompany Jutka. This young middle-level aristocrat did not even know the girl, and simply volunteered for the job out of a heroic impulse to help the Jews.

But there was one thing he had not taken into consideration – his own basically weak nature. He sat there in the train white as a sheet, his lower lip trembling. In fact, every time he so much as saw a uniform he started to shake. If the conductor stepped into the compartment to check the tickets, he scared him half to death. Sitting next to this trembling boy, Jutka also began to feel uncomfortable, even when he made rather feeble efforts to entertain her. She would happily have sent him away, but did not want to hurt his feelings by revealing that she was aware of his behavior. In fact, the poor fellow was, in his way, a true hero because he had to fight constantly against his own cowardice. Both of them were much relieved when the train pulled into Almádi and Jutka was passed on to the ministrations of the Brandeisz family.

When my wife introduced herself to Aunt Zsuzsi, she was taken aback.

'We have already prepared a place for you here,' Aunt Zsuzsi declared, embracing her.

Julia was bewildered, but, knowing from Jutka that the old lady was a spiritualist, she thought that maybe the spirits had sent a message on her behalf.

'How could you possibly know that I was coming, dear Aunt Zsuzsi?'

The answer was not in the least spiritualist, but altogether practical: 'My dear, we have so much work to do here; we are glad if someone with two strong hands drops in.'

The two girls were away in the city because their apartment had been hit by a bomb. The large yard and the numerous animals were really too much for the old lady. Julia soon came to feel very much at home with these simple, eternally kind people. She went over to their house early each morning. The two girls returned after a while and she made friends with them, too, and also got to know the numerous other people who made up their extended circle of friends. Gradually she became acquainted with their lives and their challenges.

The war made it more and more difficult to look after the

family, and little by little Julia took over responsibility for the shopping. She visited the neighboring village of Felsőörs, which was eight kilometers, or two hours' walk, from Almádi. There she not only acquired food – milk, butter, eggs, and so on – using Aunt Zsuzsi's stocks of thread as barter, but also, like a true Red Cross nurse, bound up people's wounds, recommended various home remedies, and even gave useful advice to peasants caught up in legal problems (she had learned a lot from her lawyer husband). So the inhabitants of Felsőörs eagerly awaited Julia's twice-weekly visits, and they provided her with everything that a village farmer had to offer.

Julia's letters painted such a charming and attractive picture of life in the country and the kindness of the simple people, that my younger son, George, who was still living with the good-natured Baufluss, expressed a desire to visit his mother. His decision was also influenced by the discovery that Baufluss had a Jewish wife, and her daughter from her first marriage had to wear the yellow star; poor Baufluss had enough troubles trying to save his own family.

Julia met not only the villagers themselves, in the various local villages, but also people who, like herself, were just guests – that is, other Jews in hiding. Among these was Gergely, who – not for nothing was he a book dealer – provided the community with the best books.

He often advised Julia, 'Try to act very simply and naturally. Don't be too clever. It's not always his looks that give a Jew away; more often it is his restlessness, his ambition, the fact that he knows a little about everything, or thinks he does, that he has a story for everything, speaks several languages and waves his arms around a lot.'

When Julia was asked by Baron Laky (whose wife, it turned out, was Jewish) whether she played bridge, since they needed a fourth, she would have loved to accept the invitation, but remembering Gergely's warning, 'Don't be too smart', she sadly replied that she did not play.

The arrival of fourteen-year-old George was a great surprise to

Julia. It was my definite wish that they should not live together. She could introduce him as her godson, they could spend time together, but I insisted on my original principle: that each of them had to live through these difficult times separately. They found a little cottage on the vine slopes and Jutka and George moved into its single room. Maybe it was due to this – living at such close quarters with a girl two years his senior – that the boy asked his mother one day about the mysteries of sex. Her explanation must surely have been more thorough and successful than the one I gave to Paul, his brother, some eight or ten years earlier.

I vividly remember my wife's expression, practically gasping for air, when, during an autumn walk, the boy suddenly turned to her: 'Mother, what does the father do to make a baby?'

'You'd better ask your father,' she answered, and sent him to me so that she could avoid answering the question.

I rose to the occasion. 'Have you studied the patriarchs in your religious education?'

'Yes.'

'Well then, you know that Abraham begat Isaac, Isaac begat Esau and Jacob, Jacob begat Joseph. This begetting is the father's part. Get it?'

'Yes,' he said, and that was that.

George received rather more detailed information.

After George was enlightened, his mother jokingly warned Jutka the next time he saw her, 'Watch out, he knows everything.'

But their friendship was not disturbed, although the oddity of the situation was exacerbated by their false documents, according to which George was two years older and Jutka younger than they really were. But she was his brother's girlfriend and that made her taboo. They spent the rest of the summer together in the little cottage among the vines.

There they got acquainted with Uncle Mihálcsa. This scrawny, restless, fascinating man worked in the neighboring vineyard. He considered himself a good socialist and he tried to push our two young people in that direction. He taught them about the love of humankind and about mutual respect. He assumed that these children of the middle class would be full of prejudices, and it was his particular goal to rid them of such thoughts and feelings. He was strongly opposed to anti-Semitism and lost no opportunity to instruct them accordingly. The two young people proved avid listeners to his uncommonly intelligent views, and Uncle Mihálcsa didn't let a day go by without talking with them.

'Every aspect of life should be judged soberly and objectively. To hate someone just because of this or that religious belief, or because the color of his skin is different from yours – this is contrary to sober human logic. It's the person who matters, not his race, religion or color. The Greek philosopher Democritus once said that respect for others is the highest virtue. People should keep to one basic moral principle: don't do to others what you don't want them to do to you. This is hardly my original thought: Confucius, the Chinese philosopher, said it first. It's a sure way of judging human behavior and it will always stay current and applicable.'

His topics of conversation were inexhaustible: he had all kinds of interesting things to say about greed and about lust for power, and also about miserliness and waste. His lectures were later rehashed with Julia, when Jutka and George walked with her down to Priests' Beach or relaxed under the pine trees on the hillside. Often Elza joined them, too.

Perhaps because he swam a lot, George caught a cold at Lake Balaton and apparently contracted tonsillitis. At night he ran a high fever. Since the village doctor was a local Arrow Cross leader, my wife didn't dare call him in; she was afraid that an examination would reveal not only the boy's illness but his Jewish origin as well. Ultimately he overcame his sickness without benefit of doctors, either through Aunt Zsuzsi's home remedies and special teas or because of the natural strength of a youthful constitution.

I was very much put out when I learned later from our courier that there was no doctor looking after this serious illness.

In fact, news of the goings-on at Almádi generally reached me not through letters but by way of messengers. The shifts in the

Transdanubian front made the mails very uncertain. Besides, we didn't dare to write openly in our letters. What if they got into the wrong hands – those of the fascists, for example?

Two messengers brought the news from Almádi, both rather interesting characters.

One hot July morning a well-built blonde, deeply tanned, searched me out. It was Erna Brandeisz, sister of Jutka's dance teacher, with a message from Julia. In the course of the summer she visited me on two further occasions. Each time, the messages dealt mostly with George's illness. At the time, travel required extraordinary effort; even in the city the streetcars were barely functioning. I could not imagine what prompted Erna to go to so much trouble. As we said goodbye, I asked her where she was going.

'To the blind watchmaker, from our Bible circle,' she answered.

'May I escort you there?'

'Yes, of course. I don't like walking alone these days.'

I would have liked to find out more about her, but the conversation faltered. I inquired about her trip, commented on her deep tan, and finally, feeling I was getting nowhere, asked her outright, 'Erna, forgive me for asking, but why do you make these exhausting trips to Budapest?'

'For the Jews.'

'I don't understand. What has the fate of the Jews got to do with you?'

'I used to work for the Mauthner Company. Our head gardener was Jewish. I had a great deal of respect for him, and still do. I am trying to rescue him and take him down to Almádi, but so far without success, because he has a sick mother and won't leave her.'

'And why do you feel it so important to save the head gardener?'

'Don't you know that the Jews are the chosen people of God?'

I assured her that I knew.

The other messenger was an even more unsettling individual.

Karcsi was a member of the crew of a private yacht on Lake Balaton. He got to know Jutka and invited her to come and listen to English broadcasts on the boat. Jutka took Julia along as chaperone because she didn't want to go alone. In those days, listening to English news was a rare pleasure.

Karcsi also called on me a few times. He was a boy of twenty, with tanned good looks and a slight limp. They called him 'lame Karcsi' because of his deformed foot. I think I have rarely come upon a more confused person.

'I came at Julia's suggestion because I need some advice.' He hesitated a little, looked around, as if there might be a hidden microphone somewhere. 'It's a highly confidential matter.'

'I shall treat it as such,' I reassured him.

'Well, I've hidden a great deal of ammunition and firearms in the Bakony mountains. I also have a number of good friends who know how to handle a machine-gun.'

I thought I must be dealing with some kind of lunatic.

'Where did you get it all?' I asked.

'That's a secret I can't tell you,' he said mysteriously. 'But look at this.'

He opened his backpack. It was stuffed full with machine-gun parts and ammunition.

'My elder brother works for the British Secret Service.' He pronounced the words 'secret service' as though they were Hungarian, but with his particular dialect thrown in. So it took me a good deal of time to figure out what the *'shatsrat sharvitsa'* actually was.

'But I have a problem. I don't know whether to fight on the German side or the Russian. Both sides are pretty exhausted, and a well-armed group of fighters could make a decisive difference.'

'Well, which side appeals to you more?'

'I can't decide. The fact that my brother works for the Secret Service, and the British are allies of the Russians, would point towards the Russians, but somehow I don't like them. After all, communism is still communism. But I know the Germans are pigs. So I can't decide.'

'You came to me for advice. If you really want to know my opinion, I think the time is not yet ripe for intervention.'

I suggested he should wait and see, and promised to be at his disposal any time. After he left, I got to thinking. I should have thrown the fellow out, but I didn't want to complicate things for Julia and Jutka. But perhaps I was wrong? Perhaps I could have started a rebellion which, while it might have begun in confusion, could have ended up changing the map of the world? It happened with Muhammad and Ghengis Khan . . .

Both messengers, who were so helpful to me in keeping in touch with my wife, were clearly characters obsessed in their various ways. One was a bigoted member of a Biblical sect and the other was bent on seeking adventure under the spell of his big brother's employer, the Secret Service.

Chapter 15

Cat and Mouse

The situation on the various military fronts changed only very slowly; yet gradually, decisively, the superior power of the West made itself felt. The one event to bring hope – if only for a few hours – was the attempt to assassinate Hitler on July 20, 1944; but Hitler lived on, and two hundred conspirators, German officers, were put to death. Had they succeeded, the lives of several hundred thousand Jews, perhaps even millions, would have been spared. The conspiracy showed that the German people themselves had had enough of the Hitler regime.

With the war continuing – all-out war – and with the increasing shortage of raw materials and manpower, there was more and more talk in the Hungarian press about the need for 'economic exploitation' of the Jews. Rather more than 150,000 Jews were living in Budapest in the various Jewish Houses, where there was no useful work for them. Committees were set up in these houses to compile registers of able-bodied men and women. Lists were drawn up indicating which 'human material' should be deported and which should be interned within the country. There were even rumors of the preparation of proposals to the Western powers for the emigration or sale of the remaining Jewish population.

The Jews lived in stone buildings, but they were less secure than if they had been scattered across the high seas in open boats.

Our experience so far fully justified the road that we as a family had chosen to take: it seemed the only road to salvation. But, like beasts in the jungle, we had to be constantly on the alert to save our skins. We also had to be always ready for shifts and changes in the wartime landscape. Zavics, Baufluss, the place in Eskü Square – these were now all things of the past.

My son Paul drifted from place to place. First he worked for a fountain-pen manufacturer, where he was the only employee, but the place had to close because there were no raw materials. From there he went to a radio factory, but after taking a good look around he realized that pretty much all the employees were Jews in hiding. So it seemed advisable to leave: if the police came to arrest someone, they would check everyone else's documents.

After that, to pass the time profitably, he enrolled in various technical courses – welding, driving, appliance repair, and so on.

Close to where he lived, on the right bank of the Danube toward the southern edge of the city, was the Lágymányos tennis club. Paul watched the place from outside for hours, and when he was sure that there was no one around who would recognize him, he went in. He managed to obtain the club's permission to use the courts to practice, and he succeeded in persuading the occasional girl to stay with him into the evening to play singles, with the result that he ended up playing on the unlighted courts until well after dark. Even so, various people noticed how well he played, and the people at the club got enthusiastic about having this evidently talented player get some serious coaching. (In fact, there was no mystery to the quality of his game: from his childhood he had made full use of all opportunities for practice. Since he was ten, he had spent practically all his time in the summer on the tennis court next to our garden, and every week he played with a professional coach.) It was difficult for him to turn down this honor – the opportunity to play championship tennis for the club – but of course it would have been very dangerous, since he could so easily have run into people who knew him from before as a promising tennis player.

Change of living quarters became a constant characteristic of our new life. For various reasons, none of us seemed able to stay in our chosen homes. Now it was Paul's turn to move.

He had been living in a tiny maid's room near the Technical University, in the most heavily Gentile neighborhood of Buda. His room was so small that if he stretched out his toes would have reached into the next room. His landlady worked at the National Bank and was a great admirer of her former boss, the president of the bank, Béla Imrédy, the intransigent fascist politician who went on to become prime minister. When the public learned that one of his grandparents was Jewish, he was forced to resign as prime minister, but while he was still in power the Jews had him to thank for giving them a very hard time. His own Jewish origins must have triggered his anti-Semitism: converts are always the most devout believers.

This 'patriotic' lady was completely unable to understand why such a strong, skilled sportsman as Paul had not volunteered for the National Resistance Front (an anti-communist organization) or joined the army. My own suspicion was that this fascist true believer, through her constant nagging, was trying to move Paul out, given that rents were now running five times higher than when Paul signed his lease.

Paul grew increasingly nervous at the constant calls for military recruits, both volunteers and draftees, but he made no move until a decree drafting all eighteen-year-olds was issued. Even in his assumed identity as an unattached Christian, he was now under an obligation to sign up. With the help of a document laundry we changed his birth date to make him a seventeen-year-old again, but he had no option but to leave his current lodgings. He told his landlady that he was enlisting in the army.

She was so impressed that she rented the room at the same price to the boy Paul recommended – Jutka's elder brother, who had just escaped from the Jewish Labor Service. Evidently there were still people around who believed in the rightness of the idea of fascism. But such ideas, or ideals, led only to the murder, extermination,

butchery of millions of people. So I was hard put to it to praise
her kind heart or her generosity.

My son found new lodgings – with much difficulty – in the
home of a splendid couple. The husband was a communist and
the wife ran a spice shop, thereby proving that the gap between
communism and capitalism was not wholly unbridgeable. Through
this man I learned about the underground communist movement
and read its little newsletter, sometimes two, sometimes four pages
long, which came out every week.

As the war dragged on, it became more and more obvious to
me that there was no way of saving the Jews as a group. By the
beginning of July those in the provinces had already been hauled
away. Maybe 5 percent of the Budapest Jews had got themselves
forged identity papers, but the rest looked passively to the future
with a kind of dark and resigned foreboding. Increasingly, the
cruel treatment of those drafted into the Jewish Labor Service was
becoming common knowledge. Savage 'trainers' and labor camp
officers tormented their charges to death, with the result that more
and more young men chose to escape, having lost confidence in
the notion that as members of the Labor Service they had a better
chance of staying alive until the war ended.

While all this was going on, a rumor spread that Jews who
converted to Christianity stood a better chance of reasonable
treatment than the others. A special order was issued by the
Jewish Labor Service decreeing that recent converts could wear
a white armband instead of the usual yellow one. The newspapers
announced that conversions occurring before August 1, 1944,
would be 'state-recognized'. No one, of course, had any idea
what 'state-recognized' meant.

Paul's friends and contemporaries were all in the category of
Jewish Labor Service draftees. It was not too difficult to persuade
them to leave the service if we happened to run into them. Those
kids needed help! My sons and I made a list of their immediate
needs: a bath, a few clothes, the services of a document laundry,
and a place to live – a sublet where there was no problem about

paying rent. Given that lodging was the biggest problem, I tried to come up with as many options as possible.

As long as the Avases were away, their apartment was available. Whenever I spotted an advertisement for a room to let, I immediately rented it for 'my relative from the country' and paid the rent in advance. A new acquaintance of George's, Hászka, a notary, moved into our summer house on Lupa Island, and for the rest of the summer we had the use of his house in Buda. Both Avas and Hászka had radios in their homes. In an emergency we could also place an additional person in our hideout in Eskü Square.

Our landlady also finally agreed to rent us another room next to ours. My pretext was that, given the pressure on the Eastern Front, some of my acquaintances from that area might at any moment appear on the doorstep as refugees. Furthermore, as I explained it, my godsons came to visit me from time to time, so I would like to have the use of the maid's room next to the kitchen, even though it would remain empty for a while. But I would be happy to start paying rent as soon as the lease was signed. The offer so delighted our landlady that there was nothing we could not ask of her in return for so advantageous an arrangement. Our friendship with her and her husband grew stronger, although in reality such generosity ought to have aroused their suspicions. But, even if they had second thoughts about our identity, they were evidently inclined to put such doubts aside in order not to lose such generous tenants. They now began to invite us to visit them more frequently. The main subject of discussion was always the front and the prospects for an end to the war.

After one such conversation, in which, as usual, I had taken the lead, the landlady suddenly said to her husband, 'Don't you think it odd, Pete, that Lexi, who has no military experience, can analyze these things so cleverly?'

'Clearly you don't get it,' he replied. 'Lexi has plenty of experience, but he's not allowed to reveal his identity. Don't you get it? Have you never heard of the Defense Section?'

The Hungarian intelligence and counter-intelligence operation was known as the Defense Section. Only the most reliable military officers were appointed to it. So, according to the captain I was a member of the Defense Section and was forbidden to tell anyone so. Terrific! The following day I dared to turn the volume up a bit on the BBC World Service.

Occasionally someone evicted from his home or escaped from a labor battalion would appear late at night. On such occasions we simply took them into our room for the night. On one occasion Emi, my attractive friend from the air-raid shelter at our old house on Kossuth Lajos Square, showed up with five other people. They had heard that their roommate, a pseudo-Nazi, had been arrested and they were afraid that if their apartment was searched they might get caught too. So they all had to sleep on the floor in our room.

I was very conscious of the fact that my friend Ozma, more punctilious than I, did not appreciate these unanticipated nocturnal invasions. But, weighing the pluses and minuses, I always decided in favor of the unfortunates at the door. I must admit that Ozma never actually uttered a single complaint; he preferred to suffer in silence rather than ask me to make his life a little more tolerable. Since he was willing to sacrifice his comfort, I was willing to forgive him for his insufferable penny-pinching.

I found quarters – rather a long way away from Buda – for the sister of one of the young men in the Labor Service. She was a refugee from a village in the provinces and had been recommended to me by someone I did not know. Her rent was prepaid for three months and the place was well stocked with food. I duly introduced her to the landlord as a family member who had come to the city as a refugee, and assumed that my job was complete. But a couple of weeks later the landlord called me to the telephone. It was Ella on the line. I had difficulty remembering who Ella was.

A week later she called again: something urgent had come up and she needed to speak to me in person; she had something very important to tell me. In due course, painstakingly refurbished, eye-catchingly dressed, with her hair magically transformed, she appeared at the place appointed for our meeting like a flamingly passionate rose ready for the plucking. It finally became apparent that her only problem was that she was lonely and bored and wished to compensate me for the favors I had done her. Evidently I attracted her. She seemed unwilling to believe that someone who had done a favor for someone might not want to receive a favor in return.

Hour followed hour, day followed day, in slow succession. We seemed to move through time with huge burdens on our backs. But the days were punctuated by episodes that threw a sudden, sharp light on to this masquerade, this confused world of death, fury and hatred.

One morning I was eating breakfast with my son in a third-rate café on the Kiskörút, the Inner Ring. Two young men sitting at a table in the corner caught my attention. Their tattered clothing and general appearance of having been knocked around by circumstance marked them out as likely escapees from a labor battalion. I sent my son over to them with 100 pengős and a note inviting them to join us. One of them, Miklós Schwartz, said he had escaped from Nagyvárad on the very day they emptied the ghetto and deported the inhabitants. His wife and child were among those loaded into the boxcars to be taken away.

That same day his immediate superior, a corporal, had come over to him with the following suggestion: 'Listen Schwartz, let me tell you something. Why let the Germans benefit? You'd do better to leave things to me. I'd make it worth your while.'

'What the hell are you talking about? What am I supposed to leave to you?'

'Your wife,' he replied.

'You understand,' Miklós said to me, 'that I was in a hopeless situation, but his proposal made something snap. I'm not particularly strong, but suddenly I hit the son of a bitch so hard that he lost his footing and fell six feet off the embankment we were standing on. I've been on the run ever since. Later I ran into a friend and now we're traveling together.'

This stranger from a labor brigade was not unique: it was not long before every Hungarian citizen had lived through some equally horrendous experience.

Chapter 16

The Conscience of the World

Even the most barbarous savages would have been ashamed at the obscene treatment the Germans meted out to Jews and other minorities. The history of the world contains no analogies to such brutality. As more and more details of the German death-factories became public, the civilized world slowly emerged from its lethargy and rediscovered its conscience.

The Pope energetically protested at the persecutions. Religious houses and other Church organizations struggled to lend their help, particularly on behalf of Jewish children. The Red Cross supplied food and medicine to the most needy. Still, all this help was no more than a drop in the bucket.

Even Regent Horthy tried, somewhat belatedly, to ease the situation, providing certificates of immunity to eminent Jews who in the past had performed special services for the upper echelons of society. These documents exempted their recipients from the fate awaiting other Jews and at least nominally restored them to their position in the community.

One evening, when I returned to our room I found Ozma putting the finishing touches to a letter he was planning to send to the Regent. He read it to me.

My response was blunt. 'I'm opposed to all exceptions, but if you insist on asking the Regent for an exemption, don't beg. Be forceful, and keep your tone cool and direct. That way, you won't one day feel ashamed of humiliating yourself.'

I believe Ozma never did send his petition. If he did, it was not granted, since he stayed with me and continued to live as he had before.

Several European and Latin American neutral states with embassies and consulates in Budapest started issuing certificates of immunity to Hungarian Jews, whom they lodged in buildings across the city rented for the purpose. In due course the Swiss, Swedish, Spanish and other nationalities established such safe houses. Ignoring the chance that they would be picked up while standing in line – from dawn to dusk – outside the consulates, petitioners were willing to risk deportation at the very moment of their potential salvation. Soon a black market in certificates of immunity grew up: if the owner of a certificate needed money, he could always sell it and go back and stand in line again. This was also a great opportunity for forgers, and the market in forged documents grew particularly lucrative. Soon the situation became so confused that even the people in the embassies could not say whether a given certificate was genuine or false. The hectic struggle to obtain such documents came to an abrupt end when the Nazis hauled all the inhabitants of a couple of the safe houses away to the Danube and drowned them in the river. Their bodies floated downstream.

For my part, I remained firm in my disapproval of this mode of protection: first you catch the Nazis' attention by pinning a yellow star to your chest and then you pull out of your pocket a certificate of immunity and wave it in their faces! The most rational approach, in my view, was complete separation, followed by a quiet effort to blend in with the general population. That is the way animals do it: when they sense danger, instead of presenting a clear target to their enemies, their natural mode of self-preservation is to blend with the scenery and simply disappear. Naturalists call this phenomenon 'mimicry'. Whenever friends or clients approached

Tivadar Soros with his sons and father-in-law, 1931

Tivadar Soros with his sons, 1933

Paul and George, 1934

Above: Tivadar Soros's mother-in-law who was rescued from the ghetto as a young girl

Right: Mother-in-law with George, 1931

Tivadar Soros's wife, Elizabeth, and Paul, 1927

Skiing in Austria, 1930

Summer life in peace, 1932

George, grandmother and Paul, 1943

Left: Paul, 1940

Right: George before going to school in England, 1946

Above: Tivadar and
Elizabeth Soros at the
summer house after
Paul escaped from
Hungary, 1948

Right: Tivadar Soros in
the last year of his life,
1968

War-scarred Budapest
By kind permission of Associated Press

Tivadar and Elizabeth Soros at the summer house, 1952

me to help them obtain certificates of immunity, I tried to talk them out of it and advised them to follow this other route.

From time to time we heard about other successful modes of escape. The Chorin and Weiss families, major industrialists, saved themselves, their dependents, and apparently part of their possessions by formally giving up title to their industrial holdings, and transferring them to Göring Industries, the German company in the hands of Hermann Göring. This chance of escape arose because of the intense rivalry between Göring and Himmler: Göring saw the acquisition of this industrial giant as a way of strengthening his position against Himmler and he was right. The deal was very much to his advantage: the entire arrangement cost nothing, beyond the preparation of thirty-five or forty official passports allowing the 'vendors' to emigrate from Hungary.

Then there was a group of some 1,600 Orthodox Jews and Zionists who camped in a temple yard, guarded and protected by the SS. Needless to say, it was hard to evaluate the nature of such protection. One of my uncles was a member of this group, along with his entire family. He admitted having paid a huge sum – several hundred thousand pengős – for the 'good fortune' of belonging to the group. Later I found out more about this 'business transaction' from Emi.

Emi was no ordinary girl. Her striking appearance, forthright opinions, and sharp sense of humor revealed a firmness of character but a somewhat enigmatic disposition. One summer day I waited for her, as we had agreed, at the streetcar stop outside the Rudas Baths. She failed to turn up. Over the years I had grown accustomed to the fact that women who don't work have a rather imprecise sense of time, so I patiently sat there on a bench, lost in my thoughts. Suddenly a voice startled me.

'You're Elek Szabó, right?'

Looking up, I was surprised to see in front of me a rather unpleasant-looking military policeman. How did he know my name? He wore a chain around his neck, with a serial number. I hated even looking at one of these bloodhounds. I nodded to indicate that I was indeed Elek Szabó and waited to see what would happen next.

'I have a message for you. Miss Emi sends her regards and wishes to inform you that she will be delayed until ten thirty.'

And he saluted smartly and departed. That was our Emi! Finding no one better, she simply sent a message by one of the military policemen from the detachment assigned to guard the Danube bridges. I was aware of the fact that her psychic equilibrium was not always quite normal. When she was twenty-two she fell hopelessly in love with a forty-year-old man who was in the middle of a divorce. They were not able to meet very often because he had been drafted into the Labor Service. She used all her considerable energy to keep him supplied with packages of food, so that he would not go hungry.

I did my best to explain to her that the art of living involves balancing a sense of responsibility against one's personal feelings.

'Emi, you're a sensible woman. Don't you realize the uselessness of being tied to Joska? There are plenty of intelligent, attractive young men closer to your own age.'

'If you must know,' she replied angrily, 'I happen to prefer older men. If you weren't married and I didn't know your wife, I'd fall in love with you too.'

'Very flattering.'

'Don't get any ideas. It's not that I find you particularly physically attractive, but you do always seem to have time for me when I want to talk to you. For example, this situation with Joska,' she sighed. 'Love is not some kind of rudder: you can't just turn it and head off in a different direction. Maybe I should admit to you that it's not really feelings of intimacy that draw me to him, but respect and honor. Stuck in the Labor Service, Joska is so beaten down and hopeless that I have no wish to make his life any more miserable than it is already. It would be cruel to abandon him now. It would take away his last hope: he'd simply fall apart.'

I was ruminating on this conversation when at 10.30 she

appeared. What a pleasure to see such radiant features! Only people with very delicate skin seem to shine in this way. Her eyes sparkled, and her voice was wonderfully appealing as she came up to me and greeted me.

The greetings over, she came straight to the point: 'I've come to say goodbye. I've made a decision.'

'What now?'

My voice showed no surprise. She was forever changing her mind.

She explained that Sándor Csillag, the son of one of the board members of the Jewish Council, had fallen in love with her. She thought he was nice, but that was about the extent of it. His father had arranged for him, and also for her, to be included in the list of Jews whom the SS would transport to Switzerland. This group had been assembled from among Zionist and Orthodox Jews as a result of negotiations by Kastner and Brand with Adolf Eichmann, head of the Nazi commission for the extermination of Jews.

Eichmann was a strange figure, a total thug who boasted of having exterminated millions of Jews in occupied Soviet territory and elsewhere. To broaden his knowledge of things Jewish, he had actually learned Yiddish and Hebrew. But now, with the German army's recent failures and its steady retreat on all fronts, the liberation of Europe from the Nazis seemed only a matter of time. So he now regarded the Jews primarily as a commodity to be traded as profitably as possible, while they were still alive, rather than killing them and, with typical Teutonic thoroughness, turning them into soap.

'Emi, use your head. Can you really trust the SS?'

'Of course not; but where's the guarantee that I'll live if I *don't* join the group? I can tell you confidentially that the Jewish Council has been in touch with a German Jew inside the SS and he has assured the council that the Eichmann crowd are perfectly serious about wanting to sell the Jews for dollars.'

Her reply made it quite clear that she had made up her mind: she was going where she felt she had some support. We said farewell. She turned – and had taken perhaps ten or fifteen paces when she suddenly ran back and kissed me on the cheek. I never saw her again.

And what happened to the group? They, including Emi, were transported to the concentration camp at Bergen-Belsen, where they stayed for several months. It was only after the end of the war that I learned that Eichmann and his crew, eager to prove to the foreign Jews with whom they were negotiating that they did indeed have control of Jewish lives, diverted to Austria two trains on their way to the Auschwitz extermination camp with three thousand Jews on board. These Jews survived the Nazi regime. This aside, the 1,600-person group at Bergen-Belsen was the only group allowed to cross to Switzerland, after protracted negotiation with the Jewish community in Switzerland over the ransom to be paid. A large part of the ransom, paid by each individual in the form of jewels and other valuables, had in fact been given to the Eichmann gang by the group's leaders before the departure from Budapest.

So, if we were doing a balance sheet on all of this, clearly the negotiations with the SS had the positive result of saving some 4,500 Jews from certain death in the extermination camps. But on the other side of the ledger we would have to note a much larger negative: the Jewish Council's voluntary collaboration with the authorities, combined with the ignorance of the Jews themselves, facilitated and indeed enabled the deportation of several hundred thousand Jews from Hungary to Germany. None of this could have happened without voluntary collaboration on the part of the Jewish Council.

Yes, Emi reached Switzerland successfully. She became a university student. Six months later, just short of her twenty-third birthday, she killed herself. I do not know why. Perhaps she could not endure the torment and confusion surrounding her relations with Joska and Sándor.

Later I heard about another escape attempt – a truly bizarre example of lack of forethought. One day a pilot called on a former bank director. He explained that he had a completely trustworthy contact who, in return for a large enough bribe, could secure a plane for him. Apparently two high-up people had guranteed that they would make a plane available in return for some huge sum of money. He planned to fly the plane to Cairo and could take ten people, if they were willing to pay the required amount. Preparations for the flight were begun in greatest secrecy. The price for each passenger was fixed at 200,000 pengős, which could be paid in goods (jewelry, works of art and so on) or in cash. A ten-person group ready to fly to Cairo was quickly assembled. Then, one night a limousine with curtained windows arrived to take the group to the airport.

The organizer, providing everyone with a map of the route to be followed, explained, 'I have to warn you of one thing. Magnetism is so strong in the plane that delicate and high-quality watches will certainly get broken if they're not specially protected. So we're taking a special anti-magnetic capsule with us, and we recommend that you all give us your watches for safe-keeping in the capsule.'

They duly did as they were advised. With these careful preparations completed, and after half an hour of zigzagging back and forth on city streets, they arrived at the supposed airport. As soon as they stepped out of the curtained limousine, they realized to their horror and consternation that they had been tricked: they had been driven to the Detective Center at Svábhegy. Lest there be any doubt about the fact that this was the Detective Center and not the airport, they were all viciously beaten. This center was where the planning was done for the shipment of deportees to the extermination camps in Germany.

The group was then loaded into a truck for the journey to the collection point on Rökk Szilárd Street. But, by an amazing stroke of good fortune, the truck was involved in an accident at the intersection of József Boulevard and Rökk Szilárd Street: the truck overturned and everyone was thrown out into the street. One of the people in the group was Elza Hös, a well-known and highly popular film director, who immediately realized that she had a chance to escape, particularly since her home was just a minute's walk away and she knew the area well. In this whole unhappy sequence, the accident was a kind of miraculous turn of events at exactly the right moment: she and several others were able to escape the claws of the mass-murderers. Dragging her elderly and dazed mother with her, she ran into a nearby coffee house and was able to escape.

When Elza Hös told me about this unique yet in some sense typical event, I could not contain myself. 'Elza, you're a smart woman. How on earth could you be so naive as to allow yourself to fall for such an obvious trap?'

'The plan seemed so carefully thought out. The preparations were so thorough.'

'But any child could tell you that there's no airplane in Hungary that could fly non-stop from Budapest to Cairo. That in itself should have removed any doubt from your mind that this was a put-up job.'

'I'm sure you're right,' she agreed after a moment's thought; 'but I was so eager simply to climb in a plane and get out of here that I was ready to go along with even the most risky of ventures.'

Desire guides and rules mankind, says the poet, and he's right. If we want something enough, the brain loses its ability to check the facts and our reason and logic get befuddled. Ultimately, we can't even see straight. I've become convinced of this over the years through observing my own behavior, having on many occasions judged situations too optimistically, rather than prudently analyzing all the facts and looking at what could go wrong rather than what might go right.

Chapter 17

False Dawn

n August 1944 things at last began to assume the shape I had
been waiting for so impatiently. German military failures began
to have an effect on the politics of the satellite countries. The
Allies launched massively effective bombing raids that destroyed
numbers of major military bases in Germany, and their invasion
of France pushed forward into territory formerly occupied by the
enemy. In the east, the steady advance of the Soviet Union forced
Romania into negotiations on a ceasefire.

On August 18, the King of Romania accepted the conditions
of an armistice that included an agreement to cede Bessarabia
and Bukovina, formerly Romanian territory, to the Soviets. In
return, Romania received Transylvania, previously a southeastern
province of Hungary. A further condition was that the Romanian
army would now have to fight alongside the Russian army. The
terms of this armistice were in fact the first step in what was to
become Russia's new colonialism in Eastern Europe.

These developments had a profound effect on Hungary's
national and international position and the government had
to institute some pretty drastic changes. First, in early August
Prime Minister Döme Sztójay fired three ministers from his
administration – Imrédy, Jaross and Kunder – who were more
Nazi even than Sztójay himself.

On August 18 the police beat back a demonstration in support of German Nazism. The Germans did their best to put a brake on the 'historical wheel of progress' and summoned Admiral Horthy to Germany.

On August 23, Horthy met with the Nazi foreign minister, Ribbentrop, who agreed to reduce German interference in Hungarian internal affairs. But at the same time Horthy had to declare that the Hungarian army would continue to fight alongside the Germans. Then at the end of August Horthy forced Sztójay out of office and replaced him with General Géza Lakatos.

All these events made it clear – even to the politically unsophisticated – that important changes were in the making in Hungary. By September the wildest rumors were flying all over Budapest – particularly the story that Hungary was about to break with the Axis powers. It was said that Admiral Horthy's wife and son were the chief disseminators of this sensational news, an assumption supported by the story that she was part-Jewish and her son had Jewish friends. Another rumor had it that Hitler had 'invited' Horthy to Germany and Horthy had refused to go. In a state of high excitement we listened to one piece of news after another and, amid much discussion, waited for at least one of these stories actually to come true.

But the fate of the Hungarian Jews was already largely sealed. Except for the Jews of Budapest, the others, from the provinces, had already been deported, even those living in the suburbs of the city, like Újpest and Kispest. If things were now to move in a more favorable direction, those left in Budapest – perhaps 100,000 or 120,000 – stood a chance of being saved.

As autumn advanced amid the mild glow of an Indian summer, the sunshine seemed to symbolize our own myriad rays of hope. People gained confidence and learned to smile once more. Little by little my provincial platoon returned home to Budapest. Jutka was the first to return. She could not stand the idyllic tranquillity of life on Lake Balaton when she knew that her father and elder brother were back in the city. Both had managed to escape from labor camps, and I provided them with forged identity papers from my collection, along with clothing and other necessities. Jutka was accompanied by Lame Karcsi, whom Julia asked to escort her, knowing that he was a frequent and experienced traveler. I lodged Jutka in the Avases' luxury apartment in Buda, where she was welcomed with pleasure by Avas's young sister-in-law, who had arrived in Budapest just a few days before. The sister-in-law was several months pregnant, so she was glad to have such an agreeable companion.

Karcsi, the messenger, returned to Almádi, but a couple of days later he came back with two further escorts. This time Julia entrusted to him George, who was bored with the uneventful and monotonous life of the village. George moved in with friends whom he had met through Baufluss. These friends, the Hászkas, had told him that he was always welcome to join their family. They had two children: a six-year-old boy named Otto (after the last of the Habsburgs) and a six-month-old little girl. The Hászkas were Catholics and royalists, belonging to the political faction that wished to reinstate the Habsburg rule. They simply adopted George as a third child and lavished on him all the parental love he missed and really still needed. Both Hászka and his wife busied themselves from dawn to dusk taking care of the children and tending the garden. They did not have the time to seek out any of the special foods that are important for babies.

'The Hászkas are so good to me,' said my son when I met him a few days later. 'I'd really like to do something for them. Perhaps we could do the rounds of the drugstores and try to buy some baby-food.'

We marched from one end of town to the other in search of baby-food, visiting every drugstore. Later I made trips outside the city. I discovered that in the suburban drugstores it was much easier to find special baby-foods because the population was poorer and could not afford them. Our campaign was so successful that the Hászka girl was supplied with baby-food at least until her wedding day. The parents were simply overwhelmed.

Unfortunately the baby got fed up with the stuff and refused to eat it.

Finally, on October 13, Julia and her new best friend Elza Brandeisz arrived. Elza moved into her empty dancing school, full of hope and with plans to start classes shortly. Julia arrived with a wonderful tan, looking serene, balanced and elegant. She wanted to go straight to the old apartment on Kossuth Lajos Square.

'Darling, I'm an optimist too, but trust me, it is a little too early for that. Let's wait a while.'

So she moved in with the two girls, Jutka and Avas's sister-in-law, on Tardy Street. As we arrived in the front hall of their building, we were greeted with tempting aromas: up on the second floor Mrs Avas was cooking a goose. They had returned to Budapest the previous day laden with treasures from their village: ducks, geese, pork, eggs. Evidently the good news had reached the forest, and they had hurried back to Budapest full of hope. I stayed with them late into the night, and we agreed that Julia would spend the next day with Paul. On Monday they would come back to town, and we would all meet at the Miénk Café.

October 15 arrived.

Early in the morning the news spread that Admiral Horthy's son had been killed by the Germans. A few hours later the radio announced that Horthy was going to make an important political declaration; it was read several times in the course of the morning. The text of this declaration of armistice was as follows:

Ever since the will of the nation put me at the helm of the country, the most important aim of Hungarian foreign policy has been to repair, at least in part, the injustices of the Treaty of Trianon by bringing about its revision through peaceful means. Hopes for the operations of the League of Nations in this respect have not materialized.

When the recent world crisis began, Hungary was not guided by any desire to expand its borders. We had no aggressive intentions towards the Czechoslovak Republic, nor did we wish to recapture lost territory through aggressive means. Also, we entered Bácska to defend Hungarian residents in the region only after the collapse of the Yugoslav government of the time. And as far as the Eastern territories taken from us by Romania in 1918 were concerned, we accepted the peaceful arbitration of the Axis Powers, as, apparently, did Romania.

Hungary was dragged into war against the Allies through German pressure resulting from our geographical situation. But also in this war we had no aims of conquest: we did not wish to take as much as a square meter of territory away from anyone else.

Today it is obvious to any sober-minded person that the German Reich has lost the war. All governments, responsible for the fate of their fatherlands, must draw the appropriate conclusions from this fact. As the great German leader Bismarck once said, no nation ought to sacrifice itself on the altar of faithfulness to an alliance. Conscious of our historic responsibility, I must take every possible measure to avoid further unnecessary bloodshed. A nation that, in a war already lost and in support of foreign interests, allowed the territory handed down to it by its forefathers to become a battleground for rearguard actions, would lose all respect in world public opinion.

Sadly, I must conclude that the German Reich has long since broken its obligations to us as an ally. Long since – and despite our wishes and desires – it has thrown more and more elements of the Hungarian army into battles beyond our borders.

Then in March this year, the leader of the German Reich summoned me to Klessheim for discussions, precisely because of my insistence on bringing the Hungarian army home, and there he informed me that German troops were about to occupy Hungary. And, despite my protests, he carried out this action while I was detained in Klessheim.

At the same time the German political police also penetrated the country, arresting numerous Hungarian citizens, among them several members of parliament, and even my own government's minister of internal affairs. The prime minister himself was able to avoid arrest only by seeking refuge in a neutral legation. The leader of the German Reich promised me that he would halt these offenses against, and limitations of, Hungarian sovereignty, if I would appoint a government that enjoyed the Germans' confidence. This was the reason for my nomination of Mr Sztójay's government. But the Germans did not fulfill their promise. Under cover of the German occupation, the Gestapo secret police, applying the same methods as they had used elsewhere, took it upon themselves to deal with the Jewish problem in a manner incompatible with the dictates of humanity.

When the war approached our borders and ultimately crossed them, the Germans promised appropriate support, but even that obligation was not fulfilled in the manner or the measure promised. As they retreated, they ravaged and destroyed the nation's territory.

Finally, their various offenses against the alliance culminated in an act of open provocation. General Szilárd Bakay, head of the Budapest command, responsible for the maintenance of internal order, was ambushed and abducted in the very center of the city by agents of the Gestapo, taking advantage of the poor visibility, as he left his car in front of his home on a recent foggy October morning.

Subsequently, they used their planes to scatter leaflets inciting rebellion against the current government. I have reliable information on what the troops friendly to the Germans wished to achieve by this incitement to violence: the toppling of the Hungarian government that I had established in the meantime, and the seizure of government by their own people. And in the meantime our country's territory would indeed become a battleground for rearguard actions.

I have decided that I must protect the honor of the Hungarian nation against our former ally, when it, instead of providing appropriate military help, wishes to steal, once and for all, the greatest treasure of the Hungarian nation, its freedom and independence. Accordingly, I have informed the Hungarian representative of the German Reich that I will sign an armistice agreement with our former enemies and that in return for this armistice we plan to halt all hostile action. Trusting in their sense of justice, I wish to secure, in concert with them, the continuity of the future life of our nation and the realization of our peaceful aims.

I have given appropriate instructions to our military commanders. Therefore, our troops, in accordance with their oath, and in line with newly published military orders, are under an obligation to obey the commanders appointed by me.

I call on all honest and right-thinking Hungarians to follow me on the path, beset with sacrifices though it may be, of salvation for the Hungarian people.

Everyone listened to this declaration, but there were many voices of dissent: 'Too late.' 'The horse has long since bolted.' 'We've lost Transylvania.'

'Better late than never' was the majority opinion, however. There was much rejoicing. People poured into the streets. I had not paid much attention to the weather in weeks; the only important thing was that with each day that passed we should come a little closer to liberation. Now I noticed that it was a glorious fall day: the trees competed with one another in their green, yellow and red colors. On that day not only the pretend Gentiles but the Jews as well had the courage to take to the streets, and many tore their yellow stars from their coats.

First I headed for the house on Eskü Square, where, months ago, I had begun my new life. Mrs Balázs was delighted to see me. I went down to the basement and dug out my last reserves from a hole in the wall: banknotes and ten gold coins. I was just in time, because the paper money had almost rotted away from the damp.

Balázs took me up to the stairwell where, as I discovered, they had wounded Horthy's son. The bloodstains were still visible on three of the steps. Miklós Horthy had been trying to meet Bornemissza, director-general of the Free Port, at the port's offices in the building. The Germans had learned about the plans for the meeting and on the previous evening ten plainclothes Germans in leather coats had concealed themselves in the building, threatening the building manager, Balázs, that they would shoot him dead if he told anyone. Needless to say, Balázs had no idea what was going on, but he was not pleased. The excitement kept him awake all night. In the morning, Horthy's son duly appeared, escorted by two bodyguards. Balázs heard the shots from the basement, where they had locked him up. But how badly Horthy's son was wounded, and where they had taken him, he had no idea.

And so, by a strange twist of fate, blood was shed at the building on Eskü Square in the cause of liberation from German oppression.

From Eskü Square I went to visit my client Schwartz. His big apartment on Wekerle Street was jam-packed with visitors who had gathered in excitement at Horthy's proclamation. Many members of his family were living there too, since the building was one of those marked with a yellow star. But during the day their sleeping areas were curtained off to hide the overcrowding. The old life went on under the guidance of the patriarch; even the basset hounds received their Gerbeaud bonbons as before.

The two teenage girls, as always, belied their external appearance with their derogatory remarks. The elder girl kept mentioning Paul, about whom she dreamed with all the ardor of her fourteen years, and only reluctantly talked with Jancsi Danyi, Paul's boxer friend, whom my son had delegated to the family several months earlier in his place, and who was a frequent visitor to the house. Most surprising of all: the cuisine was still first-rate. There were crêpes suzettes in my honor, better than any I have ever eaten elsewhere. The drinks flowed freely. After the meal we talked little about the past, but even less about the future, which seemed rosy in spite of the silence.

The family had four members; Gyuri (George), his wife, and two daughters. George had originally been married to a Christian, from whom he was divorced, and there were two children, a boy and a girl. The girl went with her mother, and the boy with his paternal grandmother. Among the children of the first marriage, the grandmother, and the children of the second marriage, relations were not good. Of course, I warned them not to stay in the building, with its yellow star. But when Mrs Schwartz heard my opinion, that it would be better if they all lived separately in these dangerous times, she interrupted me somewhat indignantly: 'Well, counselor, that may be your opinion. But not for a moment would I be separated from any member of my family.'

I gave up trying to persuade her.

The Schwartzes had a great deal of jewelry and asked for my advice.

'Whatever you do, don't tell anyone about it, especially not the janitor. Dig a hole in the cellar, with your own hands, and put your jewelry in it. Don't tell anyone – not even me,' I added, as if to emphasize the extreme importance of secrecy.

We sat down after the meal to play cards. Around five or six in the evening, George, my host, called me out.

'I just wanted to tell you that they've read an announcement from the Arrow-Cross Party on the radio, by Szálasi.'

Even I, a passionate listener to the radio, simply shrugged contemptuously.

'Don't worry about it. It's probably just some secret underground Arrow-Cross station.'

But George came back to the room two or three times with various alarming pieces of news from the radio: 'Szálasi has taken over . . . The Arrow-Cross Party has formed a government . . . The Germans have announced their support for Szálasi.'

But his insistence had no effect: nothing seemed capable of moving me from my indifference. I simply wanted to eat, drink, play cards. I didn't even take the trouble to turn on the radio: I was so far gone in my euphoria at Horthy's declaration. It was perhaps seven o'clock when, after abundant food and an agreeable game of cards, Danyi and I left the house together. Outside, we were greeted by a frightening silence. The street was completely deserted; the only sound was thunder in the distance. When we reached the main thoroughfare, Andrássy Street, the cause of the thunder became clear: German guns and tanks were moving through in a steady stream. My heart turned cold and a chill ran down my spine. We walked down Andrássy Street full of foreboding.

At Oktogon Square there were people. Newspaper sellers shouted, 'Szálasi's declaration! The Arrow-Crossers have taken power! Read all about it!'

I bought a copy of what was a single-sheet special edition, and, as though still living in some abnormal state, I addressed another newspaper reader, gesturing at the headline: 'What do you make of this craziness?'

When he simply looked me over from head to toe, without saying a word, I was terrified: I finally understood that Horthy's putsch had failed, that Horthy had been arrested, that Szálasi's German-supporters had seized power, that the question I had just asked was enough to have me shot. At the corner of Oktogon Square and Grand Avenue, where a crowded streetcar was just leaving the square, I could already see how innocent passengers were being treated by thirteen- and fourteen-year-olds dressed in civilian clothes with ammunition holders on their leather belts and with aged rifles that they could barely carry on their shoulders. They were manhandling and striking people as they got off the streetcar, so as to 'keep order'.

'Uncle Lexi, I really don't want to go home,' said Danyi blankly.

'Come to my place; you can stay with me.'

Danyi simply gestured and climbed on to a streetcar. Perhaps he had remembered a popular song of the time, which the actress Karádi used to sing:

No use running to liberty:
No way of escaping what must be.

I walked home feeling as though I had been beaten to death. I crept quietly into my room: I had no wish to talk with the other occupants.

I awoke early next morning to the sound of gunfire. I listened tensely, then dressed feverishly and went out to look around. A sharp chill met me when I went out into the street. In Grand Avenue I found many other early risers. I tried to discover what was going on. People just shrugged: they also didn't know what was happening. Finally someone said, 'Someone started shooting at a group of Arrow-Crossers in the street from the balcony of a Jewish House, so now they're trying to smoke them out.'

The gunfire included that of machine-guns and even occasional heavy artillery. I approached Népszínház Street. A crowd in front of the Jewish House. On the asphalt shards of glass and bits of stone. I tried to focus my attention, to engrave on my memory the faces of the Arrow-Crossers as they came out of the building – the way one of them held a club, the fury in the eyes of another. I thought that one day, when these people had to answer for their atrocities – because justice isn't just something in novels – I would be able to say unequivocally, 'Yes, he was one of them.'

I had a hard time deciding whether to be scared as a Jew or ashamed as a Gentile for allowing all this to happen.

I directed my steps toward the Café Miénk: the time approaching for my rendezvous with my wife and son. They arrived. My wife did her best to hide how depressed she was at this sad turn of events, but I recognized her tight, quiet mode of conversation, always a sign of internal turmoil and distress. Elza Brandeisz had also come. Holding a small suitcase in her hand, she explained that she was going back to the country immediately.

She turned to Julia: 'Are you sure you don't want to come?'

Julia turned to me questioningly.

From the direction of Népszínház Street a large group of Jews appeared, herded along by Arrow-Crossers. They walked with their hands in the air, like prisoners of war. A young mother clutched her baby in her right hand and held the left above her head.

Tears streamed down Julia's face.

'Go with her, dear. Go with Elza. Leave now, while there are still trains.' I knew that if she stayed, she would only limit my ability to maneuver. And I needed all the strength I could muster if we were all to survive this latest horror.

Paul, too, approved of his mother's departure for the country. 'We men can get by easier here. George has a wonderful place with the Hászkas.'

The events of that day shook me up, too, though I hid my concern and tried to seem above it all.

The women left for the station. Julia did not even stop off at Tardy Street for her suitcase. Elza would provide her with clothes if the weather turned cold.

Chapter 18

Life under Szálasi

In Budapest daily life under the Szálasi régime began. My landlord recounted, with a certain aplomb, that Szálási had appeared at the ministry and had sworn in everyone who was inclined to give his allegiance to the Arrow Cross Party. Szálasi himself had put on their armbands. The landlord was among those sworn in. Two days later he whispered to me that on his way to work that morning, along the Danube, in the area between the Ritz Hotel and the Chain Bridge, he had counted the bodies of sixty Jewish women.

'Do you realize that these poor women are lying there murdered?' he said in a tone from which much could be concluded. But his voice masked a kind of resignation, as though nothing could have been done to prevent it.

With his Arrow Cross armband on his arm, the captain was at that moment much more human, as he spoke of these horrors, than his wife when she drew her finger across her throat and clicked her tongue to show the fate of Jews driven out on to the street.

The Arrow Cross regime was visibly unpopular. Not simply because Jews were even more persecuted than under Sztójay, but because the country's fate was more firmly attached to that of Germany, about which very few people still had any illusions. But no one dared utter a word of criticism against the regime.

In fact, even if anyone did, no newspaper would publish it, so it would have no effect. Only one publication dared to print criticism of Szálasi, the weekly humor magazine *Pesti Posta.* The cover, that first week, presented a full-page portrait of Szálasi, only his head was attached the wrong way round. Underneath were the words: 'Szálasi comes as if he were going'.

The cover the following week showed a curving country road with a motorbike on it. A man was riding it, with a woman (known in Hungary as a 'gas-chick') sitting behind him, her hair flying in all directions. The caption read, 'Hang on, Malvina; there's a bend coming.'

Both captions became, as they deserved, catch-phrases all across the country. The magazine ceased publication. I have no idea what happened to the editor. Newspapers, I might add, got smaller and smaller because of the shortage of paper, but the press still had enough paper to communicate, over several days and several pages, the foreign minister's infantile theories on world politics, or corrections of statements made by Szálasi.

Szálasi did one stupid thing after another. His initial statement contained one sentence that could have upset the Arrow-Crossers themselves. As the source of his power he pointed to Edmund Veesenmayer, the German ambassador to Hungary. Chauvinism tends to run high in smaller countries. Hungary was also proud of its independence, and now the head of the Arrow Cross Party was declaring that his authority came from the German ambassador! In vain further statements were published, or statements clarifying the statements: it was no longer possible to put matters right. No one saw Szálasi as anything other than a German puppet.

A new police force had to be formed from the Arrow Cross Party because the old police officers were reluctant to participate in activities against Jews. In fact, they often saved lives by taking Jews out of the hands of the Arrow-Crossers to escort them to the police station, where they proceeded to let them go.

Each district had one or two Arrow Cross buildings whose sole purpose was torture and the 'cutting off' of Jewish lives. People suspected of being Jews were taken to these locations to assess their Jewishness. For men the assessment was extremely easy. Documents were of no importance. They had to take off their clothes, and those who were circumcised were unlikely to come out alive. Women had a better chance, because such simple criteria were unavailable.

One day I met two women who had escaped to Budapest from the ghetto in Győr and whom I knew through Emi. I tried to continue my contact with this group during the Arrow Cross period. The two of them had so many handbags with them that they could hardly carry them.

'Where did you buy those beautiful handbags?' I asked.

'We didn't buy them: we got them here in the neighborhood, at the Arrow Cross building.'

'The Arrow Cross building?' I exclaimed in surprise (though by this time I ought not to have been surprised at anything).

'Yes, the whole place is full of stolen goods. They had arrested us, beaten us up, and tried to get us to confess to being Jewish. In between the beatings, they questioned us on religion. Apart from the 'Our Father' and the Creed, we knew nothing, and even those we got wrong or stumbled over. We said that because of the constant torture we had forgotten our very names. This went on for two days, this beating and interrogation. Finally they established that we were not Jewish, and as compensation for the beating we had suffered, we were each given a wristwatch.'

One of the women held up her arm. 'Look. Isn't it nice?'

'In the end,' said the other woman, 'the Arrow-Crossers let us go with the invitation that we come back every week to choose a present for ourselves. Every Thursday, they said. This is our third visit. Come with us next week and you'll get something, too.'

The very idea offended my sense of human dignity, if for a Jew there was such a thing as human dignity any more.

It was not difficult to refuse a far more favorable proposal from the Arrow-Crossers than this when it came along a little later. The manager of the building on Akácfa Street, who had now become district party leader, sent a message by way of the Balázs family saying that he would be happy to be of assistance to me. This individual had responsibility for one of the two rental apartment buildings for which I had been the agent. He used to appear in my office every month with the accounts. He appeared as usual on April 1, shortly after the arrival of the Germans.

After handing me the money and the accounts, and as he got ready to leave, I said: 'Sit down a minute, Tóth; there's something I want to tell you. Now that the Germans are here, I really need to mention it to you. Don't think that I haven't known all this time that you are an Arrow-Crosser. People in the building have also indicated to me that you spent time in jail for anti-government activity. The law gave me the right to fire you immediately for this, but I did not do so. Why? Because I figured if the owner of a house is a Jew, at least the janitor should be a Nazi.'

Maybe this speech had some lasting effect, and for that reason he kept sending me messages that I should not forget him if I needed help.

It was my firm belief that it was impossible to deal with the Nazis or with the SS, let alone come to an agreement with them. I regarded them as fundamentally untrustworthy. It's perfectly possible that this man's good intentions toward me were sincere, but he might come under such ideological influence that he would be obliged to act differently from his original intentions. Among my lawyer colleagues several were notorious anti-Semites or Arrow-Crossers. It was said of one of them that he had Jewish blood on his mother's side. Some time after the Arrow-Crossers came to power I ran into this colleague on the street. He was clearly delighted to see me.

'My dear Tivadar, I'm in a leading position now. I'm in charge of economic affairs for the Arrow Cross Party. I'm going crazy with all the work. Wouldn't you like to join us as deputy director? After all, in these economic matters "we" are the experts.'

That was all I needed, to become a party official for the Arrow-Crossers. I declined the offer politely but firmly.

He insisted. 'Look, I'll give you my phone number. Perhaps

you'll change your mind. In a position like this, you'd be completely safe.'

There were indeed some people who sought their salvation within the Party. One time I visited the refugees from the Győr ghetto. Seven of them, boys and girls together, were living in a single room. When I came in, one of the boys was just putting on the Arrow Cross armband and the rest of the Arrow Cross insignia.

'He's going to work,' his friends explained.

This was not a unique case. The Prónay Detachment announced the execution of five Jews who had been found among their ranks, and the story was written up in the newspapers. Sometimes Jews owed their lives to the miraculous intervention of such pseudo-Nazis. I had heard of Jews in SS uniforms and now here was one with an Arrow Cross armband.

My own fake-Gentile life can be compared, as I have already suggested, with the natural phenomenon called mimicry: the animal takes on the color of its surroundings so that it is hard to detect and can escape its tormentors. The fake Nazis were like those butterflies whose majestic style of flight imitates that of another species, which happens to give off a penetrating odor. This smell is so powerful that it keeps enemies away. The imitators resemble them in coloring and flight and, although they don't have the ability to exude a strong odor, they are left unharmed by the birds.

The Arrow Cross government made no secret of its intention to deal radically with the Jewish question. They looked around for home-grown methods of mass extermination. At the end of October they mobilized able-bodied young women. Later, they gathered everybody from the Jewish Houses, young and old, men and women, and dispatched them to the Újlaki brickworks, where they were divided into groups and herded toward the Austrian border. Those unable to walk, and those who fell or sat down by the roadside, were massacred by their guards. One short fellow I know told me afterwards that he had never been more grateful in his life for his shortness than on that march from the brickworks toward

Vienna. Several of the Arrow Cross guards amused themselves by vying with each other as to who could shoot the most tall people among the marchers. And so the tall people fell one by one under their bullets. The road to Vienna was soon lined with bodies.

When they reached the frontier at Mosonmagyaróvár there were plans to put the forced marchers in boxcars, but by this time the German railroad system was falling apart and no train was available. After three days of waiting, everyone was allowed to go. Some of those returning home were recaptured by the Arrow Cross guards and taken to party headquarters. The lucky ones were allowed to leave after a thorough beating; the rest were taken to the banks of the Danube and shot.

On this occasion I received a message from the 'English' group. That evening they told me that I was to be ready for a night assignment. My assignment was on a truck, sitting next to the driver. We covered the highway to the Austrian border twice, to pick up those staggering home. We gathered up only those who could not walk any more, and children. We lifted the unfortunates silently into the little truck and drove them to the Jewish hospital at Bethlen Square in Budapest. I was kept so busy with this work and with handing out the sandwiches we had taken with us that I hardly had time to be scared. Though hot with the excitement of it all, I still shivered in the cold of the night.

In November a ghetto was finally established in Budapest. It was in the seventh district, and consisted of Dob, Rumbach and Síp Streets and their immediate surroundings, an area already densely populated with Jews. Here the frightened, bewildered Jews were gathered together, generally one family to a room, but in some places with as many as twenty people jammed into a single room. The hygiene of the ghetto was vastly better than that of the brickworks, since at least they were in buildings intended for human habitation and not in the open air. Thanks to the efforts of the Red Cross there was also an irregular and limited supply of food.

The ghetto posed a new problem for me. My mother-in-law,

who had returned to Budapest, was swept into it: I received the news one morning from Balázs, along with her new address. On the fate of the ghetto I was full of foreboding, so I saw it as my responsibility to get her out as soon as possible. Jews, of course, were required to live in the ghetto, but the evacuation of the Christians living within its confines, while it had been planned for some time, had not yet been carried out, because of the shortage of means of transportation and of suitable places to house the evacuees. Given that there were numbers of Christian residents in the ghetto area, some free traffic between the ghetto and the outside had to be maintained. So Christians were able to come and go as they wished.

My first task, then, was to get word to my mother-in-law that we had received her message and would take care of her. A sixteen-year-old Gentile boy, Imre, served as our courier. Initially my younger son ran errands for us, but later, to reduce the risk involved, I gave the jobs to Imre. He was trustworthy, with a good memory, a sense of adventure, much agility and an eagerness for money. He lived with his old mother and was the breadwinner for the two of them. So first of all I obtained the address of an acquaintance of mine, a Christian, living inside the ghetto, so that if Imre were stopped he would have an adequate excuse and could say where he was going. Imre's first task was to go to my mother-in-law and tell her that she should telephone me at the Café Miénk the following morning between nine and ten o'clock from one of the public phones in the street.

The following day I heard a voice from another world on the other end of the line.

'Mother?'

'Yes, it's me.'

'How are you?'

'How do you think I am, stuck here?'

'Listen, I want to get you out of there and place you somewhere better, as Rozália Bessenyei. Imre, who visited you yesterday, will come for you.'

'And where will he take me?'

'To Paul, and Paul, in turn, will escort you to your new lodgings.'

'And where will that be?'

'I can't tell you yet, but it will be a decent place, I promise.'

'I refuse to go anywhere if the people don't know who I am and I have to pretend I'm somebody else all the time.'

'Mother, please, don't be difficult. You're not thinking about this the right way. If someone knows there is a Jew in his house, he acts more embarrassed if there's any danger. If he doesn't know his tenant is a Jew, he acts much more naturally when they ask him whether there's a Jew living with him.'

It was no use. My mother-in-law insisted that the landlord should be told she was Jewish and was living under an assumed name.

For two days I spent my entire time running around looking for a place, even though wandering around the streets was not without its dangers at the time. I did not have to face the moment of declaring to a startled landlord that I was looking for a place for a secret Jew, since I found no place of any description.

After these vain forays I suddenly had an idea. I remembered a family I visited some months ago. I had been struck by the size of their apartment and the relative lack of furnishings it contained. I looked for their address and went and visited them. I explained the situation. There were three of them living in a three-room apartment, and they agreed to provide one room on the condition that I paid them not with cash but with food. In this way, my mother-in-law would not only be given a place to live but could also take her meals with the family. At the time there were various items of food that could not be bought for ready money: they had simply disappeared from the market. Over the past few months I had succeeded in buying a lot of provisions, either through the black market or in the stores, so I didn't haggle, but simply stipulated that they would have to provide the transportation to get the goods, since transportation was impossible to find. They determined how much firewood, cooking fat, lard, rice, coffee, tea, chocolate, and so on, I would have to provide. I had no idea who the Molnár family were, nor what they did for a living, but I suspected that one of them – or perhaps all of them – was a pseudo-Christian. I was happy that finally I could get my mother-in-law out of the ghetto.

Everything went according to plan. Imre, pretending that he was leaving the ghetto with his mother, simply walked out with her. At the appointed place he met Paul, who paid him the equivalent of $15 in bills as his fee. Paul took his grandmother to her new place. He told her when Gran could call Lexi – and wrote down my telephone number for her.

I took a deep breath. One less thing to worry about.

My happiness was short-lived.

Some eight or ten days had passed when the phone rang.

'How are you, Mother? What's new?'

'I'm in big trouble. A young man came to my room yesterday, introduced himself as the representative of the owner of the building. He told me that the owner had learned that there was a Jew in the building and had given the offending individual twenty-four hours to move out or he would call the police.'

'And what did you say?'

'What could I say? He said I was a Jew. It's true.'

'But, Mother, don't you know that you are a Hungarian lady related to Baron Bessenyei? Why didn't you throw the guy out? How dare he accuse Rozália Bessenyei of being a Jew? You should have spat in his face at the insult.'

'Ladies don't spit in people's faces,' she replied quietly.

'True, but even a lady gets outraged when she is hit with an insult like the one you received. You must learn how to behave on occasions like this – with dignity, but forcefully. If you can, kick the person who makes such an accusation, or try to tear his eyes out. Or, at the very least, say that you'll tell your brother, the colonel of hussars, who'll cut them to pieces with a rapier.'

'You're always joking with me, Lexi. You don't really mean it?'

'Actually I do; I'm perfectly serious. I'm beginning to suspect that Mama is not a real Bessenyei. A Bessenyei girl would not stand for such an offense! And how are you getting along with the Molnárs?'

'I don't really know. They're peculiar.'

'How do you mean, peculiar?'

'When I enter their room, they immediately stop whatever they are doing. If I ask a question, they seem to answer reluctantly. Send someone for me and let me move to another place.'

'Please, Mother, try not to worry. This business yesterday was just a bad joke: there's no real danger. I take the responsibility; you just stay there. You have my telephone number; call me if anything happens.'

And so we said goodbye. In my mind's eye I could see the situation. The Molnárs were clearly forgers or 'laundry operators'. My mother-in-law must have noticed some of their activities and, being bored, must have started asking questions: 'What's this for? Why are you doing this?' And since they had no intention of sharing their secret with her, they had a difficult time answering. They began to regret the deal they had made and wanted to get out of their part of the bargain, so they asked a friend to scare the old lady into leaving. A week later I had another phone call.

'I tell you, Lexi, I can't stay here any longer. These people are very impatient and they won't even talk to me any more.'

I could tell from her voice that she was having a hard time and I began to feel very sorry for her. I promised to find her a new place and said I would call her as soon as I had something. Recent experience had shown that apartment-hunting was hopeless, so I tried the hotels. I was lucky: after a brief search I found a room at the Hotel Carlton, one of the better hotels in town. Even more surprising was the fact that my mother-in-law accepted my proposal right away. She was convinced not because the Carlton was a good hotel but because it was only about a minute away from her apartment in Eskü Square. So she was pleased. My son escorted her to the hotel, where she registered as Rozália Bessenyei. My son gleefully reported that when she was handed the registration blank, she exclaimed, '*Shema Yisroel*, I can't fill it out already. I've forgotten my new name!'

More likely, this was simply a grandson's warped sense of humor: my mother-in-law was not in the habit of breaking into Hebrew. And so, for the moment, I considered myself very lucky that I had found such a good place for her and had this problem squared away.

Chapter 19

Further Horrors

As the Szálasi regime continued, the overall situation of the Jews worsened day by day. The fate of those living in the ghetto grew progressively more cruel. Words like 'terrible' or 'horrible' little by little lost their significance: there is no language to describe the daily sufferings of concentration camp or ghetto. They were tormented not only by the overcrowding and the hunger, but also by the hopelessness, the lack of any prospect of improvement. The Arrow-Crossers turned up from time to time and simply shot all the inhabitants of a given building. They didn't even bother to herd them down to the Danube. No one knew when their turn would come, which house would be next, and so the terror was unrelenting. More and more stories leaked out about the German mass-extermination and cremation camps, and even the most optimistic people realized that there was no route to salvation. People became lethargic, without faith, despairing. Their will to live was ebbing away. They lost their appetite, refusing even the little food they could get. They died like flies in autumn.

Of course, unhygienic living conditions and rampant malnutrition encouraged disease. Eventually there came a time when death no longer shocked the spirits of the living, becoming simply part of the routine. There was an epidemic of a particular kind of diarrhea that affected people psychologically as well: it made those suffering from it feel constantly dirty. They kept demanding to be washed, asking for their clothes to be changed. It was impossible to keep them in bed: even those close to death crawled to the faucet to try to wash themselves, and it was there that death frequently overtook them.

Even people who had been exempted for economic reasons were driven into the ghetto by the Arrow-Crossers, but there were some who had the special privilege of being exterminated in their own homes. The whole city knew Muki Knapp, who was famous for his skill as a businessman, with the result that the Germans also used his services. Neither he nor his wife wore a star. At the behest of the Germans, Knapp made several journeys to Portugal to obtain vital industrial commodities. He and his wife lived in Kossuth Square, in the apartment where they had always lived. One day, two armed Arrow-Crossers went to the apartment and shot both of them.

People under the protection of foreign embassies were not pushed into the ghetto. They lived in 'protected' houses, that is, houses provided for foreigners. On several occasions such houses were surrounded, and the inhabitants were hauled off to the Danube, where they were shot dead.

The Red Cross, and representatives of foreign diplomatic missions, visited the ghetto regularly, but there was little they could do. It was rumored that the Arrow-Crossers would blow up the entire ghetto one night. There were indeed plans to do so, but they were not put into effect, presumably because the Christians had still not been moved out.

A new decree from the Arrow Cross government required 'spouses of Aryans' to move to the ghetto. In Hungary there was a high level of assimilation and over time this had resulted in a great many mixed marriages where one partner was Christian and the other a converted or active Jew. The Jewish partner was known in Hungarian as an 'Aryan-spouse' (*árja-párja*). Even Mrs Horthy was a descendant of such a Jewish–Gentile marriage, and so was the infamous anti-Semitic politician Béla Imrédy. Up to now, members of mixed marriages had been exempted from the anti-Jewish regulations, but this now changed. New tragedies ensued. Sometimes, out of solidarity with a marriage partner, the Gentile partner moved to the ghetto too, but there was also a wave of suicides.

Some time later, I had occasion to meet a heroic member of the aristocracy, who had been committed to the ghetto because of her efforts to help escaping Jews. Baroness Orczy was not easily intimidated, even in the ghetto, and since she knew the secret phone number of the minister for internal affairs, she called him and terrorized him with denunciations and threats. Nothing works better against terrorists than terror.

Shortly after the new regulation came out, an Arrow Cross journalist, a regular visitor to the Ministry for Internal Affairs, created a sensation by telephoning the Telegraph Office, without authorization, and telling them that the publication of the decree was done in error and needed to be corrected immediately in the *Official Gazette*. On the basis of the call, the Telegraph Office duly published the correction and announced that the favorable treatment for 'Aryan-spouses' would continue. The resulting confusion was enough for Baroness Orczy: she used the occasion to gain liberation for a number of the 'Aryan-spouses' through telephoned threats.

As had happened frequently in the past, they hauled this blue-eyed, solemn-faced, restless woman off to the Arrow Cross headquarters, where they had already knocked out one of her teeth. An Arrow Cross detective beat her with his fists and whipped her – and then, suddenly, he had a new idea.

He interrupted the beating and offered the baroness a cigarette. 'Would you like a smoke?'

'Very much.'

'This isn't the first time I've knocked you around. It doesn't seem to work. You answer back as though you weren't really in our power at all. Why not take the step of joining us in our propaganda work? The pay is good. We need persistent, self-assured women like you, always ready with an answer. What do you think?'

'You must be joking. That's my answer.'

'Why?'

'Don't you know, poor fool that you are, that you and your pals will hang within two weeks?'

The detective struck her across the face with his whip.

My personal contact with the ghetto stopped after we got my mother-in-law out. Once in a while I was able to send in food and cigarettes by way of Imre, but later, with the food situation in the city getting worse, and the constant bombings, he and his mother moved in with relatives in a little village on the Danube.

Ozma and I stayed together. What else could we do? He and I had completely opposite temperaments, but we complemented each other in many ways: we needed one another. We had our little differences. Lajos asked me, for example, to obtain a forged birth certificate for the actress Kerényi, who was a friend of his wife. I delivered the document and Lajos asked how much he owed me.

'Two hundred pengős.'

He gave me the money and said with a sour smile: 'Sometimes I just don't understand you, Lexi. You give documents to people you don't know at all for free, and then you charge me two hundred pengős.'

'You're so thrifty, Lajos, that you won't miss two hundred pengős. Do you know the story of Mayor Lueger of Vienna? He was a notorious anti-Semite, but he was once seen walking down Kärtner Street arm in arm with a Jew. A friend asked him how he, an anti-Semite, could walk around in public with a Jew? "*Wer Jude ist, bestimme ich* (I decide who is a Jew)," he replied. I do the same with the prices of documents: I decide who pays.'

These small skirmishes at least took the boredom out of our relationship.

In the autumn, when the theaters opened for the season, we bought four season tickets for the National Theater and for the Opera. Most often I gave these tickets to boys who had escaped from labor camps, and insisted that during the intermissions they eat some of the particularly good Gerbeaud pastries served at the buffet. This was my way of helping them rediscover a little human dignity – my third front, as it were.

After my wife had left for the country, I went to visit the Avases. The sister-in-law had been taken to the hospital because of a premature birth, brought on by Szálasi's proclamation and the fear and terror it produced. Jutka had moved to Pest because the sister-in-law's family was also now living with the Avases and the apartment was very overcrowded. I was concerned that so many people were living in the same apartment, particularly because the others in the building also seemed to be Jews in hiding. While I was visiting, there was an air-raid warning and we all had to go down to the cellar. Sitting in the shelter, I had the impression that the whole group was Jewish.

Avas reassured me with one of his *ex cathedra* sentences: 'Nothing bad will happen.'

The Avases had been back in the apartment for some four or five weeks when one evening four young men came to their door. A knock on the door. A request for identity papers. There were four people in the apartment at the time – the Avases, the sister-in-law and her mother. When he was asked for his papers, Avas stood up quite quietly, to his full and imposing height, and slowly and deliberately removed his wallet from his pocket to show his card. But before he could do so, his knees suddenly crumpled and he fell to the floor. The women rushed over to help. The thrashing of his legs as the apoplexy seized him and the frightened cries of the women so upset the Arrow-Crossers that one after the other they stole away, not just out of the apartment but out of the building. I had always admired Avas as a model of coolness under pressure. But it seems that even people so outwardly cool have their emotions: a little check of identity papers and they collapse. Paradoxically, the stroke saved Avas. Somehow they managed to find an ambulance and get him to the hospital. Eventually he was taken to the sanitarium at Budakeszi, where he remained quietly for the rest of the Arrow Cross period, along with his wife as his nurse.

A few days later I learned of a worse tragedy, a visitation of fate that befell my best clients, the Schwartz family. George and his family had a newly built rental apartment building on Ipoly Street. The agent suggested that the family move into the last vacant apartment in the building. They called me to ask my advice. Although I insisted that it would not be prudent for the family to remain together, they decided to go ahead. Their household staff remained in the old apartment and a maid carried a hot dinner over every day. She was very pretty, and the policeman on duty at the corner noticed her and struck up a conversation. This blossomed into friendship, and the girl happened to mention that she was taking dinner to her Jewish employers. The policeman was a member of the Arrow Cross Party and immediately reported the matter. One night the Arrow-Crossers arrived and took the husband and wife, their two young daughters and the building superintendent to the Danube and shot them.

Another client of mine perished at about the same time, Pauer, the vinegar manufacturer. One day in December I was walking along Rákóczi Street and noticed with great amazement that his factory was still in business. So I went in and asked the secretary, 'Where's the boss?'

'In the office.'

Pauer was a bachelor, a very wealthy man. On several occasions he had hired me, as a lawyer, to make inquiries at foreign embassies about whether there were ways of purchasing special awards from the Red Cross, the Knights of Malta, and so on. I walked into his office, where he greeted me very cordially. I could not hide my surprise at finding him in his own house, in his own office.

Assuming that he would listen to my friendly advice, I confronted him: 'Look, you're tempting fate if you live this way. The Arrow-Crossers won't stay in power for more than a couple of months. You have a good Swabian face: no one will bother you if you disappear and live somewhere as a pretend-Christian for a while.'

He was the type of client whom I would have charged handsomely, had he ordered documents from me.

'My dear sir, that's really not necessary in my case.'

'Why? Don't the Jewish laws apply to you?'

'Of course, but I have influence with certain kinds of people, so I really don't need to disappear. Please don't repeat it, but the Budapest chief of police keeps me apprised of the situation on a daily basis.'

And while I stood there he called the chief of police, apparently to prove to me that he had good relations with the right kinds of people. The police chief assured him that there was no change in the situation.

Three days later, they shot him and his mother in a corner of the factory yard. This man valued his good connections more than his life.

The disasters overtaking my close friends had a profound effect on me, despite my efforts to cultivate a thick skin. I often wondered how I would behave if I fell into the hands of the Arrow-Crossers and faced certain death. I imagined I would not wait to be executed but would try to escape, try to get out in whatever way I could. In any case, it would be better to get shot by the guards, to perish in a life-and-death struggle, than simply to give up.

The big question, though, was whether I would have the strength to act. It was surely this question that brought on my nightmares . . . A door would open and I would find myself staring into a huge 45 revolver in the hands of an Arrow-Crosser . . . Someone would be sitting on the edge of my bed, trying to tie my hands. I would try to cry out, but no sound would come . . . Often I dreamed that I was in the hands of a firing squad. At the very moment of the command to shoot I would wake up. Waking up after a dream like that, needless to say, always filled me with relief – but not just because the dream had come to an end. Above all, I was pleased at how I had behaved. Within my dreams, I was never overcome by fear, never gave in, never begged forgiveness. I always checked to see whether my heart was beating faster than normal.

According to Adler, a psychologist whose views were opposed

to those of Freud, dreams represent not so much the subconscious rising to the surface as the desires of the dreamer. My dreams were no guarantee that I would hold up when faced with the real thing. I never seemed to be concerned in my dreams with the possibility that something might happen to my sons or my wife. But I decided to be more careful and attentive in future. A little self-criticism caused me to condemn my conduct when, on a recent occasion, in what must have been a fit of cockiness or maybe spite, I took nine Labor Service Jews to dinner at Gundel, a famous restaurant, at a time when they were cooking for only forty people a night because of the food shortage. Furthermore, we were pretty loud and undisciplined.

On December 9, Lame Karcsi came to visit for the last time, sent by my wife. He had come by in November, bringing a big basket of fresh mushrooms, sour cream and a big fat goose, gifts from Aunt Zsuzsi and Julia. From Julia he brought a long letter. The mails were no longer working, and only this adventurous, confused young man got any pleasure from the terrible journey. Julia gave a faithful account of her life in Almádi. When she returned from Pest, she went back to the retired school principal and rented the same room. But she failed to observe that the room had neither stove nor fireplace. So when, a few days later, the autumn rains began, she caught such a terrible cold that she had no option but to move in with the Brandeisz family, in their one-room home. 'But you won't believe it,' she wrote.

A miracle has happened. Every evening, in the pitch dark, I walked back to my room at the principal's house, at the other end of the village – a half-hour walk at least. At that hour there was no one on the street. And for the first time in my life I was not afraid. My steps echoed in the silence, and occasionally dogs barked at me, or one of them followed me part of the way. When the doctor told me I had a bad case of sinusitis and needed to stay in the warm, Elza invited me to move in with her, as though it was the most natural thing in the world.

When a neighbor of hers, who has a three-room house, asked
Aunt Zsuzsi how she could possibly make room for me, Aunt
Zsuzsi replied, 'We can fit her in because we're used to living
in one room!' Elza let me share her bed: the two of us sleep in
opposite directions on a pretty large sofa, each with our own
eiderdown. I'm not sure whether I would ever have shared my
bed with someone in the old days. I don't know whether you
realize what a different world I'm living in now. Every evening
Zsusza reads from the Bible and sometimes sings psalms. On
the slopes of Káptalan Hill there are thick pinewoods. Now
that I am friendly with several of our neighbors, we go up
there to pick mushrooms. The mushrooms emerge from the
forest floor a few hours after rain, when everything is still
wet. They smell so wonderful! You have to look for the
path the mushrooms follow – the mushroom-stream, we call
it. Because in the place where you find a given kind of
mushroom there are always more: they 'flow' under the dead
pine-needles. And their colors! You can see for yourself how
unusual they are! Pink, bright blue, yellow. And these are
all definitely edible mushrooms. I can now recognize them
with absolute certainty and tell the difference between these
mushrooms and the various poisonous ones. I am still going
to Felsőörs, to the country folk there, and I stay friendly with
Uncle Mihálcsa . . .

Karcsi's December journey was full of difficulties. The German–
Russian front was by then moving towards the south of us and
he had to make a detour all the way up north and come in from
Győr, on the only possible road, getting rides on military trucks.
Even so, he produced a big roasted loin of pork from his knapsack.
Julia said in her letter that she went to Veszprém, where a radio
repair shop fixed her little short-wave radio; so now, at night, she
could listen to the German-language program of the BBC. The
trip to Veszprém was full of adventure: there was no train, so for
part of the way she went by cart and most of the trip she did on

foot, with the radio in her knapsack. She wanted news of everyone – her mother, the children, Jutka. And did I know what it meant, and why they kept repeating, '*Le baton du maréchal est en bakélite*' on the French-language program?

Through Karcsi I sent Julia a gold necklace, a brooch and lots of cigarettes, so that if Aunt Zsuzsi's supply of yarns ran out, she too would have something to trade.

Our adventurous messenger was just able to make his way back, through the front and the lines behind it, and Julia received my letter and package – but I found this out only much later. In the meantime, for several long months, we were cut off from one another. The Germans occasionally retreated from, and then recaptured, the area around Lake Velence. Lake Velence is on the road to Balaton.

Chapter 20

Raid

E very day I went across to the Café Miénk, which was close
to my apartment. I grew accustomed to its atmosphere
and stopped by even when food shortages meant they had
almost nothing to offer their customers but a cup of hot
tea, and sometimes not even that.

Of late, I had been surprised how often you heard French
spoken in the café. At the time, I spoke French well, so I soon
made friends with a Frenchman, who in turn introduced me to
the other members of the French colony.

It was a curious group of people, consisting of French soldiers
or labor camp inmates who had escaped from Germany, similar in
status to ourselves. Like us, they were careful not to fall into the
hands of the authorities. As I got to know these people, I found
the notion of the decadence of the French truly absurd. It's true
that they were not fond of war, or of taking unnecessary risks, but
that's understandable.

These slim, active boys were devilishly smart and full of ideas.
Although they didn't speak or understand Hungarian, they found
ways to fight their way through the hard times and even live well.
The French call this talent, this ability to get by even under the
most difficult of circumstances, *se débrouiller*. The prewar notion
of *savoir vivre*, knowing how to live, was transformed during and

after the war into *débrouillardise*, resourcefulness. The French were brilliant practitioners of the art of resourcefulness.

In Hungary, French was spoken by educated and well-to-do people, because it was the chic thing to do, and by people who had worked in France before the war. So the French could get acquainted with numbers of Hungarians and find help among their new friends.

These French boys, who had battled their way out of some German prisoner-of-war camp or labor camp and made their way, thin and in rags, to Budapest, reappeared within a matter of days well, or even elegantly, dressed, perhaps with a whiff of cologne to complete the effect. Even more remarkable was the speed with which they acquired a girlfriend or a wife.

This was a time when the middle classes were generally extremely worried and pessimistic about the future of Hungary. For women, the main object was to find a mate. A Frenchman, belonging to the winning side, was a particularly desirable catch. That explained why the French boys, when they reappeared a few days later, no longer sat alone at their café tables. They presented the women who were with them as '*ma femme*' or '*mon amie*' or '*ma fiancée*'. To their credit, you never saw any of them with an unattractive woman: in this regard they had high standards. Evidently they held to the principle that if you are going to conquer a woman, she should be beautiful. The energy required is the same, whether the girl is beautiful or not. When wartime conditions caused a shortage of bridge partners, there was always a Frenchman who, siege or no siege, cried, '*Pourquoi pas?*' and sat down to play.

I do not know how they supported themselves, but I do know that if I asked them to obtain anything for me – medicines, food, whatever – they always managed to find it, almost as though they controlled the black market. Let me cite just one example.

Mentioning Emi's name, a Jewish woman, in hiding, came to see me. She wanted to sell her gold bracelet for 6,000 pengős. I didn't know much about jewelry, but as soon as I saw this piece I would willingly have given her the money there and then had it not been for the fact that I was short of cash and, if I used up what I had, I would have been hard put to it to get my hands on more. So I promised only that I would try to sell it for her. I was thinking of the French boys. They did not disappoint me, and immediately agreed to try to make a sale. I introduced my younger son to them as my representative. While his knowledge of French was very limited, his only task would be to accompany them while they looked for a buyer.

Hours passed and the boy did not return. I began to get concerned. The mechanism of human patience operates on principles that are the exact opposite of reason, as we can all of us easily establish from our own experience. For example: you wait for a streetcar. It doesn't come. You get more impatient every minute, although, logically, the chance of the streetcar's arrival increases every minute. So if I had been thinking logically, the longer my son stayed away, the less anxious I should have become.

The problem is that you can't get rid of worry with logic. Over the years, I have come to realize how irrational the connection between time and events is. Take the problem of old age. People get old, become bald, full of wrinkles, but it is precisely when we are older that we need an attractive exterior, need to stay the same on the outside as before.

It was already afternoon when finally I heard someone at the door. It was George, excited, happy. He deposited a little pile of money on the table.

'What took you so long?' I blurted out, giving voice to my earlier concern.

'It was really interesting. I would never have believed that there were still so many cafés in Budapest. And so many unbroken mirrors in them. The one thing that worried me was that they kept taking the bracelet away with them and leaving me in the café waiting for them to come back.

'And how did you make out with their French?'

'Quite well, because they made pretty effective use of their hands. "*Je prends le bijou*" – and the Frenchman pointed to his pocket. "*Mon ami*" – and he pointed to his friend – "*reste ici*" and he pointed several times at the floor. In other words, he left me one Frenchman as a guarantee, which reduced my concern but hardly eliminated it. Each time, they ordered an aperitif, but because I wasn't quite sure what that was, I played it safe and ordered raspberry syrup. I've learned more French today than in two weeks with Aunt Lili.'

The transaction, in all its sordid detail, went something like this: the Frenchmen sold the bracelet for 20,000 pengős (George heard them say the words '*vingt mille*' several times). George got 12,000. I gave the seller 7,000 because my own sense of honesty required that I increase the 6,000 requested by a further thousand, at my expense. No doubt a true businessman would find my behavior very unethical, since I paid 7,000 for something that could have been bought for 6,000.

We were still good friends with the Frenchmen, when one day, unexpectedly, something happened that made me quite worried about the future of some of them.

One evening in December, the military police surrounded the Café Miénk. There were guests at every table, many of them French. I was sitting by myself. Suddenly, everybody froze. It was as though, without anyone saying it out loud, the word 'raid' flashed through the room. A collection of beefy police officers, their uniforms smelling of sweat and their heavy boots thundering on the floor, moved from table to table. The people the leader pointed to had to leave their places and go straight to the police guarding the doors. Only the selection of examinees took place in the café: the actual examination would occur in the notorious Hadik Barracks, the counter-espionage office. Without stirring from my place, I knew these things immediately: I could tell from the whispers of the waiters and the guests, from the movement of their mouths. Each minute brought the police closer to my table. Several of the Frenchmen had already been fingered. Two tables away a fine-looking man, in a lieutenant's uniform, with delicate features and the look of an intellectual, was made to stand up.

When people were slow to respond to the finger pointed at them, the police reacted with savage crudity. 'Move it, or I'll kick your fucking balls so hard you'll never get up again.'

Never in my life have I heard officers address people so obscenely. Several Frenchmen were sitting with fashionably dressed women who were aghast and horrified at such filth. The police reached my table. I sat quietly, but with all the concentration I could muster.

'How old are you?'

'Fifty-two,' I said, in line with my identity papers (I was actually fifty).

They moved on. Evidently they were looking for deserters and so had no interest in me, because fifty-two was the upper age limit for military service. I breathed a little more freely. I have no idea where she came from, but I suddenly became aware of a woman, a charming brunette, standing at my table.

She spoke to me imploringly: 'Allow me, sir, to join you. I see that you are alone. They've taken away the lieutenant I was with. I'm really scared.'

I don't know why, but – perhaps because of my own uncertain situation – I refused. 'I am sorry. I have to say no. Don't ask me why, but I have my reasons,' I whispered, as firmly as I could.

I happened to look at the clock: 7:30. I was supposed to meet Paul here at eight. If he walked in now, while the raid was going on, he'd be dead meat. Somehow I had to call him.

I'd be tempting fate if I tried to get to a telephone. Surely I'd immediately attract the attention of these animals? But I couldn't just sit there: I had to make the call. I could put my own life on the line by taking risks, but I had no right to put my son's in danger. So I went to the telephone. I spoke to him and told him not to come. The whole thing went like clockwork. I went back and sat down at my table. What luck!

After the raid, people came together to talk. Such experiences tend to bring people closer. We went back over the events of the evening. They had taken away a total of seven Frenchmen, all of them of draft age.

Around nine thirty the crowd began to thin out. At that point, instead of going home, and on a sudden impulse, I went over to the table of the woman who had talked to me earlier and offered to escort her home, if she so wished.

When we were out on the darkened street I explained myself, 'Now I can tell you why I didn't let you sit at my table.'

'I'd like to know that – though some people from the police department gave me a seat at their table right away.'

'It's quite simple: I'm Jewish.'

'You're Jewish and you go to cafés!' Her voice showed her surprise.

In the course of our conversation I discovered that she had a two-room apartment on József Boulevard. She took such pity on me that she generously invited me in. I declined the invitation, but I asked her if, in a pinch, I could use her address and apartment for one of my friends.

Next day, my first order of business was to go round to the café and inquire after the Frenchmen. I was delighted to learn that four of them didn't even reach the barracks before they made their escape, aided by the darkness. For my part, I decided not to visit the café in the evenings any more. I also decided to leave home less frequently, and again only in the mornings. But I ran into fewer and fewer people I knew.

But one morning someone ran after me, out of breath and shouting, 'Doctor, Doctor!'

The thin, haggard man seemed familiar, but I could not place him.

Seeing my embarrassment, he introduced himself. 'You defended me in my race-debasement trial a couple of years ago.'

At the time, sexual relations between Christian and Jew were punishable by law. Because I dealt with relatively few such cases, I remembered him at once.

'What happened to you?' I asked, with considerable interest. 'As I recall, you lived in Újpest.'

'I didn't dare go back. Too many people knew me,' he replied with a sigh. 'You can't imagine what I've gone through.'

Always interested in people's stories, I encouraged him to tell me his. Perhaps I could be helpful in some way.

'I was in jail, but because of the Russian offensive, thank God, they had to evacuate the place. They simply let us loose to go where we wanted. Other guys in the jail had told me that, if you're homeless, the place to go is Szív Street, where the Salvation Army has a hostel and there's a free place for everyone. So I set off towards Szív Street. It was a cold, peaceful day. Having been locked up for a year and a half, I thought that it would be good at least to walk along one nice street, to enjoy my freedom, so I turned into Andrássy Street. I marched along the snowy street, taking deep breaths of the fresh, cold air.

'Suddenly, in front of a building, some kind of armed guard spoke to me. "Aren't you Jewish?" "Sure, I'm Jewish." Only when I got inside did I realize that I was in 60 Andrássy Street, the Arrow Cross headquarters.'

'But didn't you know what was happening to the Jews?' I asked in surprise.

'You know, jails are funny places. In my eighteen months in jail, I heard nothing about the German occupation, nothing about Jews wearing yellow stars, or the ghettos, or the murders. In the prison we didn't know any of this. Nobody cared about your nationality or your religion; nobody called you a yid. We all wore the same sackcloth, and we were interested in only two things: the food, and how soon we were getting out. Believe me, only in jail is there true democracy.'

'And what did the Arrow-Crossers do to you?'

'I got hit across the face a few times, but the guards didn't really treat me badly. I think they were more in a joking mood. "Don't worry Jew, you've got a great dinner invitation tonight, with some top people." "Where?" I asked hesitatingly. "In the next world," they cried, exploding with laughter. I didn't appreciate the joke. At midnight they lined us all up. We had nothing on our feet and were wearing just our underwear. They lined us up two by two and tied each of us to our companion. There must have been fifty or sixty of us, men, women and children.

'We set out on foot along Andrássy Street toward the Danube. A layer of soft snow covered the asphalt, but although we were barefoot I did not feel the cold. On the way, I whispered to my companion, an accountant about your age, forty-five or fifty, "Let's loosen the cord, at least enough to get our hands out if we have to." "What's the point?" he asked apathetically. "At least it won't hurt to do so," I replied. He didn't stop me when I loosened the cord. Though we marched slowly, we seemed to reach the river quite quickly. They stood us two at a time on the steps leading down to the water. The guards shot the two on the lowest step; if anyone was not killed immediately and did not fall into the water, they pushed him in with their rifle-butts. And so the next two people moved down to the lowest step. No one cried out, or at least I did not hear them. The group dwindled, and I realized that we were third in line. Then there was a commotion. A ten- or twelve-year-old girl was next. One of the guards took pity on her: "Let's leave the girl. Let's let her off." The disturbance caused more of the guards to move to the front of the line. Suddenly I pulled my hand out of the cord and, like some phantom in my white underclothes, amid the white snow, I ran off in the direction of Kálvin Square. They didn't even shoot at me. When I had no breath left, I slowed down.

'Then I heard the steady sound of marching in the distance. Only German soldiers march like that. So I ran as hard as I could – harder than a hunted animal, even. By this time it was perhaps three o'clock in the morning. Finally, I saw an open gate. I ran in and looked around. I was in a courtyard, maybe belonging to a horse-drawn freight company. A large pile of fresh manure was steaming at my feet. I inhaled deeply: perhaps it would warm me up. Now I began to feel the cold. I tried in vain to warm my naked feet.

'I don't know how long I was there. It seemed like a long time, because I was shaking with cold. Then a light came on in one of the windows. I crept over to it. Finding a nameplate next to the door, I ran my fingers over it in the dark and puzzled out the letters: superintendent. I hid myself again, waiting impatiently in the darkness, in the hope that the shadowy figure moving around inside would leave. It was still dark when the superintendent came out through the gate. At last! I rushed into the room. Before I could even turn around, I heard the frightened cries of a woman: "Help! Help!" I tried to quieten her: "Don't worry, I'm not going to hurt you." But she just kept shouting. I didn't dare use force, so I decided to leave the warmth of the room and run outside again.

'At the gate I ran full-tilt into two members of the National Guard, on their way back from night duty. They glanced at my feet, at my lack of clothes, and stopped me. I had to explain what had happened. I had hardly got started when they invited me up to their apartment on the second floor, and there I told the rest of my story. The two guardsmen were brothers, and the elder was married. The table in the apartment was laid and the wife was preparing food for the guards' return. They barely touched their meal, though: they were so busy filling me with food. After supper, they didn't let me leave until they had provided me with a complete set of clothes, from head to foot. Look at this coat I'm wearing! I got it from them.'

So this sad story had its elevating side too. The human heart still had some warmth. I loaned him a few hundred pengős, as a sign of my own human solidarity.

Chapter 21

Passing the Time

The air raids grew more frequent. Russian planes were now involved, and they did considerable damage to the brick buildings of the city. The frequent air raids also damaged the electric power lines, so the streetcar service deteriorated and, more to the point, all the lights went out. On such occasions we had to stop reading and could not listen to the radio. Our building received its power from an auxiliary substation, with the result that the power came back on from time to time when the rest of the city had none. In many houses the water system stopped functioning too, because the pressure dropped: at best there was a trickle of water on the ground floor. Many restaurants didn't even open, or, if they did, didn't stay open for long and could serve nothing because there was nothing to serve. I concluded that the time had come for my sons to move in with me, because it was getting more and more dangerous to be out on the street. My decision was influenced in large measure by the destruction of Margaret Bridge. The bridge had been mined: evidently the Germans planned to blow all the Danube bridges up when they retreated. But this explosion went off much sooner than they intended, for reasons we do not know. At the time the bridge was full of pedestrians, and a two-car streetcar, packed with people, was on its way across. All the passengers died in the river.

My younger son got to my apartment by taking a long detour. I did not let him return to the Hászkas.

My sons continued in the role of godsons: others in the building knew them as such from earlier visits, and had been told that they would be moving in.

Ever since the throat-slitting incident, I had been doing my best to avoid all unnecessary conversation with our landlady, but now I had to turn on all my charm to find a solution to this new situation. I wanted her to cook a hot meal for us every day. The woman was fond of money, and so, even though at first she showed reluctance, she couldn't refuse when I said that, in addition to paying her, I would keep her supplied with all her household needs, so that she wouldn't have to take care of these things herself. Later, in connection with this cooking arrangement, it transpired that there were two refugees living in the maid's room next to the little kitchen. This was the same room that I had already rented from her, as a reserve, a couple of months earlier.

The landlady explained that she had taken pity on the two refugees and given them kitchen space and somewhere to live. Maybe I was wrong: perhaps she had a good heart after all. Or maybe not. Perhaps she simply wanted to get double rent on the maid's room.

'With all this new activity in the kitchen, perhaps we should invite them to eat dinner too,' she added.

We could hardly refuse the request, and so at the first dinner we met the refugees. One glance and I saw that they were in the same boat as we were. The woman was a likable person, fortyish, with a nice smile. She was registered as a war refugee and talked constantly about the good life she had once enjoyed – living in a well-appointed house, with a big household, lots of servants, in fact like a countess. So we simply named her the countess. Her friend, whose shaving habits left something to be desired, was a tall, intelligent-looking man of around sixty, whose outward behavior betrayed internal anxiety. This anxiety reached a level of downright torture if anyone at the table asked him questions.

'Where are you from?'

'From Nógrádverőce,' he said, after a moment's thought.

Ozma suddenly sat up, his local patriotism stirring. 'Who do you know in Verőce? I have a summer house there; that's why I ask.'

The man's embarrassment was so palpable that he made me uncomfortable too, and I felt the need to intervene.

'Mr Fényes lived in Verőce fifty years ago, when he was a child. And you've lived there for only two years. He's hardly likely to know you as a local celebrity.'

Ozma must have grasped the situation from the way I snapped at him, because he fell silent. We went back to discussing the countess's wealth.

After the meal I took the man aside. 'You have no reason for fear, at least not from us,' and he almost fainted when he learned that we also were Jews.

For the most part we led our lives confined to the apartment. One night I discovered some unexpected guests. Turning on the light, I happened to look at the wall. There, walking quietly and with dignity across it, was a bedbug. My captivity in Russia had taught me how to deal with these wild creatures without having to touch them. With the help of a strip of paper and a match, I was able to incinerate our little bloodsucker. This was generally the best way of exterminating them, but it did of course leave a mark on the wall.

I decided not to mention my discovery to the landlady for fear that she would attribute the arrival of bedbugs to my various illegitimate overnight guests and forbid me to let them in. Because pest-exterminating firms were no longer functioning in the city, we could not get outside help. With no other options available, I took to turning on the lights several times during the night, when everyone else was asleep, and using my tried and true method for eliminating the insects. The burn marks on the wall increased from day to day. But finally one of these hunting expeditions had its glorious culminating moment: there were no bedbugs on the wall. But true happiness is lasting happiness. Even after several days there were still no bedbugs to be seen: they had evidently retreated, but the burn marks on the wall bore witness to our previous struggles. It occurred to me that I could use two wall-maps bought some months before, one of Hungary and one of Europe, to cover the burns. I delegated responsibility for this enterprise to my son. I was a great believer in shared labor.

The two maps with their bright colors lent a certain unaccustomed freshness to the room. Hanging there, they looked like two surrealist paintings. But later they became not just interesting decorations but the basis for an exciting, not to say impassioned, game.

With the city under siege it was almost impossible to leave the house, and so to pass the time we began to ask one another questions based on the maps.

'How many villages in France?'

'How many rivers in Italy?'

'How far from Budapest to Munich?'

The winner was the person whose guess came closest to the information provided by the map. Afterwards, as tends to happen with such games, precise rules developed, along with certain rewards, in addition to the glory of winning. We had in reserve three boxes of Gerbeaud cookies (before the war Gerbeaud made the finest cookies in Hungary). We each took one of the boxes and from here on the winners were rewarded with cookies. This new game led us to abandon chess, in which my older son was already so proficient that no one but he stood a chance of winning.

The new game had its moments of crisis. I was pretty lucky with my answers, with the result that one day my younger son asked, 'Don't get angry, Uncle Lexi, but are you preparing your answers in advance?'

'What do you mean by that?'

'Well, for example, before asking us the distance from Paris to London you check the map so that you end up with the best answer.'

'You mean, I cheat?'

'Not normally, but maybe in games.'

I felt that self-defense would be beneath my dignity, so I simply said, 'In my regiment I was the best judge of distances. You've heard me say that before, so I didn't just invent it. Let's do things a different way: we'll take it in turns to ask the questions, which will give everyone the same chance.'

For several days our games continued in harmonious tranquillity, using the new rules. But luck continued to favor me.

One morning, as we were about to start playing, my elder son spoke: 'I speak not just for myself but also for George. Godfather, your approach to the game is not entirely above reproach.'

'I don't understand. What are you complaining about now?'

'Ever since we started, you've been winning. In itself, there's nothing wrong with that. The trouble is, you eat your winnings.'

I was taken aback by his remark. 'As far as I know, there's no prohibition against eating what you win. You know I like sweet things.'

'It's true it's not actually prohibited, because no one thought of it. But it *is* unfair, because you reduce the chances of our winning the cookies back.'

George chimed in, 'From our perspective, this is more a moral than a material question.'

His remark showed that he wanted to hang on to the moral high ground. I tried without success to explain that, even if I didn't eat the cookies, there was no certainty that they would win them back. And if they lost their entire stock, how would they continue the game? On credit? With an IOU? At what point would it be permissible for me to eat my winnings? We could come to no agreement on these matters and so the game ended. To restore peace, I magnanimously proposed that we play chess for cookies. I had accumulated enough and so I felt able to make the proposal. We began to play. But it became clear that my sons, generally better chess players than me, played less calmly than usual now that their last cookies were on the table – with the result that they lost more often than they won. So we had to abandon the contest and go back to playing for glory alone.

Paul now rediscovered his skill at chess and began to beat me more soundly than before. Our landlord the captain was already in despair: he had not won a game in weeks. In fact, he no longer dared play chess with Paul. So I had to play some consolation games with him to bring back his good humor.

One December day we had a wonderful surprise.

Danyi, Paul's friend, came to visit, unwashed, unshaven, but with a big knapsack on his back.

'How are you doing, Jancsi?'

'Not too well. Imagine, I've walked all the way from Soroksár. The Russians have got that far. Our whole ditch-digging team simply ran away. As soon as they heard the Russians had arrived, they took to their heels. It occurred to me that everyone would have abandoned the village office as well, but that they would have left their rubber stamps behind, so I went round and picked them up, thinking, Uncle Lexi, that you might be able to use them. I've brought them all.' And he proudly put on the table a total of thirty-seven different rubber stamps.

'Thank you for thinking of me.'

But secretly I was a little concerned. What on earth would I do with so many stamps, especially now, when everything was coming to an end?

'Anyway, go and wash up, and eat something, to get your spirits back.'

Danyi became the terror of our landlady: he was so fond of eating that he ate everything that was put on the table. I enjoyed watching his hearty appetite: he was able to put away two pounds of sausages without a bit of bread. For Christmas I gave him a set of ration coupons, valid as of January 1. The nearby black market in coupons was still in operation.

Two days before Christmas, the Russians advanced as far as Széna Square, in the heart of Buda. Members of the Szálasi cabinet and other prominent Arrow-Crossers had been hastily packing up everything they could find and moving westwards in commandeered trucks and taxis. There wasn't a rental car or a taxi left in the city.

On December 24, the radio announcer read a new decree whose brutality and cruelty exceeded pretty much anything we had encountered before:

> Everyone sixteen years old or older must report for military service.
> Anyone who fails to obey this general mobilization *is to be shot*.
> Anyone who hides Jews *is to be shot*.
> Anyone who hoards merchandise, or sells at a higher price, *is to be shot*.

At the end of each statement the words 'is to be shot' appeared (actually the Hungarian words were more like 'is to be butchered').

In other words, anyone who disobeyed the decree would not be tried by law, not even by court martial, but simply murdered on the spot. The text of the decree showed that the Arrow Cross government had lost the game, and also its collective equilibrium: its only hope was to buy a little time through out-and-out terror. The desperate tone of the decree only reinforced our hopes.

'This is no longer the end of the beginning, but the beginning of the end,' said Ozma.

Our hopeful mood prompted us, and not just our Christian landlords, to celebrate Christmas. We had one can of food with no label on it: the label had come unstuck over time. So we didn't know what was in it. The shining can, mute as to its contents, was a steady source of fantasy to us. We speculated constantly on what it might contain: goulash with paprika perhaps? or corned beef?

We decided to celebrate by opening the can. Lacking a can-opener, we used a hammer and chisel to cut round the top of the can and opened it with much excitement. To our great surprise the two-pound can contained pineapple, which even in more peaceful times was reckoned a rare delicacy. We had not seen pineapple in years, let alone eaten it. We decided that we would each eat one piece a day, and, because there were five of us, we could brighten our lives with it for the next four days.

In the course of my life, whenever I have tried to economize, I have come out the loser. It was the same on this occasion: on the third day our exquisite pineapple pieces went bad on us and we had to throw away the last day's supply.

The landlord and his wife invited us to Christmas dinner, but they did not seem to be in a holiday mood, in fact seemed downright gloomy. I thought this might be because the landlady's stepdaughter, who was an Arrow-Crosser, had just left to escape to the west. But it turned out that their unhappiness had a different cause. While we were still at dinner the landlord pulled me aside. He was visibly flustered and evidently did not know how to start the conversation.

'Lexi, what do you think? Will I get into trouble for having furniture taken from Jews?'

'Why would you get into trouble? You got it from the government, didn't you?'

'Yes, but what if the Arrow Cross government collapses?' he whispered.

'It won't collapse,' I said, to cheer him up.

'But what if it does?' he went on insistently, evidently looking for further reassurance.

'Do you have a receipt, to show that you paid for the furniture?' I asked, pretending to be an expert on such matters. The captain scratched his head.

'I would be happy to pay, but so far nobody's told me how much.'

'Try to get a receipt,' I advised.

'I'm afraid it's too late for that,' he said despairingly.

'Surely you can get one. You have such good connections,' I assured him.

He made a long face and, with a gesture of hopelessness, turned back to the dinner table. We sat down again.

It's amazing how easily one loses one's common sense when greed takes over. My landlord had, in middle-class terms, a perfectly decent apartment, and he had no need for the collection of beat-up old pieces of furniture that he had acquired. Getting them there had required a great deal of energy: they had transported them through the streets on a tiny handcart because there were no other means available. In the apartment there was hardly enough room for the furniture, which effectively blocked free movement around their room. A stouter, big-bellied person couldn't have even got into the hall. It was perhaps just as well that they spent relatively little time in the apartment anyway: most of the time they were in the air-raid shelter. And now they were frightened that a change of regime would bring some kind of trouble: fear was written all over their faces.

The Russians' military victories and their gradual advance on the city gave me hope and a measure of secret joy. But our sense of celebration was short-lived: we had to figure out what to do about the emergency decree.

The proclamation of general mobilization meant that every man between the ages of sixteen and fifty had to report for military duty. My son Paul clearly belonged in that category. His biological age was eighteen, and his identity papers indicated that he was seventeen. Tall and well-built, he looked more like nineteen than seventeen. There was no way we could rearrange his identity papers to make him sixteen or younger. I carefully studied the decree, looking for exceptions, but none of them seemed applicable to Paul. There was nothing for it but to order him to stay in the apartment for the time being. For some time now we had not been going to the air-raid shelter in the basement, because our ground-floor apartment was at almost the same level as the shelter and in some ways a better place to be if the building got hit: it was easier to dig people out of a ground-floor apartment than out of an air-raid shelter.

Because we did not spend time in the shelter, it was hardly possible that Paul would catch anyone's unwanted attention because of his age. But since our building had no running water, it was now George's job to carry buckets of water to the apartment from the basement of the neighboring market. Up to now, the job had been shared by the two boys, depending on who 'owed' a work assignment. I should explain the system. Between seven and ten o'clock each evening the electricity was turned off. Our passion for betting had taken over again and during the day we laid bets on the exact time the current would go off. The person who came closest to guessing right was declared the winner for the day. If we had no chocolate or cookies to bet with, we could offer relief from an hour's work assignment in place of a Gerbeaud cookie. Sometimes we had enough manpower stored up to last for days or even weeks.

In the evenings, sitting in the dark, we realized how hungry we were. As we sat round the tile stove that heated the room, one of us suggested that we could bake potatoes in the ashes. The experiment was such a success that it became a nightly routine. We invited the landlord and his wife too, and our potato baking became the high point of the day. Baked potatoes smell wonderful. We never investigated whether it was the smell of the potatoes or the word of the landlord and landlady that caused the entire building to learn that Lexi Szabó and his family baked potatoes every evening, but not an evening passed without one or two people dropping in, on one pretext or another, to sample our potatoes.

Even the new threat of summary execution, like all bad things, had its good side. Café and restaurant owners were so terrified about food hoarding that they opened up again. Even though they kept their shutters closed, one door was always open, and, if nothing else, you could always get a cup of hot tea, though sometimes without sugar.

The merchants were frightened, too, and sold whatever merchandise they had left. One of them, in our neighborhood, was shot to death for selling beans above the official price. The streets presented a depressing scene. On József Avenue, hoisted on a lamp-post, hung two men. Attached to the neck of one of them was a piece of paper saying: 'This is what happens to a Jew who hides.' Around the neck of the other a paper said: 'This is what happens to a Christian who hides a Jew.'

The wind shook both papers with the same indifference.

Passers-by turned their heads away as they hurried past, their faces blank, but there were a few who gathered in groups to comment.

I also stopped and risked a remark: 'Maybe it would be better to let the law courts deal with people we think guilty.'

A red-faced fellow glared at me so angrily that I felt it best to keep quiet.

Chapter 22

Siege

Life in the city grew more and more difficult. For weeks we had seen no German planes. Anyone who has done military service knows how much easier it is to fight when you don't have to worry about enemy planes. Not only did the Germans have no planes – or none that we could see – but their anti-aircraft guns didn't seem to be working either. Russian planes flew in from time to time at surprisingly low altitudes and strafed the streets.

On one occasion I was walking with George over to the neighboring market for water. On the way back he suddenly said: 'Dad, look how low that plane is flying, and look at those red flashes!'

I looked up and with one motion yanked him under our gateway. We flattened ourselves against the wall of the staircase entrance. With a great roar and a *pick-pick-pick* sound, the plane thundered over our building. When we looked out afterwards into the silence of the street, two people lay dead on the sidewalk.

The number of people dead in the street, and of horses too, kept increasing. The horse carcasses turned out to be quite useful: an occasional diligent housewife would run out into the street with a sharp knife, cut off a piece of meat and head back home to her hungry family with her loot.

Public services fell apart almost completely. Only one thing operated smoothly – food inspections by our landlord, the captain. Not a day went by without bread. However little the bakeries baked, somehow the inspector always got his loaf. For us this was important: we received our daily bread; we did not have to go hungry.

Jutka, my older son's girlfriend, moved in with us. Her father was stuck in some village on the Great Plain. He had gone there in search of food, when the Russians suddenly occupied the place.

One day I accidentally touched her hand and noticed that it was unusually hot. We got out the thermometer: 104 degrees. We looked for a doctor at once, and found one in the neighboring building. He came and examined Jutka carefully.

The diagnosis was very disheartening: 'An advanced case of pleurisy. If you feed her well, she may have a chance.'

Jutka was an extraordinary little person. Her soft voice, her wisdom, her constant smile filled everything around her with a kind of harmony. Her personality charmed everybody.

'Do you know, little one, what the doctor said?'

She looked at me with her lovely eyes. The doctor's sad warning was still ringing in my ears as I said to her with intentional severity: 'If you don't eat normally, you'll die.'

'You're just trying to frighten me, right?'

'Not at all. You know that I never joke about serious matters.'

We decided that we would not let her go back to her old lodging. She would receive my bed, and I would sleep on the floor with the boys. To tempt her to eat, we took out our secret reserves. She always ate remarkably little when she came to visit us, but I attributed this to her good manners: she didn't want our food supplies to be depleted on her account. But now she took matters seriously. It was clear that she was trying to eat. Apparently my directness with her had an effect.

Her illness cast a shadow over the entire family: we all loved her very much. She had been with us for several days when a chance conversation revealed how she had become so ill. From the Avas family, she had moved over to Pest, to stay with a girl-friend who was also part-Jewish. I had assumed that Jutka was well situated there, but apparently from the time of the recent draconian decree the girl's parents didn't want Jutka around any more: they felt that with their lack of 'racial purity' the risk was too high. They lived on the top floor of their building. When the apartment next door was hit by a bomb and the tenants moved out, the family put a mattress in among the ruins and made Jutka spend the night there. The wind whistled through the bare walls and rain poured in through holes in the ceiling. Jutka had been sleeping there for the past several weeks. She had said not a word about it to us because she didn't want to cause us more trouble than we already had.

And now, as she lay ill in our room, I never heard her complain. Even Lajos was gentle and kind to her, though he really suffered from the fact that we were now five in the room. Paul became more and more fretful under his imprisonment in the room. He kept reproaching me for not 'arranging' matters for him. I suggested that, if he was so impatient, he should obey the decree and sign up for service as József Balázs. At least he would then be legally registered and we would gain some time to find a way out before he was actually called up. But this did not appeal to him. The solution we finally found was to have the village of Soroksár certify that he was employed as a baker and therefore exempt from military service. The only defect in this excessively official-looking document was that Soroksár had been in the hands of the Russians since before the recent decree came into effect in Budapest.

Dr Katona, Jutka's doctor, came to visit her daily. Penicillin was unknown at the time, but even if it had been available abroad, it was impossible to obtain medicine of any description during the siege. The doctor gave the last of his dwindling supply of drugs to his young patient. This good-humored, balding man was quite scathing in his comments on the Arrow Cross regime, but since I had not known him before, I had no way of telling whether this was his long-standing opinion or merely a symptom of the recent crisis. As the fall of the Germans got closer and more certain, more and more people tried to put some distance between themselves and the Arrow Cross Party, the Hungarian variant of Nazism.

This phenomenon has its roots in human nature. In general, people believed the slogans of the Arrow Cross press about a Jewish–Bolshevik–Plutocrat front – which seemed to prove that the Jews were the most powerful people on earth: at one and the same time they held in their hands, through their diabolical cleverness and their web of contacts, the Western capitalist countries and Russian Bolshevism. Consequently, whichever of these groups reached Budapest first – the Western capitalists or the Russian communists – their first move would surely be to punish or reward people for their mistreatment of the Jews at a time of crisis. So a trend began – one might even say a secret movement – aimed at providing people with suitable alibis. Everyone tried to exonerate himself in advance. People lined up witnesses and contacts designed to show how they had sabotaged the regime, and how many Jews, and particularly how many Jewish possessions, they had saved. Rumor had it that some people began to visit the ghetto, and look up the occasional Jewish neighbor. Wags called this sudden enlightenment '*alibi-baba*'. The term really described a characteristic latent in all humankind: a tendency to turn towards the party in power. It was precisely the opportunists who now believed that the Jewish sun was rising.

It is certainly possible that Dr Katona was looking for an alibi, because, when I heard his remarks about the regime, I discreetly told him I belonged to a secret society whose goal was to help Jews in hiding, and he at once offered his services. I promised him only that I would pass his offer along. A few days later I told him that the society needed ten hospital certificates indicating that the bearer had undergone an operation for phimosis. I gave him a model text. Within forty-eight hours he put the ten certificates in my hand, with spaces for the names.

Why the need for documents on operations for phimosis?

In Hungary, the circumcision of boys was not common practice, except that the Jews circumcised their young sons in accordance with their religious beliefs. Accordingly, when carrying out male identity checks, it was most important to the Arrow-Crossers to establish whether someone was circumcised or not. There exists a medical condition known as tight foreskin, or phimosis, which can be dealt with through adult circumcision, and a hospital would provide a certificate in such cases. The certificate was of doubtful value. I knew of a case where Arrow-Crossers shot a Christian despite his perfectly genuine certificate, and of another case where someone managed to get out of the Arrow Cross headquarters with a forged certificate. The true value of the certificate can be summed up as follows: there's a good chance that if you have to use it it won't work, but it certainly does no harm to have it.

So I handed out the certificates. I gave one each to Danyi, and to Ozma, and of course to my sons. In this way the foreskin problem, a constant threat haunting our pseudo-Christian lives, was quietly laid to rest.

Paul read the text of the certificate carefully and shook his head in disbelief: 'Godfather, don't you think they would find it a little odd if they checked our papers and all five of us Christians produced certificates indicating medical removal of our foreskins? Isn't that rather a lot?'

I didn't reply, but I might have pointed out that some problems in this life cannot have perfect solutions.

The severity of the 'summary execution' decree had exactly the opposite effect from the one intended. It simply hastened the collapse. Everyone tried to jump from the sinking ship. Even the people who registered for service, then obeyed the call-up papers and were sent out to the edge of the city to dig defenses, deserted within a matter of days. If you looked around a shelter during an air raid, half the men in the room were deserters. I became friendly with a sergeant living in the neighborhood, and invited him over for a glass of brandy. Before setting out, he hung a machine-gun round his neck.

I pointed to it. 'What do you need that for?'

'Look, brother, it's always a good idea to have something to prove that you're on duty.'

He came over to see us on several occasions. I liked his amusing way of talking and his sense of irony. On one occasion we were saying goodbye to one another at the door and he was on his way down the hallway when I noticed that his gun was still in the room.

I ran after him. 'Brother, your machine-gun!'

'Never mind, I'll be back for it,' he said casually.

'But I can't let you go without it; something might happen to you out on the street.'

Scratching his head, he came back reluctantly to get it. I could hardly let him go without his favorite 'guitar'.

Discarded guns and bazookas (anti-tank weapons) were by now scattered in the streets; but nobody bothered to pick them up. Arrow Cross insignia disappeared; no one wore the armbands any more.

My mother-in-law, our matron, was having trouble again. The hotel where she was staying was full of rootless people of various descriptions. There were people trying to get to Yugoslavia and unable to continue their journey, or aristocrats who couldn't get to their country houses, or pseudo-Christians doing their best to hang on during difficult times. The residents of the hotel were such a mixed bag that it was no surprise when one night the authorities selected from among them the people they suspected were Jews, with the intention of marching them off to the Danube. My mother-in-law was among those selected.

Although she did not follow my earlier instructions to give the Arrow-Crossers a thorough tongue-lashing, she did declare decisively, 'I am not a Jew.'

She repeated this several times, and finally her firmness had the desired result. The rest were marched away: she alone was set free.

I discovered all this when she visited me at the apartment on Vásár Street, at a time when everyone avoided going outside.

'But how did you find me, Mother?' I asked.

'Balázs gave me the address.'

I had given Balázs strict orders to reveal my address to no one. I could imagine how my mother-in-law must have tormented the poor man into disobeying my instructions.

'Do sit down, Mother, but talk quietly' (Jutka was just then asleep). 'Tell me, what's new?'

'There's trouble,' she said, scarcely audibly. 'The doorman at the hotel has told me that the German commander has ordered the hotel evacuated. I have to find a new place.'

'The doorman can say what he likes. One thing we know, Mother: you mustn't leave the hotel. You can't come here: there are five of us in the room already, Jutka and Lajos in the beds and the rest of us on the floor. This is no time for apartment hunting.'

'But this is an order from the Germans!'

'The Germans should get used to not giving orders.' By this time, half of Budapest was in Russian hands. 'The siege will be over in a matter of days. Here's a piece of advice, Mother. Tell the commander that you're a Red Cross nurse and that you'll tend to the injured, but don't move out of the hotel.'

'I can't say that. I don't know anything about nursing.'

'But you know how to peel potatoes, right? Go into the kitchen and start peeling potatoes. There's not an army in the world that doesn't need potato peelers.'

It was clear from her face that she was hardly in love with the idea.

'If you don't want to peel potatoes, try cleaning. What matters is that you stay in the hotel. And now Paul will take you home, and he'll also talk with the doorman.'

My mother-in-law did not object. Paul later told me what happened. The doorman got very embarrassed when Paul asked him where in the hotel he could find the German commander's office: he wished to speak with him about the evacuation. It turned out that none of the other guests had been told to move. The doorman had made up the whole story in an attempt to obtain a room for someone, for a fee.

It's remarkable how people always exploit the weak, the unprotected, the uneducated. These are the people who get charged exorbitant interest rates, who end up buying miracle drugs that don't work, or get tricked into buying copper rings instead of gold. Our hotel doorman, good psychologist that he was, figured that my mother-in-law was the type who would fall for the idea of a German order. Afterwards he would be able to give the empty room to someone else and clean up in the process.

By the time my mother-in-law turned up, the Arrow Cross days were coming to an end. As we heard by way of the BBC, the Russians were moving forward day by day to occupy further Budapest streets and neighborhoods. Their advance was not as fast as I kept hoping it would be, but the progress was steady, and there was no doubt that the city would soon fall into their hands. They had already taken Margaret Island, in the heart of the city. Along with those living on the island, some fifty German soldiers surrendered to the Russians.

Day by day the cruelties perpetrated by the Arrow Cross executioner-soldiers intensified. They realized that they didn't have much time left. Not just at night, but now in full daylight, in sight of everybody, they continued their crimes. Remarkably, there was always someone who managed to run away and spread the message of their atrocities. At the end of December they murdered all the patients in the Jewish hospital at Városmajor and Maros Streets in Buda; they also tortured some of them before killing them. The operation was directed by a psychotic former monk, Father Kun. The patients and pseudo-patients in the Jewish hospital on Bethlen Street lived in fear of their lives, not least because the hospital had a special section for the wounded who succeeded in swimming ashore from the Danube. On one occasion, when the Germans raided the hospital, the patients retreated to the attic, since there was nowhere else to hide. The Arrow-Crossers did haul various patients away from the Bethlen Street hospital as well, but they left the rest of them alone.

In contrast to Father Kun, the monks and nuns of the city worked hard to save Jewish children. At the convent on Vörösmarty Street some fifty Jewish children were housed, along with a handful of Christian children. Convent discipline was strict. Many of the previously spoiled children did not like the discipline, the lock-step teaching, the education based on authoritarian principles. One little ten-year-old boy actually ran away. Out in the street, torn apart by the siege, was a world quite different from the one he had imagined. Afraid to go further, he waited outside until someone came to visit the convent, and crept back inside.

Somehow, the Arrow-Crossers learned that the convent was hiding Jewish children. Early in January, four armed Arrow-Crossers herded the children to the bank of the Danube and massacred them, using the established method. Here again, two boys managed to save themselves. One of them had lived on an island in the Danube and from infancy had been a strong swimmer. He didn't wait for the shot but simply jumped into the water. In January the water in the Danube is freezing cold, and of course he caught pneumonia – but he lived. The other boy was wounded in the arm, but managed to swim away.

They also began to murder the residents of buildings under foreign protection. On December 30 they murdered most of the people living in the Swedish house at 16 Katona József Street. On January 3, 1945, the foreign Jews were transferred to the ghetto because it seemed safer for them there.

The activities of the Arrow Cross government, in addition to the butchery of Jews, seemed to consist largely of putting up posters around the city to encourage the despairing inhabitants. I still remember one of their posters because of the sheer oddity of its design and text. It looked a little like an illustration from an anatomy textbook. The picture showed a person whose skin had been removed, with bleeding body. To make it look more natural, bunches of black hair were sticking out from the body.

Underneath, in big letters, stood the words: 'THEY WANTED MY WATCH!' The purpose of such posters was to stir up anti-Russian sentiment.

The sole topic of conversation in our building was what would happen when the Russians took the place over. Tenants known and unknown asked my opinion. I did my best to reassure them to the extent possible. I told them that for many years I had been a prisoner of war and I spoke good Russian. The Russians were generally a good lot, I said, and there was no reason to fear them, because they were decent guys, even if sometimes they were quick to anger.

One thing I could not say: that my first and only wish was to see them arrive on the doorstep.

The story soon got around in the air-raid shelter that I spoke Russian, and soon I received a visit from the commander of the local anti-aircraft unit, along with two of his trusted colleagues.

'We would like to discuss with you what arrangements should be made for the reception of the Russians, when they get here.'

I had no advice to offer, but I did promise to be at their immediate disposal if they let me know when the Russians arrived. I said I would do everything I could to prevent any harm from coming to anyone.

We no longer ventured out into the street, at most going as far as the courtyard for a breath of air. We were the only ones in the apartment: the rest were living in the shelter.

The noise of machine-guns grew steadily louder and steadily closer. The windowpanes in our room broke one after the other. We covered the windows with cardboard. Fortunately we had an adequate supply of cardboard and thumb-tacks in the room.

Explosions or stray bullets no longer broke the glass but tore the cardboard. My younger son was eager to repair the rips in the cardboard as fast as possible, to keep the place warm. He prepared strips of paper so that he could cover the holes quickly.

'George, stop that hammering!'

As a former army officer, I had long since noted that in one part of the room we could remain quite safe, but anyone in the vicinity of the window could easily be struck by a bullet coming through the window at an angle.

George was lost in his work, and didn't hear, or pretended not to hear, my command.

I raised my voice: 'Leave the window alone!'

There was no way he could not hear me this time.

'Why don't you just let me finish, Father?'

How easy it would have been to say the obvious: because I'm afraid for you. But something stopped me – some inhibition, some principle of child-rearing, who knows? So I just said: 'I don't have to answer that question. Just do as you're told: Stop it!'

George sullenly retreated from the window, as if to say, 'Now Dad and I can't understand one another either.'

Chapter 23

January 12, 1945

For three days we stayed in the house, most of the time in our room, except for occasional visits to the courtyard for air. We were dressed more warmly than usual, as if we were going skiing, because cold air was pouring in through the window. From the direction of the street came the frequent sound of machine-gun fire. We didn't feel like reading, but we had plenty of time to think. The state of war I had lived through since the Germans invaded had changed my emotional world. Living as a victim of persecution had heightened my sense of empathy: the condition of all such victims of persecution became my affair, a part of my condition. The atrocities of the Japanese government made *me* ashamed; the measures taken against South African blacks were offenses against *me*. It was as though I felt responsibility for the whole world. The residue of this feeling stays with me today here in America. It is what makes me give up my seat for the old black lady in the overcrowded subway, when she looks tired; and it fills my eyes with tears when someone tells me a story of some spontaneous manifestation of generosity.

I have never been slave to hatred. Hitler's Nazism annihilated many of my dearest friends and two of my brothers. But I cannot identify Hitler and what he stood for with the German people. I have tried to bring my two sons up in this same spirit.

As though fate wished to put this belief to the test, from the direction of the bathroom came a loud crash. What had happened? One of my sons looked in.

'There's a German soldier in the bathroom!'

We all went in. There stood a fair-haired, blue-eyed German boy in full military equipment, his chin as smooth as a baby's. The bathroom window, which had frosted glass in it, was normally never opened. Now it stood open.

Chance had so arranged things that this solitary German soldier, representative of the power and might of Germany, now stood before four Jews, who had the opportunity to treat him with the same senseless barbarity and malice that the Germans had used on millions of Jews. With his blue eyes and blond hair he seemed the very embodiment of that Aryan-ness whose fanatical adherents had sought to enslave peoples and exterminate races. Should the *lex talionis*, the principle of compensation, of an eye for an eye and a tooth for a tooth, apply? Was he himself guilty? Was it right to punish him for something he had perhaps not done himself, not even approved of? And did the 'Aryans' weigh such matters with similar exactitude?

We did the boy no harm.

'*Wie alt sind Sie?* [How old are you?]' This was my first question.

'I'm seventeen,' he declared, eager to please.

'Do you smoke?'

'Yes.'

He took my offered cigarette, lit it, and inhaled eagerly. He explained that there was a Russian tank in front of our building. This was evidently the source of the machine-gun fire we had been hearing. He had run from the Russians into the basement of our building, and, looking for a way out, had gone from there to the air shaft. Our bathroom window looked out on this air shaft, so he had broken the glass of the outer window and pushed at the inner one. When it gave way he tumbled into the room.

We talked for perhaps a quarter of an hour. The question then was what to do with him.

The eyes of fourteen-year-old George seemed filled with tears. I put a handful of cigarettes into the Aryan soldier's fist and gave him his orders: 'You're to go out the same way you came in.'

The boys helped him climb on to the window-sill, and the armed representative of the German Reich exited Jewish-occupied territory.

Perhaps we treated him roughly when we committed him to fate, sending him off neither with good advice nor with a few bits of clothing that might have helped him escape the Russians, disguised as a civilian. But, as pseudo-Christians, we had not quite reached that level of Christianity where we were willing to return bread for stones.

To return to the fate of the Germans.

How steep the path that led down from the Germany of Goethe, Schiller, Beethoven, to the pathetic little soldier of Hitler's Germany! When the Hitler regime began, no one could have anticipated this cataclysm. Maybe not even Hitler.

In 1933, the day before Hitler was appointed chancellor, Goebbels, at the time minister of internal affairs, later minister of propaganda, called into his office, one by one, the Jewish lawyers of his acquaintance and told them that next day the Nazis would take over power. He advised them to leave the country as soon as possible. One of my lawyer friends who was there at the time told me this. So, even in that dark soul there was hidden a little human kindness, or something like it.

At the beginning of the Hitler period, the Nazis continued to support emigration to Palestine, and they even allowed Jews to take their possessions with them – after payment of the Reichs-fluchtsteuer, the Refugee Tax. In Hungary, the Arrow Cross program declared that recipients of the Silver Medal of Honor in World War I were not to be treated as Jews. What *inversio in peius*, what decline to the lowest common denominator, took place

in ten short years, when the final solution became the extermination of Jews by all means at the Nazis' disposal!

But extermination affected other groups too. One encyclopedia I saw recently says that the Germans killed:

15,000,000 Russians
2,000,000 Poles
1,000,000 Greeks
1,000,000 Yugoslavs.

Their theory of racial purity resulted in the butchery of:

5,000,000 Jews
2,000,000 Gypsies and others.

Is our collective sense of human solidarity strong enough to prevent similar mass murder in the future? I don't know. We can only hope that it is.

If you wait for something too long, you can't fully enjoy it when it finally happens. So much energy gets used up in the waiting that, when the day arrives at last, all you feel is a simple lifting of the heart.

This was the situation now, when, in quick succession, several people ran in with the same message: 'The Russians are here!'

The date was January 12, 1945, and the hour two o'clock in the afternoon.

We had survived the most difficult adventure of our lives.

I rushed outside. In front of the door stood three Russians. Despite their torn clothing, it was clear that they were officers.

I spoke to them in Russian. 'Come in and have some tea.'

Those were the literal words, but to a Russian they meant, 'Make yourselves at home.'

And they did.

Thanks to my knowledge of Russian, my room became the base for the battalion command. There were three or four battalion leaders, responsible for some four or five hundred men. The group was clad in worn-out, greenish, fleece-lined uniforms. They looked tired, but in good spirits. I did my best to act as a good host, trying to get Moscow on the radio (I finally succeeded) and putting wine and cookies on the table. One of them took a whole plateful of cookies.

Another immediately jumped on him: 'You have a nerve eating all these people's food! Come on! They may be putting their last mouthful in front of us.'

He silently put the cookies back.

A heavy-set Russian, with a scarf round ⟨ ⟩, called me into the courtyard. I left the closet open ⟨ ⟩ wristwatch next to the radio and headed out with ⟨ ⟩ asked me to show him the tunnel that led in the dire⟨ ⟩ was pointing. I explained to him that you could only ⟨ ⟩ one shelter to another underground, and only within th⟨ ⟩ lock.

He looked at me reproachfully. 'I thou⟨ ⟩ were our friend. Now you don't want to help.'

'I can only tell you the truth. If a t⟨ ⟩ esn't exist, it's no help to tell you it does.'

It occurred to me that very close ⟨ ⟩ uilding, barely two blocks away, was the most notorious ⟨ ⟩ ow Cross buildings, the one on Rökk Szilárd Street. I wou⟨ ⟩ o be there to see how the Arrow-Crossers behaved when t⟨ ⟩ ins arrived.

'You know what? If you want to ⟨ ⟩ r the most important building in this neighborhood, ov⟨ ⟩ kk Szilárd Street, I'm willing to lead you there, but onl⟨ ⟩ of the street.'

My proposal mollified him, bu⟨ ⟩ y also disillusioned him, and nothing more could be done ⟨ ⟩ We said goodbye. I went back to our room. A few minutes ⟨ ⟩ o Russian soldiers led in a tall Hungarian, about forty year⟨ ⟩ ey had brought him from a workshop in the area, where ⟨ ⟩ and a whole collection of anti-tank guns. They wanted ⟨ ⟩ estion him.

Imploringly, tremblingly, h⟨ ⟩ d: 'For God's sake, brother, help me. It's true, brother, ⟨ ⟩ were anti-tank guns there, but I swear to you, brother, that I wanted to use them against the Germans. I'm a supporter of the communists; I even went to jail because of it. I swear it, brother.'

I let him talk. Every tenth word was 'brother,' and this word 'brother' was precisely the word that the Arrow-Crossers used among themselves – which would suggest that he was no friend of the communists but an Arrow-Crosser. What to do? If I communicated this impression to the Russians, they would undoubtedly take him out and shoot him. This did not fit my lawyer's mind-set. You can hardly take a man's life on the basis of his speaking style. So I gave a favorable report and they let him go. Later, I took the trouble to make some inquiries and discovered that in fact he was telling the truth.

Around four o'clock, as dusk was falling, the battalion leaders marched away. The wristwatch lay in its place untouched: they had taken nothing. They even offered to help me out, but I declined their offer. Personally, I never had any trouble with the Russians.

The events of the previous couple of hours made me the natural choice for house interpreter. That evening, the residents urgently summoned me to the shelter. I was greeted by a young fair-haired Russian soldier, no more than nineteen or twenty years old. As he talked, he kept rotating his revolver under my nose, as if he had stepped out of a Western movie. I had difficulty understanding what he wanted.

'. . . all the men must assemble for a work assignment . . .'

I got quite angry at the routine with the revolver, but kept myself under control. With apparent calm, I said: 'If you want something from me, son, put away your revolver. I'm a nervous man and I don't like talking with a gun in my face.'

Perhaps he sensed the determination in my voice; at any rate, he slowly lowered his gun.

Gathering the men together with considerable difficulty, he took them off to some kind of work assignment. They walked six or eight kilometers to the outskirts of town, where they waited at a suburban train station. Nothing happened. Eventually the Russian guards disappeared. At daybreak the men decided to walk home again.

But not all such excursions ended so happily.

A few days later I learned that some of the people rounded up for *malenki robot*, small work assignments, had been transported to Soviet Russia as 'prisoners of war'.

The Russian soldiers, like most soldiers, also indecently attacked women. In fact, rape and deportation became everyday events.

So the Hitler regime came to an end and life went on. But there was no return to tranquillity. The Russian occupation brought new and menacing dangers. Regimentation, the ideology of class warfare – these required a new dance, a new masquerade, to make everyday life tolerable. Again we had to play a game whose rules we didn't know but had to learn.

Hitler's Grand Guignol had ended. Yet the new show was to have its exciting moments, too.

But that's another story.

Editor's Afterword

'Tivadar Soros's powerful influence on his sons is clear: George's numerous public references to his father and Paul's statements in family memoirs and again in the foreword to the present volume confirm it. *Masquerade* is the principal public record of that influence – a personal history of Budapest under the Nazis and a telling portrait of its author. Tivadar Soros was a charming, exasperating and supremely resourceful individual, for whom a life of adventure in wartime and of discriminating comfort in peacetime was merely a preparation for the test of survival that was thrust on him and his family in 1944 by the arrival of German soldiers on the familiar streets of the city where he had once felt so at home. 'That was my father's finest hour,' George has written, 'because he knew how to act. He understood the situation; he realized that the normal rules did not apply . . . I had a father whom I adored, who was in command of the situation, who knew what to do and who helped others.' In short, Tivadar Soros, his insouciant optimism masking a wary and canny protectiveness, was the father every boy dreams of when peril is near. To the 14-year-old George, this time of peril was a great adventure – a time when he and his family had to live on their wits in order to survive. Years later, reminiscing about the boys' childhood, their mother Elizabeth spoke of their father's extraordinary love for his children, and of the way in which he never talked down to them, tried always to challenge and encourage them. 'You see,' she recalls her husband saying, 'I wanted to have them always on my level . . . I wanted them to understand things as they are.' Tivadar had learned the lessons life taught him well, and these lessons helped him and his family survive.

Elizabeth's memories, recorded in New York in the 1980s, at about the time she was honored (in her eighties) as the oldest student at Fordham University, bridge two worlds – the old and vanished world of middle-class Central Europe between the wars, and the new postwar world of opportunity in America. Her two sons crossed that bridge between the old world and the new, and met success. If *Masquerade* helps explain their achievement, more importantly it offers a fascinating portrait of a man who found a mission and of the challenges that beset him. As editor of this volume I do not pretend to have a complete understanding of the man called Tivadar Soros, but I do believe that the book reveals those aspects of Tivadar's character that he wished to share with posterity, and that the unusual history of its publication offers a story worth telling, both about Tivadar and about the times. Tivadar combined clear and simple values with a willingness to compromise and persuade. He wasted no time fighting battles he knew he could not win, nor in ethical debates where lives were at stake. There is little moralizing in this story, and little hesitancy: only the optimistic urgency of one who felt he had a job to do, a task that he had been given, and who assumed that task gladly and with single-mindedness.

Masquerade focuses on a period of less than a year in Hungarian history, but a year in which hundreds of thousands of Hungarian Jews, and many other Hungarians besides, were destined to perish. The eleven-month period between the German occupation of Hungary in March 1944 and the liberation of Budapest by the Russians, completed in February 1945 falls into three distinct phases. Hungary's Jewish population had long endured various forms of discrimination, of a kind, sadly, not uncommon in the Central Europe of the day. Hungarian Jews had, over the years, learned to live with such restrictions, and there was a kind of comfortable understanding among all parties that, while the restrictions would not go away, neither would the balance between the classes be seriously upset. Jews had long played a prominent economic role in the country, as financial and industrial leaders. But in the late 1930s, as Hungary moved gradually into the orbit of Germany and as Germany intensified its official anti-Semitism, the balance began to tip: the so-called Jewish Laws pushed the Jews further and further away from the center of political and economic power. Protected by its nominal independence, Hungary for a while was spared the anti-Semitic horrors of Germany and Poland, and other Nazi-occupied territories – until March 1944, when the pent-up desire of the leaders of the Final Solution to get their hands on the Jews of Hungary joined with German military reversals in the Balkans and worries about Hungary's loyalty, persuading Hitler to seize power in Hungary. Adolf Eichmann traveled on one of the first trains to arrive in Budapest from Germany, and the Final Solution came with him. Deportations began in late April, and by early July almost half a million Jews – more or less the entire Jewish population outside Budapest – had been carted off to slaughter.

Eye-witness reports reached the West and resulted in energetic protests by Western and neutral leaders – at least considerably more energetic than they had mustered earlier. Although in June the Jews had been herded into so-called Jewish or Yellow-Star Houses scattered across Budapest in preparation for deportation, the Hungarian head of state, Admiral Horthy, felt strong enough to resist Eichmann and his henchmen and was largely successful in halting the planned deportations, at least for the time being. The Germans, needing Hungarian support on the crumbling Eastern Front, did not intervene to reverse Horthy's order. So ended the first phase of the eleven-month period, and there followed, from mid-July to mid-October, the second phase: a period of continued outrages, but at least on a lesser scale than before. In late August,

Romania switched sides to the Allies, Horthy dismissed his prime minister and brought in a somewhat more moderate government, and Eichmann left Budapest.

A third, horrendous and chaotic phase began in mid-October, when Horthy, in an ill-timed and unprepared move, announced Hungary's withdrawal of support for Germany. Within hours the Germans arrested him and a virulently fascist government was installed in Budapest. As the Russians advanced across the Great Hungarian Plain, an orgy of killing began. Eichmann returned and began organizing forced marches to Austria, fascist gangs roamed the streets, and anarchy descended on the city. It was not until January that the Russians, advancing inexorably across the city, reached the apartment where Tivadar, Paul and George Soros were living, liberating them as Jews but making them spoils of conquest as Hungarians. The city was in ruins. The book ends as the Russians seize control.

The first and only priority for the Soros family was survival. While many Jews sought somehow to negotiate with the authorities, to seek to mitigate their privations and avoid deportation, Tivadar chose a different path. This most devoted of family men, this loving parent, saw the family unit not as a means of survival but as a potential target: he advocated invisibility. A supremely talented negotiator, who, with his apparently easy-going style, readily drew others into his friendship, he acquired, as we have seen, false identity papers for each member of the family and proceeded to make arrangements to lodge them in various locations in the city and beyond. He did the same for many of his friends and family members, and he acquired the material means that he needed by dealing in false papers on a broader scale. He himself set up a secret hiding-place in one of his apartment buildings, enlisting the help of an architect friend, Lajos Kozma, in its design, and living there with Kozma in the early months of the Nazi occupation. In characteristic fashion, however, he did not spend all his time hiding out: he lived the life of relative freedom that his identity papers in effect empowered him to lead, visiting the local swimming pool, frequenting cafés and restaurants, and even going to the theatre.

And the family survived – Elizabeth and Paul and George and Elizabeth's mother – though many other more distant family members perished, and both Elizabeth and Paul suffered ill-treatment at the hands of the victorious Russians. As George Soros suggests, it was indeed Tivadar's finest hour.

Such is the immediate historical scope of this book, but behind it lies what was in effect a lifetime of preparation. As George Soros points out in his foreword, this was by no means Tivadar's first adventure. To understand, we must begin at the beginning. Tivadar Soros was born Tivadar or Teodor Schwartz in the town of Nyíregyháza, in northeastern Hungary, in 1894. He was the second oldest of some ten children of relatively prosperous, largely secularized Jewish parents who ran a general store and wholesale business. Sent to a good school in Sárospatak, he went on to study law, apparently spending some time at Heidelberg. When war broke out he joined the Austro-Hungarian army. He did so, as he put it, largely in search of adventure: 'I was just twenty years old. I headed for the front immediately, volunteering while still a student, before my studies were completed. It was not patriotic enthusiasm that drove me to enlist, but fear that I would miss out on the war. I was sure that this was the last world war: if I let it go by, I would miss a unique opportunity.'

Life at the front was initially relatively easy. The young man whiled away his time in various activities, writing (according to Elizabeth) occasional newspaper articles, and also learning the international language Esperanto, created some thirty years earlier by a Polish Jew, Lazar Ludvik Zamenhof, who believed that a neutral, easily learned second language would help create understanding among the nations. A young man in search of adventure, Tivadar was also an idealist.

All too soon, his idealism was put to the test. The Russians surrounded his unit and he was taken prisoner. Moved from place to place across Russia, he ended up at Khabarovsk, in the

Russian Far East. And there, regrettably, he stayed. Meanwhile the allies landed an expeditionary force in Vladivostok, whose purpose became not the successful prosecution of the war so much as the provision of support for Admiral Kolchak, leader of the Whites against the revolutionary forces of the Reds. For the allies, the Austro-Hungarians were now an irrelevancy. Marauding bands of Cossacks, rabidly anti-Semitic, swept through the Russian Far East. When Kolchak was turned over to the Reds by the Czech Brigade and the Red advance eastwards began, the Reds were equally disinclined to treat the remnants of a foreign army well. With the surrender of the Germans and their allies at the end of 1918, Soros and his companions found themselves prisoners-of-war representing an imperial Austrian government no longer in existence. There were no plans for their repatriation: a civil war was raging in the vast tracts of territory separating them from their homes, and, besides, no one much cared. As for Soros himself, he was a Jew in territory not known for its kindness to Jews, and a leader in his prison camp at a time when the Reds, arriving in the camps, routinely butchered the leaders. So he escaped, crossed the frozen Amur River to Khabarovsk, and set out for home. Now began a journey of epic proportions through a war-torn and uncertain Russia. For the first two weeks he traveled uncertainly by train along the Trans-Siberian Railway, reaching the area of deepest wilderness through which the railway passes, the mountain ranges north of the Amur River, a region where in those days there were no human settlements at all. Unable to go further because of the hostilities, he and his companions traveled on foot through the mountains, ultimately reaching a mining settlement on the other side by rafting down one of the rivers that drain into the Arctic Ocean. Later Tivadar was to make a joke of his seeking civilization by rafting towards the Arctic, but in this, as in so many other matters, he knew exactly what he was doing.

We do not know how Tivadar reached Irkutsk, but it is as Schwartz from Irkutsk that he is identified in reports in Esperanto magazines in 1920 as one of the founders of a national Esperanto organization in the Soviet Union, apparently the only foreigner in the leadership. By this time he was already in Moscow, where, as he tells us in *Masquerade*, he finally managed to obtain passage to the West by posing as an Austrian army officer from the city of Linz (as we have seen, he committed the Baedeker guide to that city to memory in order to answer the questions of the repatriation committee).

Apparently detained for a while at the repatriation camp at Csót, he re-entered Hungarian civilian life later that year. Although he also had many other interests, he continued his spirited involvement in Esperanto – at a time, right after the Béla Kun regime, when Esperanto was regarded with a certain amount of suspicion as a leftist pursuit, particularly in the provinces, where local clubs sometimes had difficulties with the authorities.

He was some 28 years old when he and his Esperanto-speaking friends Kálmán Kalocsay and Gyula Baghy launched the literary journal *Literatura Mondo* (the first issue was dated October 1922). Soon his account of his Siberian adventures, *Modernaj Robinzonoj* (called *Crusoes in Siberia* in English translation), began to appear in the journal in serial form, and later, in 1924, it was turned into a book (recently republished). Unlike Kalocsay and Baghy, prolific writers in Esperanto throughout their lives, in *Crusoes in Siberia* Soros is quite explicit in disclaiming literary pretensions, and his narrative is unvarnished and unassuming. Little political and military detail finds a place in the story: the narrative seems suspended in political space. While there is little overt criticism of the new order in Russia, it seems clear that he had little time for the Bolshevik view of the world, though his internationalist and humanitarian views hardly put him in sympathy with the other side, such as it was, either.

Crusoes was Soros's only significant literary contribution to *Literatura Mondo* during the two years he remained closely associated with the magazine. While Baghy and Kalocsay were occupied with its content, Soros was primarily interested in the business side: it was his subsidy as publisher and owner that launched the enterprise and kept it alive. Despite its paper losses, he shrewdly saw the enterprise as an investment. With hyperinflation raging, the inflow of foreign exchange from subscriptions was very helpful to him personally: he used it primarily to invest in real estate, betting on the eventual stabilization of conditions in Hungary. In September 1924, however, he announced that he could no longer continue his subsidy and the journal was taken over by the Hungarian Esperanto Institute. His name continued to appear in the list of collaborators until the end of 1924, when it dropped from sight.

It was at this time that Tivadar married Elizabeth, a second cousin ten years his junior. Curious about the world, the two of them traveled abroad frequently: Elizabeth describes a particularly memorable Esperanto trip to Italy in 1924, when, in Padua, they heard radio broadcasts for the first time. Later the radio was to become Tivadar's constant companion. Following the completion of his stewardship of *Literatura Mondo*, Tivadar moved away from the Hungarian Esperanto scene, as other interests commanded his attention. In 1926 Paul was born, to be followed by George in 1930, and life settled down to a rather easy routine, with Tivadar practicing law in Budapest, managing real estate, writing the occasional newspaper article, and losing no opportunity for travel, particularly in pursuit of his favorite sporting activity, skiing. Summers were spent at the family's little summer house on Lupa Island, north of the city. During the rest of the year the family lived comfortably in an apartment on Kossuth Lajos tér, on the east bank of the Danube, close to the Parliament Building, with views of the Buda Hills. The coming of World War II did little to change the rhythm of family life, though the pressure on Hungarian Jews increased steadily as the government limited Jewish access to the professions, and anti-Semitic rhetoric, always a feature of Hungarian life, became increasingly strident.

Elizabeth talks of how World War I had changed Tivadar. The

young, ambitious, devil-may-care army officer who left for the
front returned from Siberia less eager for material success, more
inclined to enjoy life for its own sake, more devoted to the people
around him. The youthful enthusiasm for Esperanto, at least as it
related to the journal *Literatura Mondo*, gave him an opportunity
both to exercise his entrepreneurial talents and to serve a greater
cause, but in due course his family took the place of some of this
idealism, though his talent for deal-making and his enthusiasm
for athletics, and the open air, and the pleasures of the city, never
left him. He also continued to travel, making two trips to the
United States and even writing a number of newspaper articles
in Hungarian. This was the Tivadar Soros who confronted the
horrors of Nazism and survived.

Following the war, life in Hungary was hard, and the old ways
were gone. Taking advantage of his knowledge of Russian, Tivadar,
with customary resourcefulness, almost immediately got a job as
legal counsel in the American Interests section of the Swiss embassy.
The convening of the 32nd World Esperanto Congress in Bern in
1947 presented an opportunity: Tivadar was given responsibility for
assembling the twelve-person Hungarian delegation, and succeeded
in including not only himself but George as well. At the end of the
Congress, George stayed behind, moving on to become, eventually,
a student at the London School of Economics. Later, Paul, as
a member of the Hungarian national ski team (and despite a
severe leg injury that he somehow succeeded in concealing from
his teammates), also succeeded in leaving Hungary, for the 1948
Winter Olympics in St Moritz, Switzerland. He defected and, after
a year in occupied Austria, arrived in New York in December 1948
on a student visa.

Tivadar perhaps began work on *Masquerade*, his second and
more ambitious memoir, following his own arrival in the United
States eight years after that of his son. In 1956, in the wake of
the abortive Hungarian Revolution, he and Elizabeth, on their
second attempt, crossed the border into Austria, They considered
the possibility of taking up residence in Vienna, where Tivadar

still owned property he had acquired in the 1920s, or perhaps dividing their time between Vienna and New York, but finally made the trip across the Atlantic and remained, more or less continuously, until Tivadar's death in 1968 and Elizabeth's twenty years later. Paul of course, had lived in the States since 1948; George made the move from London shortly before Tivadar and Elizabeth arrived.

Although Kalocsay told me (when, as a student, I recorded an interview with him in Budapest in the summer of 1963) that Soros had plans to publish his memoirs, the earliest written mention of Tivadar's project for *Masquerade* I have found is contained in a letter of October 23, 1963, to the Esperanto publisher Juan Régulo Pérez. The letter is signed 'T. Schwartz', the name he always used in the Esperanto movement but had given up in other spheres in 1936 when the family adopted a Hungarian name as a kind of protective camouflage against being labeled foreign or Jewish, both liabilities in the xenophobic and anti-Semitic Hungarian environment of the day. It was written from Langegasse 11, one of the Soros family properties in Vienna, where he and Elizabeth were staying for three months before returning to the United States. By March of the following year, an agreement on publication had evidently been reached with Régulo, and the book appeared, in a print run of one thousand copies, in 1965.

Paul Soros believes that the first draft of *Masquerade* may have been written in Hungarian, though concrete evidence is lacking. Tivadar probably eventually chose to write in Esperanto because of his earlier experience with *Crusoes in Siberia* and because he could enlist the help of the network of Esperantist friends, some of them Hungarian, whom he met through the New York Esperanto Society. For political reasons, the Hungarian-language publishing market was unavailable to him, and the Esperanto market was certainly not negligible: there were at least hundreds of thousands of speakers and users of the language scattered across the world. Later, he enlisted the help of a family friend, Sophie Bogyo, in an English translation, which, according to a letter to Régulo, was finished in 1966. The text survives, and helped me as I prepared my own translation, but the quality is uneven: Sophie Bogyo was not a native English speaker. Shortly after Tivadar's death, Elizabeth received a call from a publisher asking for a copy of the manuscript, but chose not to pursue the opportunity. So the book remained relatively unknown in English-speaking circles and the present publication will come as something of a surprise to many readers.

The Esperanto book, with the title *Maskerado čirkaŭ la morto: Nazimondo en Hungarujo* (Masquerade Around Death: The Nazi World in Hungary) appeared in time for the World Esperanto Congress in Tokyo in the summer of 1965. Tivadar was among the attendees, and a year later made the trip to Budapest for the 1966 congress, his first visit to Hungary since his departure ten years before. The book, something of a new departure for Régulo, most of whose fifty-or-so titles up to that time had been volumes of poetry or fiction, appears to have sold reasonably well. Régulo was perhaps attracted to it because it dealt with the here and now: here was a book that gave the lie to those who argued that Esperanto was a form of escapism – a direct, gritty, deeply disturbing story about matters that many people in Europe and beyond were still disinclined to confront.

Masquerade was, in its way, breaking new ground – something that is perhaps hard to appreciate in today's environment in which personal accounts of the Holocaust run into the thousands and World War II constitutes not just history but a kind of cultural industry. 'When I think about those years, I realize how little direct observation [of the Holocaust] there was,' remarks the protagonist of a recent novel, Bernhard Schlink's *The Reader* (1997: 147–8), referring to the 1960s. 'We were familiar with some of the testimony of prisoners, but many of [the accounts] were published soon after the war and not reissued until the 1980s, and in the intervening years they disappeared from publishers' lists.' The same was true of accounts of survival outside the camps: in fact, *Masquerade* was among the earliest survival stories to reach a general international public, its significance long unrecognized by the accident of language and a short print run.

The diary of Anne Frank, of course, had been published in Dutch in 1947, and the first translation appeared in 1952. While a few other accounts appeared in various languages in the late 1940s and 1950s, in the years following the war most people's eyes were on the future, and on rehabilitation: remembering was too painful. The Nuremberg Trials had told the world something of the nature of the beast that was unleashed on Europe in the 1930s and 1940s, but it was the capture, trial and execution of Karl Adolf Eichmann between 1960 and 1962 that brought to the world's attention the full measure of the atrocities committed against the Jews. Following the Eichmann trial in Israel came the Frankfurt trial (1963–5) in Germany, in which twenty-one SS officers who worked at Auschwitz were accused of various crimes and eighteen were convicted. The evils of the Holocaust were there for all to see.

While this was going on, Soros was writing, or may indeed have completed, his first draft. Régulo, a survivor of Franco's persecution, perhaps saw in Soros a comrade-in-arms, certainly a possessor of a story that needed telling. His comments in the foreword to the 1965 edition suggest as much, and the blurb for the book, probably Régulo's own work (his publishing house was a one-person operation), reinforce this impression.

As in his earlier book, Soros approaches his subject in unpretentious style. His comments there bear repeating:

> In providing this brief account of what occurred, I have no intention of writing an enduring work of literature. Lacking such power of the pen, I will merely offer a true account of my experiences and my reactions to them. My aim is simple: to provide a remembrance of human pain and suffering experienced in this twentieth century, the so-called 'century of humanity'.

Crusoes is also clearly a story about the indomitability of the human spirit and the resourcefulness of the human intellect, surely characteristics that come through in *Masquerade* as well. Soros would have been the last to suggest that *Masquerade* was great literature, but he would almost certainly have claimed that it was intended as 'a remembrance of human pain and suffering experienced in this twentieth century'. And if the so-called 'century of humanity' looked anything but humane in 1924, it was surely even less so when Soros sat down, thirty years later, to write his memoir of this new sadness.

The response to Tivadar's volume in the Esperanto press is a microcosm of 1960s responses to the emerging details of the destruction of the Jews. Readers were particularly struck by the sharp contrast between the huge events rumbling around the Soros family and their oblique chronicling in the day-to-day survival of family members. They noted Tivadar's defiance, his humor, his refusal to give up. Somewhat bemusedly they recognized that irony and humor were really the only way not only to humanize accounts of the horrors but also to survive as they were going on: to stare unflinchingly into the void was to be drawn into it. Reviewers noted the relative lack of introspection: the book focused on action rather than reflection, on narrative rather than feelings, and they wondered at the sheer brazenness of Soros's defiance of the authorities – 'at the risk-filled way' in which he 'frequented swimming pools, theaters, cafés and other public places'. The young German historian Ulrich Lins echoes these sentiments:

> Sometimes one is inclined to forget the circumstances in which the masked participants in the masquerade actually lived, so easily does our author chatter about his efforts to make life more agreeable . . . He succeeds in laying his hands on ten barrels of the best wine when others scurry around looking for the most basic provisions; he allows himself to succumb to the cheerful indifference of a group of fun-loving

Frenchmen . . . while at night he hunts down and kills all the
bedbugs in his room, giving details on how best to carry out
the extermination.

'The persecution of the Jewish population of Budapest along
with the world political conflagration towards the end of the
war clearly cries out for passionate narrative,' another reviewer
writes, 'but the author rightly and fairly understands that there
is something banal in the simple condemnation of the detailed
crimes of the greatest genocide in history. At a time of abnormal
and general madness . . . exaggerated sentiments of solidarity can
be more dangerous than carefully analysing all the options in
each situation and acting independently, looking for ways round
problems, observing the smallest hole that offers escape.' So the
great strength of the book is precisely its undramatic quality,
precisely its refusal to engage in histrionics. Such simplicity –
and we should not ignore this – is itself art. Tivadar's strength,
both in life and on the page, was conveying the impression of easy
control while planning each move, freighting each encounter. And
his mode of writing helped set the tone for others' later accounts
of similar events.

Reading the book today, I would add that it is the moments of
contrast and of quiet that impress me most. Julia's letter from Lake
Balaton, and the pastoral life that it describes (picking mushrooms,
visiting the next village), sits on the page next to the story of
the inadvertent betrayal of Tivadar's clients the Okányi Schwartz
family, discovered by the police through the loose talk of a servant
carrying food to them and carted off to be shot. As Lins suggests,
Tivadar does battle against bedbugs even as the Nazis exterminate
human beings – and there comes a day when the bedbugs are fully
eliminated, though the marks of their incineration are still there
on the wall, to be hidden, I should add, from the landlady.

And there also comes the moment, amid the exploding shells of
the advancing Russians, when a 17-year-old German soldier finds
himself at the mercy of Tivadar and his sons, having just tumbled

through a window into their apartment. How easy it would be to blame this young man for the horrors perpetrated on the Jews by the evils of Nazism, how easy just to beat him to death, right there and then. But would revenge relieve the pain? Would it even the score? Would it restore a sense of humanity? The questions are not asked, in so many words, nor are the answers given. But they hover unspoken over the episode, and it is for us, gentle readers all, to ask and to answer. So there are no histrionics, no accusations, no struggles to the death – just a conversation and the gift of a few cigarettes:

> We talked for perhaps a quarter of an hour. The question then was what to do with him.
> The eyes of my 14-year-old son seemed filled with tears. I put a handful of cigarettes into the Aryan soldier's fist and gave him his orders:
> 'You're to go out the same way you came in.'
> The boys helped him climb on to the window-sill, and the armed representative of the German Reich exited Jewish-occupied territory.

The author's final comments on the episode leave irony to the reader, in this story of war among Christian nations:

> Perhaps we treated him roughly when we committed him to fate, sending him off neither with good advice nor with a few bits of clothing that might have helped him escape the Russians disguised as a civilian. But, as pseudo-Christians, we had not quite reached that level of Christianity where we were willing to return bread for stones.

If in the 1960s people were still feeling their way with their narratives of the Holocaust, in many respects Tivadar Soros's story was a step along the road to the more sophisticated understanding of these events today. Even as I was translating his words, *Life is*

Beautiful, a film in which slapstick comedy collides with the darkest of prison-camp tragedy, was playing in the local movie-houses, and down the street at Borders bookshop, Victor Klemperer's diary of the Nazi years was telling a story not too dissimilar from that of Tivadar Soros: 'It's not the big things that are important, but the everyday life of tyranny, which may be forgotten. A thousand mosquito bites are worse than a blow on the head. I observe, I note, the mosquito bites.'

Whether we are closer to preventing the evils that Soros enumerates I do not know, but I do know that we have learned much about how the canny survive and how human values live on. 'Life is beautiful,' writes Tivadar Soros, beginning his story; 'but luck must be on your side.' Cleverness and blind luck must go hand in hand. Ultimately, though, as Inge Clendinnen (*Reading the Holocaust,* 1999) points out in her examination of writing on the Holocaust, 'this is not what we want to hear.' She quotes Lawrence Langer, who suggests that 'one of the deepest instincts in the civilised mind' is 'the need to establish a principle of causality in human experience.' We find that principle in the words of Paul and George Soros: they survived because their father made it possible. But, on the other hand, replies their father, whose gift to them was precisely the causality that Langer refers to.' 'Luck must be on your side.'

Notes

A NOTE ON THE TRANSLATION. The present text is based largely on the Esperanto version published in 1965. I have, however, supplemented it with some material found only in Sophie Bogyo's English translation. In fact I have generally included in my translation everything that appears in either of the two versions, and have sought to reconcile any discrepancies in the two texts (the significant ones are identified in the notes below). The Bogyo translation rearranges some of the material in the 1965 version, and I have largely followed this rearrangement. A note at the end of the 1965 volume states that 'the publisher . . . conscientiously respected certain curiosities of the author, for example the numerous names for a single person . . . the double orthography of the same names . . . the hybrid rendering of others . . . the unusual Latin renderings of several words . . .' I have taken the liberty of eliminating most of these oddities. Latin texts are rendered in the customary Latin words. I have tried to be consistent with names, using the conventional Hungarian forms wherever possible, except that in referring to the Soros brothers I have rendered *Pál* as *Paul* throughout, and *Gyuri* and *Gyurka* as *George*. All translations of Esperanto texts in the notes and the introduction are mine. H.T.

1 Some History and Geography

Page 1 The pengő, divisible into 100 fillér was introduced in 1927 and remained Hungary's basic unit of currency until 1946, when it was replaced by the forint. At the beginning of 1944, the weekly salary of a factory worker was perhaps 20–25 pengős. The cheapest cinema ticket was 20 fillér.

Concerning the remark, 'You give as though your money will be always yours', 'The remark is ironic,' Soros wrote to Régulo (August 4, 1964). 'You give this amount because you don't realize that in a short while you'll lose everything.'

Page 2 'We have become breakers of contracts out of cowardice . . .' Teleki wrote to Horthy in a letter found near his body. 'We have become grave-robbers. The most despicable nation. I did not hold you back. I am to blame.' Churchill declared that in the peace conference following the war an empty chair should be kept for Teleki (Lázár 1989: 179–82). The most famous earlier example of 'political' suicide was that of Count László Teleki (1810–61), an associate of the great Hungarian patriot Lajos Kossuth and Pál Teleki's great-grandfather: László Teleki took his own life rather than retreat from the principles of the revolution of 1848.

The Yugoslav Pact actually lasted for a little over three months after it was signed on December 12, 1940. While it brought Yugoslavia rather more firmly within the German orbit, Teleki saw it as a way of preventing total German domination. On March 27, 1941, the Serbian army overthrew the Yugoslav government. Teleki insisted that the Pact also applied to the new regime, but in early April the Germans invaded Yugoslavia, with the cooperation of the Hungarian army, which joined in without waiting for Teleki's approval (Ignotus 1972: 187; Mikes 1957: 24–5).

By 1939 there were already anti-Jewish laws on the books. In fact the notorious *numerus clausus*, used to limit Jewish access to universities, had been put in place at the time of Hungarian independence and was the first formal anti-Jewish measure of the inter-war years in Europe, earning for Horthy a reputation as an anti-Semite (Sakmyster 1994: 79–80). The law, accepted by Parliament in September 1920, stipulated that the number of students of the various 'races and nations' of Hungary could not exceed their percentage in the general population. The first of the so-called Jewish Laws in Hungary dated from May 29, 1938, and essentially broadened the concept of *numerus clausus* to cover the professions (Gilbert 1985: 56; Braham 1981: 122–7). It was in connection with the second such law (the one the author has in mind here), submitted to Parliament on the day before Christmas in 1938, that prime minister Béla Imrédy uttered the words that were to be his downfall, when he declared that 'one drop of Jewish blood' was enough to call into question an individual's character and patriotism, only to have his political opponents unearth (on somewhat questionable evidence) a Jewish great-grandmother in his own ancestry. This gave Regent Horthy the excuse he needed to get rid of him (Ignotus 1972: 185–6). The Second Jewish Law was adopted on May 4, 1939 (Gilbert 1985: 79; Braham 1981: 147–56). Horthy refused to sign it, but was finally persuaded to accept it in modified form. In August 1941 a third Jewish Law was added (Braham 1981: 194–5). On Hungarian Jewry throughout this period, see Lévai 1946 and 1948.

Page 3 Kamenec-Podolsk: now Kemenets-Podolskiy, in Ukraine, just north of the Moldovan border, close to the River Dnestr. The group of eleven thousand or more forced laborers consisted, according to Gilbert (1985: 186), of 'Hungarian Jews, mostly from the areas annexed by Hungary from Czechoslovakia in 1938 and 1939.' At a meeting in Vinnitsa on August 25, 1941, the German authorities demanded that Hungary take the group back. When the Hungarians refused, Lieutenant-General Franz Jaeckeln of the SS informed the conference that he would 'complete their liquidation' by September 1. The murders were carried out by machine gun at a series of bomb craters outside the city (not in the river, as our author suggests) over a three-day period. Gilbert quotes a harrowing eye-witness account. See also the narrative of Gábor Mermelstein in Braham (1995: 6–8). Mermelstein adds that, although the SS systematically carried out the mass-murder, members of a German regiment on the other side of a nearby building actually protected sizable numbers of Jews. A detailed account of the event and its background, and an examination of the question of whether the Hungarian authorities knew about it, is provided by Braham (1981: 199–207). Gilbert (1993: 69) raises his own estimate of the number of killings to 14,000.

Page 4 Miklós Kállay (1887–1967), prime minister from March 9, 1942, to March 22, 1944, was a patriot who tried to maintain the old life-style of the Hungarian elite, seeking to steer the country, somewhat naively, between the excesses of Nazism and the dangers of Soviet communism. He held a doctorate in political science, was a personal friend of Horthy, and was distinctly conflict-averse. When the Germans arrived, he took refuge in the Turkish embassy, but was later arrested by the Gestapo and transported to Mauthausen, where he survived the war. Despite his aversion to conflict, he resolutely refused a June 1942 request from the Germans that the Hungarians begin the segregation and deportation of Jews. Szinai (1998) maintains that if Kállay had given way, the result would have been a steady and complete deportation not only of Hungarian Jews but of those of the Balkans as well.

Page 5 Nikolaus (Miklós) Horthy de Nagybánya (1868–1957) was regent of Hungary from 1920 to 1944. A naval officer under the Austro-Hungarian Empire, he became commander-in-chief of the Austro-Hungarian fleet in 1918. With the disintegration of the empire at the end of World War I, he was named minister of war in the 'white' government, opposing Béla Kun's communist régime and suppressing it in 1920 with assistance from Romania. He was sympathetic to Hitler and supported the Axis powers. He fell from power in an act of defiance of the Nazis in October 1944, when he sought to dissolve the German-Hungarian alliance and appealed to the Allies for an armistice (see Chapter 17). Imprisoned in the castle of Weilheim, Bavaria, he survived the war.

Horthy's visit to Klessheim, near Salzburg, for the meeting with Hitler would have been farcical were its outcome not so catastrophic. Hitler lost his temper with the Admiral, accusing him of preparing an Italian-style betrayal of Hungary to the Allies. Horthy vehemently denied it. When Horthy ordered that his special train be made ready for the return trip to Budapest, Ribbentrop organized a fake air-raid to delay his departure. When the train did eventually leave, an extra car was secretly attached to it carrying Hitler's new representative in Hungary, SS Brigadier-General Edmund Veesenmayer, named as Germany's minister plenipotentiary but in fact far more than that, and his staff. Horthy had essentially acceded to Hitler's wishes for the establishment of a new government in Hungary, though it was already too late: Operation Margarethe, the code name for the Nazi occupation of Hungary, was well underway. See Macartney (1957: 221–9); Yahil (1990: 504–5); Braham (1981: 369–70).

The Germans sought to make the take-over as quick and quiet as possible. They delayed Horthy's train to postpone his arrival until the middle of Sunday morning. Meanwhile, German troops crossed the frontier from four different directions, and soldiers were parachuted in to take over airfields and other strategic locations. Yet Sunday morning was much as it always was: 'In Budapest itself the cafes and restaurants had opened as usual, the trams, buses and suburban trains were running according to schedule, the ordinary organised amusements of the day had not been called off. Most of the population only learnt that their country had been occupied when they strolled out of doors after completing their long Sunday lie-in and consuming their leisurely Sunday breakfasts' (Macartney 1957: 245).

Page 8   Endre Bajcsy-Zsilinszky (1886–1944), politician and editor, 'last and most genuine of the romantic patriots', was allegedly the only leader to confront the Germans with firearms. In captivity for several months, he was eventually released. He took leadership of the so-called Freedom Committee of the Hungarian National Insurrection, and was rearrested, along with his fellow committee-members, on November 21, and executed on December 23, 1944. He began his career as a convinced rightist (and anti-Semite), entering parliament as a member of the National Radical Party. See Ignotus (1972: 189).

Page 9   On March 24, Roosevelt issued a statement (quoted in Braham 1981: 1102) condemning the Nazis for their crimes: 'As a result of the events of the last few days, hundreds of thousands of Jews, who while living under persecution, have at least found a haven from death in Hungary and the Balkans, are now threatened with annihilation as Hitler's forces descend more heavily upon these lands.' Tivadar finds no mention of this in the US press because the Voice of America, as a government-run foreign broadcasting service, was specifically forbidden by Congress from operating within the United States.

2 Meet the Germans

Page 12 The Arrow Cross (Nyilas) Party, with its emblem of crossed arrows, was founded in 1933 as a coalition of several rightist parties.

Page 13 The Sztójay prime-ministership was a compromise: the Germans favored Béla Imrédy. Horthy tried to veto the most unacceptable cabinet nominees (Sakmyster 1994: 338), but in the end the leadership consisted exclusively of pro-German rightist extremists, with the sole exception of General Lajos Csatay, whom Horthy succeeded in retaining as minister of defense.

Regarding denunciations, the Germans were apparently themselves surprised by the number of tips that reached them in the first days of the occupation: some 35,000 (Yahil 1990: 509).

3 The Jewish Council

Page 16 Gilbert (1985: 89) traces the origins of the Jewish Council, or *Judenrat*, system to the notorious Berlin meeting of September 21, 1939, on the future (or lack of it) of Polish Jewry. See Gilbert *passim* for the subsequent history of its use. Yahil (1990: 238–9) discusses its effectiveness.

Page 18 The National Institute for Rabbinical Training was established in Rökk Szilárd Street in 1877. As of March 21, 1944, it served as one of the 'relocation points' where the Germans held some two hundred well-known Jews as hostages, changing the composition of the group every month or two. Those no longer needed as hostages were shipped off to Auschwitz (Frojimovics-Komoróczy 1995: 310).

Summonses were sent to journalists, lawyers and other pro-
fessionals. For many people 'this proved to be the first stop to
Auschwitz' (Braham 1981: 407).

Page 19   The execution story appears in the Bogyo translation but not
in the published Esperanto text.

On the question of resistance, Yahil (1990: 508) remarks:
'Wittingly or otherwise, even though the circumstances had
been revolutionized, the Jews [of Budapest] continued to
conduct themselves as though they were still confronted by
the ambivalent Hungarian attitude to which they had grown
accustomed over the decades. Somehow they did not grasp
that with a wave of the hand the Germans had swept away
all the old conventions and together with their Hungarian
collaborators were now operating on completely different
assumptions.'

Tivadar's tour of the Swift and Armour stockyards took
place on a trip in 1928. In 1939, the author paid a further
visit to the United States to negotiate the sale of the family's
property in Berlin. He returned by way of Switzerland, where
he met the family, and serious discussions took place about
the possibility of emigrating from Hungary to the United
States. The idea was finally rejected, primarily because no
agreement could be reached within the family on the Berlin
sale. The best offer on the property was perhaps half of its
peace-time value; Elizabeth's mother was unwilling to settle for
this low figure.

Page 20   The Latin saying is attributed to Pompey the Great (Gnaeus
Pompeius Magnus – 106–48 BC).

Page 21   Schiller, *Wilhelm Tell* 2.2.

Page 22   Lukacs (1997: 156–7) supports the view expressed by Tivadar,
citing Maser (1971: 254), 'As early as November 1941 – that is,
before the failure of the German army before Moscow, and
before the event of Pearl Harbor – Hitler knew that he could
no longer win the war: more precisely, *his* war, the war he had
planned to wage and win.'

Page 23   Kurt von Schleicher (1882–1934), minister of war under Franz von
Papen, succeeded him as Chancellor and was in turn succeeded
by Hitler. Ernst Röhm (1887–1934) was an early Hitler supporter
and an organizer of the paramilitary stormtroopers who helped

create the climate needed for Hitler to seize power in 1933. Both were executed on charges of treason.

4 In Search of an Identity

Page 26 The Latin saying is attributed to the first-century Roman rhetorician Quintilian.

Page 27 *The Fall of Berlin* was a documentary film directed by Yuri Raizman, made in 1945. In 1950, Shostakovich composed music to be added to the film.

Page 28 On the remarkable contribution of Jewish athletes to Hungarian sport see Handler (1985). Our author may well have had the great Attila Petschauer in mind here. Handler, describing how many Jewish athletes 'starved, were beaten, and died ignominious deaths,' writes (102–3): 'The most frequently recounted . . . was the fate of Attila Petschauer, one of Hungary's world-renowned fencers. The happy-go-lucky Bohemian and eternal optimist struggled to retain a semblance of humanity and dignity amid deprivation and brutality in the labor service that took him to the Ukrainian town of Davidovka. He nearly succeeded. Staggering exhausted and starving on the street, the labor servicemen passed a group of Hungarian officers. Petschauer recognized one of them. It was Lt. Col. Kálmán Cseh, an equestrian, who, like Petschauer, participated in the Amsterdam Olympics of 1928.' Far from gaining Cseh's support, Petschauer was persecuted on Cseh's orders. Although Petschauer survived to be liberated by the Russians, he died soon afterwards. For a Jew to excel at so characteristically aristocratic a sport as fencing perhaps constituted too clear an example of hubris to be ignored (Zeke 1995). *Sunshine*, a recent film by István Szabó, was inspired in part by Petschauer's fate.

Kálmán Rózsahegyi (1873–1961) was a long-time member of the National Theatre and also appeared in a total of 59 films. Irén Varsányi (1878–1932) was a member of the Comedy Theatre (Vigszínház) in Budapest. Her performances of Chekhov and Molnár were legendary (see *Új Filmlexikon*, Budapest: Akadémiai Kiadó, 1973).

5 A Little Jewish Philosophy

Page 31 Yahil (1990: 506–7) comments on the particularly fragmented
nature of Hungarian Jewry, which was widely dispersed and
represented many different traditions and social classes. The Germans exploited this fragmentation. In her chapter on Hungary,
Arendt (1963) comments on Eichmann's contrasting relationship
with the Jewish Council on the one hand and the Zionist
movement on the other.

Page 32 The insult was widely used in Central Europe in pogroms and
other attacks on Jews, apparently beginning with the anti-Jewish
riots in Hamburg in 1819. On the blood libel legend see Dundes
1991, Handler 1980.

Page 33 The communist regime was led by Béla Kun (1866–1939),
with the support of many of the prisoners of war recently
returned from the newly established Soviet Union. The regime
moved too fast in its revolutionary fervor, and the result
was strong resistance, ultimately forcing Kun's flight, early
in August, to Austria, and the collapse of the regime. In the
counter-revolutionary zeal which followed, and which made
Jews its particular targets, thousands of Jews perished (Braham
1981: 18–20). Kun himself was of Jewish background, as were 32
of his 45 commissars (Braham 1981: 35, quoting Rothschild).

Page 35 Jules Verne, *Kéraban le têtu* (Keraban the Inflexible, 1883); Heinrich
von Kleist, *Michael Kohlhaas* (1808). Prince Nekhlyudov is the hero
of Tolstoy's novel *Resurrection* (1899).

Page 37 Giovanni Papini (1881–1956) published his *Storia di Cristo* in
1921. Martin Buber (1878–1965), Austrian Jewish theologian
and philosopher, was particularly interested in the Hasidim.
Probably the author had in mind *Tales of Rabbi Nachman*
(1906) or *The Legend of Baal-Shem* (1907).

6 Initial Experiments

Page 38 The author was editor-in-chief of *Literatura Mondo* from 1922
to 1924. The identity of the unfortunate Esperantist is lost
in time.

Page 40 Advances by the Russian army in the course of 1944 led to the complete conquest of Romania by August and the capitulation of Finland in September. By the time of Germany's occupation of Hungary in the spring of 1944, many observers already regarded the loss of Romania and Finland as inevitable unless the Germans somehow succeeded in reconfiguring the political context of the war.

Page 41 The yellow star decree was in fact published on March 31 and came into effect on April 5. Macartney (1957: 278) describes the various enactments as copies of the Nuremberg Laws in Germany. They came into effect through ministerial decrees rather than acts of parliament, since Horthy had said he would sign no anti-Jewish laws. Everyone subject to the anti-Jewish enactments 'had, if 6 years old or over, to wear a yellow Star of David on his breast. Jews were dismissed from all branches of the public or municipal services, and also debarred from holding licences of profit, including those of chemists. They were forbidden to practise as teachers (except in the special Jewish schools), lawyers, actors, publishers or journalists, except the staffs of two purely Jewish newspapers (all other Jewish organs were closed down). As, however, there was a shortage of doctors, they were allowed to exercise that profession until June, when they were forbidden to treat other than Jewish patients. They were expelled from all bourses and from the transport trade. They might not be directors of businesses, and it was announced that they would be expelled from banking, from the Federation of Hungarian Employers, and, indeed, from any other branch of gainful employment.'

Page 43 As Ignotus (1972: 155) explains, the Order of Heroes (Vitézi Rend) was established as 'a new kind of lesser nobility' following the ousting of the Red regime. It was intended to reward 'persons who have specially distinguished themselves in the war, the counter-revolution, and other patriotic services.' 'Members of the order were granted inalienable landed property: to the ordinary folk just enough to secure the subsistence of a peasant family, but to officers four or five times as much.' The title was inheritable by the eldest son. 'Horthy ... recalled with pride that he had never allowed even the most patriotic Hungarian of Jewish extraction to join this order, as he was determined to keep it racially as well as morally pure.'

Page 48 The extermination camp at Auschwitz, in operation from 1941 to 1944, was the principal destination of the Hungarian Jews deported in the spring and summer of 1944. Nearby, in the Birkenau (Brzezinka) Forest, a second camp was set up towards the end of 1941, initially for Russian prisoners.

Page 49 Walters (1988: 289) describes how Jews in labor battalions were sent to the Eastern Front. 'Though behind the front-lines, they suffered heavy losses from the cold, malnutrition, artillery and air attacks, and even partisan raids.' The labor service was not a new creation: it had been established in 1939 for 'all those who were unfit or ineligible for military service, including Gypsies, Jews, and people regarded as enemy nationals. By 1941, there were 260 labor units in which 52,000 Jews served' (Yahil 1990: 348). Braham (1981: 285–361) provides a detailed history of the Labor Service system.

The Lukács Spa is situated on the west bank of the Danube, immediately north of Margaret Bridge – one of numerous hot springs in the city (the guidebooks speak of a total of 123). The world-famous Gellért Hotel and Baths are also close to the west bank of the river, in the southern part of Buda.

Page 50 Eskü Square was situated at the Pest (eastern) end of Elizabeth Bridge, one of several bridges crossing the Danube in the center of the city. These bridges were blown up by the Germans at the end of World War II and subsequently rebuilt. The Rudas Baths, a complex containing a swimming pool, a hotel, and other facilities, were in Buda, right across the bridge from the square. The baths were one of several famous Turkish baths in Buda. The Rudas Baths still retain the cupola erected by the Turks at the time of the establishment of the baths.

Identified as Ozma in the book, the eminent architect Lajos Kozma (1884–1948) was a neighbor of the Soroses at their summer home on Lupa Island. Kozma had worked closely with the path-breaking architect Béla Lajta (1873–1920), who combined Art Nouveau designs with Hungarian motifs in an effort to create a Hungarian idiom in architecture. Although never executed, Kozma's design for a new Orthodox synagogue in Buda (1928) created a major sensation. He went on to design the famed Glass House, headquarters of the Weiss glass company (1935), a building filled with light, whose glittering interiors were later to become a refuge for hundreds of Budapest Jews, after Arthur Weiss turned the building over to the Swiss embassy during the war. In 1941 Kozma (as Ludwig Kozma) published *Das Neue Haus* (Zürich: Girsberger). In 1908 he had been involved in the founding of the literary magazine *Nyugat* to which the poet Endre Ady was the chief contributor. (See Frojimovics 288 and 353 on the Buda synagogue, 408–11 on the Glass House, and 471–3 on the collaboration with Lajta.)

Page 52 On air raids, 'there had been a tacit agreement between the Hungarian regime and the British and American air forces operating from southern Italy, to the effect that their planes would cross over Hungary largely unvexed and that Hungary would not be bombed. Now that was over. Beginning in early April British and American planes would drop bombs on the industrial ring and on the railyards of Budapest' (Lukacs 1988: 217). The Bogyo translation and the Esperanto text differ significantly here in their emphasis. I have tried to combine the two. On the basic facts, however, they do not differ: many people believed the Jews were behind the raids. While there were perhaps some non-Jews who believed that if people stopped persecuting the Jews the Allies would stop bombing the city, it seems likely that the majority believed, if anything, that the Jews were somehow behind the attacks. Bierman (1995: 62) quotes a report by three members of the Jewish Council who escaped to Romania in August, in which the authors say that every air raid gave rise 'to the most ridiculous stories with only one theme – that the Jews had signaled to the bombers or given the enemy information by wireless.' Magda Denes, in her sad but winning memoir of growing up Jewish in Budapest, describes one such incident, when the Arrow-Crossers accused her family of using Morse code to signal to Allied planes (Denes 1997: 55–7).

On the program of extermination, Braham (1998) points out that at the time of the occupation in early 1944, Hungary was the only country under Germany's control whose Jewish population was relatively untouched. The German extermination program in Hungary was faster and more intense than in the other occupied countries.

7 Among Forgers

Page 55 On the production and use of forged documents, see the interesting discussion in Yahil (1990: 644).

The Western Station is on the Pest side of the river just north of the city center, on what is now known as Nyugati Square but was then Berlini Square (and became Marx Square after the war).

8 Provincial Ghettos

Many of these 'ghettos' were no more than holding pens – barracks, brickworks, timber yards (Gilbert 1985: 670). The first significant deportations of Jews from the Hungarian provinces began in late April, and the first deportations specifically to Auschwitz, in Poland, on May 15 (Yahil 1990: 510). The operations in the provinces led to the establishment, Yahil tells us, of a total of forty ghettos and three concentration camps containing 427,400 Jews. Lukacs (1988: 96) points out that 'Most Jews in Hungary were dispersed, many of them assimilated within the Magyar population in the small towns of the provinces.' This demographic pattern was in complete contrast to, say, Austria, where the vast majority of Jews lived in Vienna.

Page 60 Nyíregyháza is situated some 150 miles east of Budapest on the northern edge of the Great Hungarian Plain, in rich agricultural country, known particularly for its fruit trees. Today the city has something over 100,000 inhabitants. Braham (1981: 547–8) provides an account of the ghettoization and deportation of the Jews of Nyíregyháza. The rounding up of Jews in the villages around the city began on April 14, and on April 24 the Jews of the city were ordered into the ghetto. By May 10 the ghetto population stood at 17,580. Shortly thereafter the entire population was moved to three staging areas outside the city to prepare for deportation. They were subjected to particularly vicious searches for valuables, Braham says. Deportation began on May 17 and was completed on June 6. Susan Rubin Suleiman, whose mother came from Nyíregyháza, describes a recent visit to the city (1996: 175–81). Some 437,000 Jews were deported from the provinces between April and July (Gilbert 1985: 701).

Page 61 The Levente movement was a form of military education for young men below military age, a way of getting round the Trianon Peace Contract, which placed strict limits on the size of the standing army in Hungary. Membership was compulsory.

Page 64 The German physical chemist and polymath Friedrich Wilhelm Ostwald (1853–1932), recipient of the 1909 Nobel prize for physics, was particularly interested in electrochemistry and in what he called 'energism'. His 'energetic imperative' states: 'So act that the crude energy is transformed into the higher with the least possible loss.' He saw this as not only a principle of applied physics, but also as a social principle. Ostwald also had an active interest in linguistics, and gave part of his Nobel prize money for the development of Ido, a derivative of Esperanto (Sikosek 1999: 129; and see Becker and Wollenberg 1998).

Page 65 The Nazis went to extraordinary lengths to disguise the actual condition and final destination of their deportees. The first deportation from Hungary to Birkenau took place on April 29. Jewish leaders in Budapest were told that the group, from the town of Kistarcsa, had been taken to the pastoral-sounding 'Waldsee' in Germany. When they expressed surprise that none of the deportees had communicated with their families back home and asked where Waldsee was, Eichmann's staff was evasive (Gilbert 1985: 671). Later, the SS forced some of the deportees to send postcards back home, saying that they 'were well, were working, and lacked for nothing.' Gilbert (1985: 672) reports: 'Even in the undressing rooms at Birkenau, some Jews were given postcards to write. Each had to contain the same brief message: "*Es geht mir gut*, I am well."' In short, 'Waldsee' was Auschwitz-Birkenau. The deception was apparently first used during the deportation and destruction of Greek Jews in 1943 (Braham 1981: 63).

The 'statement at the Council office with details of the German atrocities' was probably the report (the so-called Auschwitz Protocols) that ultimately helped bring a halt to the deportations (Braham 1981: 710–11). Gilbert (1985: 681) writes: 'Inside Birkenau, two Jews who had witnessed the first ten days of the Hungarian arrivals escaped on May 27. One, Arnost Rosin, was a Czech Jew, the other, Czeslaw Mordowicz, was Polish-born. They managed to reach Slovakia, and their report, combined with that of two earlier escapees who had fled before the Hungarian deportations, reached the West towards the end of June. The two earlier escapees were the young Slovak Jew, Rudolf Vrba, and an older Slovak Jew, Alfred Wetzler. In their report, Vrba set out the fate and the statistics of the deportations into Auschwitz-Birkenau since the summer of 1942, when he himself had arrived from Slovakia.' See also Yahil (1990: 638).

Page 66 Győr, a city in northwest Hungary, was the scene also of the massacre of hundreds of death-marchers later in the year, in November. On the Győr ghetto, see Braham (1981: 621–3).

Page 67 On the passionate policy debates in the Jewish Council and elsewhere, see Braham (1981: 626–32 and 691–724). No entirely satisfactory explanation has been given for the fact that, despite the abundant proof of the mistreatment and extermination of the Jews, months passed (precisely the months of the major deportations from the provinces) before the Hungarian Christians finally grasped the dimensions of the horror and at last began their efforts to intervene.

9 Exodus

Page 71 Kornfeld (1882–1967), financier and converted Jew, was a member of the upper chamber of Parliament and was arrested, along with numbers of his colleagues, when the Germans arrived in March 1944. His family was part of the Weiss-Chorin group who in May successfully negotiated with the SS the transfer of their assets to the Germans and their safe passage to Portugal (Braham 1981: 515–24; see Chapter 16, below). In 1939 Kornfeld founded the Association of the Holy Cross (Szent Kereszt Egyesület) to protect the interests of Jews converted to Catholicism (Braham 1981: 1050–1). The Kornfeld and Weiss (or Weisz) families were heavily intermarried.

Gugger, or Gucker, Hill, in the north of Buda, was officially known as Látó Hill (Lookout Hill), on account of its lookout tower, constructed in 1929.

Page 72 The Sonderkommandos, Special Detachments, consisted of male Jews customarily assigned to work in the extermination camps. Their normal duty period was four months, after which they were shot (Snyder 1976: 324–5).

Page 73 Zavics is presumably the traveling salesman mentioned in Chapter 6, who brought papers from Nyíregyháza.

Page 75 The Piarist School, run by the Roman Catholic Piarist fathers, was on Eskü Square. Pál Sándor Schlesinger (1860–1936) was in fact known as a rather enthusiastic duelist. He entered Parliament in 1901, where his friends encouraged him, and his opponents mocked him, with this expression. The expression gained wider currency in 1924 in a song by the popular composer Imre Harmat.

Page 77 The 'English resistance' were presumably associates of Col. Charles Telfer Howie, a South African who had escaped from prisoner-of-war camp in Germany and had been recaptured in Hungary in September 1943. With the help of Regent Horthy's son, he was allowed to remain at liberty and went into hiding, periodically emerging to play a part as a liaison between the Horthy government and the Allies. He remained in Hungary until September 1944, when he left for Italy on an unsuccessful mission to discuss Allied intervention. See Macartney (1957 passim); Szent-Miklosy (1988: 52–3). Concerning the 'one occasion' on which the author was able to assist, see his discussion of the November death marches, Chapter 18. On other British and American infiltration, see Ungváry (1998: 252).

10 June 6, 1944: D-Day

Page 91 Belvárosi plébániatemplom, the Inner City Church, lies at the Pest end of Elizabeth Bridge. Dating from the twelfth century, it is the oldest building in Pest. Under the Communists, the square on which it is situated was renamed Március 15 Square, celebrating the outbreak of the 1848 revolution on March 15 of that year. The apartment building where the author had his secret lodging was on the north side of the square.

11 Julia's Adventures

Alag is a suburb just north of the city; Városliget, the so-called Woodland Park, lies to the northeast of the inner city. Érd, also a Budapest suburb, lies twelve miles southwest of the city, on the Danube. Lake Balaton, southwest of Budapest, is the principal summer resort for people from the city; Balatonalmádi (Almádi for short) is situated on the northeast edge of the lake.

12 Swimming Free

Page 104 Endre and Baky, members of the Hungarian radical right and 'unabashed anti-Semites', 'were installed in the Interior Ministry by Ernst Kaltenbrunner, the head of the RSHA, as chief aides to the minister, Andor Jaross, in all matters related to the Jews' (Yahil 1990: 505). Endre was named Secretary of State for administration and Baky was made Secretary of State for political affairs. Baky was also responsible for the Hungarian police (Arendt 1963: 199–200). The RSHA was the Reichssicherheitshauptamt, the Reich Central Security Office, which was headed by Reinhard Heydrich until his assassination in 1942. One branch of the office, known as Amt VI, was headed by Adolf Eichmann. On the transportation shortage, see Yahil (1990: 511). For background on Endre and Baky and the composition of the Sztójay government, see Braham (1981: 400–17).

The lies perpetrated to hide the extermination of the Jews were of staggering proportions. Eichmann told Horthy that 'the provincial ghettos are like sanitariums. Finally the Jews have started living in the fresh air and have exchanged their old way of life for a healthier one.' Endre, writing in the Arrow Cross journal, declared that the Jews 'suffer no injury. They may live among themselves, after their own racial and popular laws ... I have given instructions that their personal safety should be carefully guarded' (quoted by Yahil 1990: 512).

Page 105 On Jewish Houses see Yahil (1990: 512, 517), Braham (1981:

732–42). By October there were some 2,000 Jewish Houses in the city. According to Braham (1981: 733), the government official in charge of the plan to establish the Jewish Houses, József Szentmiklóssy, 'an extremely decent individual', did his best, in cooperation with the Council, to derail the project. At the very least, the situation was more complicated than it appeared. Regarding the number of Jews in wartime Budapest, Soros's figure of 150,000 is clearly too low: see his rather clearer statement at the beginning of Chapter 15. At a meeting of the Council of Ministers on August 2, 1944, Interior Minister Andor Jaross put the number of Jews living in Jewish Houses (presumably what Soros is referring to here) at 170,000 and the total Jewish population of the city at 280,000 (Braham 1981: 742). When the war was over, perhaps 130,000 Hungarian Jews remained, almost all of them in Budapest (Suleiman 1996: 108 quotes the figure in the 1949 census, the last census that asked about religion: 133,862).

The publication date of the new regulations was in fact June 17 (Braham 1981: 735), with initially a three-day period for implementation, subsequently extended to eight days. On June 25, the day after the relocation was complete, a further regulation drastically limited the free movement of Jews.

13   Vásár Utca 2

Vásár Street is a short street on the northeastern side of Rákóczi Square, which in turn lies halfway along József körút, part of the ring of avenues encircling Pest on the eastern side.

Page 106–7 The village of Tállya is in the Tokaj (Tokay) region in northeastern Hungary, famous for its wines, and Pincehely is a small town southeast of Lake Balaton. Budafok, a suburb to the south of Budapest, was once famous for its vineyards, and its labyrinth of cellars and subterranean passages is still used in part for the storage of wine.

Page 113 The Zurich publisher was presumably Girsberger, who published Kozma's 1941 book *Das Neue Haus*. I can find no evidence that *Moderne Baukunst* ever appeared.

14 Life in the Country

German troop movements across Hungary continued throughout the summer as the Russians pushed steadily southwards and westwards into Romania. So Tivadar's communication with his wife might have been much hindered. With Romania's change of government in late August, the Russians moved into Hungarian Transylvania and also advanced along the Danube, gradually cutting Budapest off from the south and the east. The Bakony mountains, mentioned by Karcsi, are northwest of Lake Balaton.

15 Cat and Mouse

Page 123 On the numbers of Jews in Budapest see the notes to page 105, above. The major initiative on the emigration of Jews took place in April, when Eichmann proposed, by way of his Jewish emissary Joel Brand, that the Germans 'sell' a million Jews to the Allies. Brand's efforts to convince the Allies that this was a serious proposal were unsuccessful. See Braham (1981: 941–51); Gilbert (1985: 682); Yahil (1990: 632–4).

Page 125 Béla Imrédy (1891–1946) was, according to Ignotus (1972: 185), 'a devout Catholic, a believer in high dividends and soldierly obedience, a "Salazar type", as his admirers said. He was the great hope of the magnates, bankers, priests, and other respectable anti-Nazis. But under the impact of Munich he turned Nazi overnight.' On his fall, see notes to page 2, above.

Page 126 Braham (1981: 988–91) believes the activities of the Communists to have been very limited and ineffectual, despite revisionist praise of their efforts after the war.

Regarding Jewish conversions, early in July, at about the same time as the halt in the deportations, rumors circulated that those Jews who converted before July 11 (this appears to be the operative date) would be immune from further persecution. A veritable 'conversion fever' followed. See Braham (1981: 779–81).

Page 129 Nagyvárad, in northern Transylvania, now the Romanian city of Oradea Mare, was noted for its strong Jewish cultural life. Some 30 per cent of its inhabitants were Jewish, and its ghetto was the largest of those set up by the Nazis in the provinces in

April and May. Deportations from Nagyvárad began on May 27 and were completed on June 3 (Braham 1981: 579–83).

16 The Conscience of the World

On June 24, 1944, news of the extent of the deportations of Hungarian Jews, provided by eye witnesses (see notes to page 65, above) was telegraphed from Switzerland to London and Washington, leading to protests not only from Britain and the United States, but also from the King of Sweden, the Pope, and the International Red Cross (Yahil 513–14, 640–1; Braham 1981: 754). On July 7, Horthy agreed to stop the deportations and on the following day they did indeed stop. Adolf Eichmann's plans had been to begin deportations from Budapest in the second week of July. Eichmann was furious, and made two attempts in the following days to continue the deportations in defiance of Horthy: on July 19, he managed to hoodwink the Hungarian authorities and send a further train to Auschwitz, filled with prisoners from the Kistarcsa concentration camp. Another deportation took place from the concentration camp at Sárvár on July 24 (Braham 1981: 771–4). Eventually Eichmann left Budapest, returning only after Horthy's fall and the coup of mid-October (see Gilbert 1985: 700–1; Yahil 1990: 514–15).

A decree issued on August 21 declared that special immunity would be given to people who had made major contributions to the nation in certain fields and professions, including the arts, science, and the economy. 'Provisional' certificates of immunity were issued even before this date, but after the fall of Horthy, almost all of these exemptions were revoked by the new regime. See Braham (1981: 783–6). While the Hungarian government certificates restored their grantees to their place in society, those of the neutral countries put their owners under the protection of the government of the country in question. The history of the efforts of neutral countries to save Jews has been told many times. (See, for example, Bierman 1995.) During this period, Raoul Wallenberg, the Swedish diplomat, was active in Budapest, having arrived there from Sweden on July 9 with a list of 630 Jews for whom Swedish visas had been granted. This idea was invented (Rosenfeld 1995: 26), and the effort was initiated as early as May 1944, by the courageous Valdemar Langlet (1872–1960) of the Swedish Red Cross, an enthusiastic adept of Esperanto (see Nina Langlet 1982, 1995). On Langlet's partly forgotten heroism, see Joseph (1982: 105–9), and the article by Nina Langlet in the journal *Esperanto* (Langlet 1995).

Switzerland had a list similar to that of the Swedes, and within a few weeks, under the leadership of Charles Lutz (Grossman 1986), it set up a special immigration department in what had been a Budapest store, registering several hundred Jews as Swiss-protected persons (Gilbert 1985: 701–2; Yahil 642–8). This building, the Glass House (see the notes for page 50, above), ended up housing as many as 3,000 Swiss-protected Jews, despite several attacks against it by the Nyilas gangs, for example on December 31. Efforts were redoubled after the collapse of the Horthy regime (Gilbert 1985: 752–3). According to Yahil, some 17,198 certificates were issued, with at least the tacit consent of the Hungarian government, most of them by Switzerland and Sweden, but also by the Vatican, Portugal, Spain and El Salvador. On the other hand, as many as 120,000 illicit copies of Swiss documents were printed, according to Yahil (1990: 645).

Page 132 The attacks on the safe houses took place after Horthy's removal in October, during the Szálasi regime that followed. Even at this stage, however, Swedish 'Schutzpasse', as they were known, continued to save lives, as Wallenberg continued to distribute them to numbers of people driven out of Budapest on forced marches.

Page 133 While Göring had been successful in this kind of maneuver against Himmler before, on this occasion it was Himmler who succeeded: his representatives signed an agreement with the Weiss (Weisz) and Chorin families (along with the Mauthners and the Kornfelds) before Göring had a chance to learn of the matter. The deal was to transport fifty members of the two families to Lisbon and to provide them with three million marks, mostly in foreign currency. Ribbentrop tried to intervene to stop the arrangement, as did the Hungarian government, but part of the group did in fact reach Lisbon (with only some of its money). See Yahil (1990: 519–20); Braham (1981: 514–24). Braham notes (526) that 'the rumor that the Weiss-Manfréd Works was to be consolidated with the Hermann Göring Works persisted not only during the negotiations with the Himmler group, but also after the conclusion of the agreement on May 17, 1944.' (On the Weiss and Chorin families, see McCagg 1972.) The agreement was possible because the families included non-Jewish members to whom they had deeded much of the property, thereby giving them leverage with the authorities. Among the fifty members of the group were several non-Jews. As for the people who gathered at the synagogue on Aréna út (and other locations: see Frojimovics (1999: 380)) under the protection of the SS, Eichmann allowed the group, totaling 1,686 people, to leave Budapest by train on June 29. They were taken first to Belsen. On August 22, 318 of them reached Basle from Belsen, and a second group of 1,368 people reached Switzerland on December 7, 1944 (Gilbert 1985: 682, 884).

Page 135 On Brand, see note to page 123. Rudolf Kastner (Rezső Kasztner) met with Eichmann on June 3 to try to negotiate the release of some six or eight hundred Jews from the provinces to the relative safety of Budapest. 'Your nerves are too tense, Kastner,' Eichmann declared. 'I shall send you to Theresienstadt, or perhaps you prefer Auschwitz' (Gilbert 1985: 682). For Eichmann Hungary was a new challenge, and he and his team moved to Budapest at the very beginning of the occupation, getting to work immediately. It is now generally believed that the stories of his knowledge of Hebrew and Yiddish were exaggerated (see Arendt 1963: 41, Bierman 1995: 63). It was claimed that he was born in Palestine and had picked up his knowledge there. In fact, he was born in Solingen, Germany, and raised in Linz, Austria, and was no scholar. He may have picked up a few Hebrew tags along the way, and gained some control over the Hebrew alphabet, but his knowledge of Yiddish (even when combined with his knowledge of the Hebrew alphabet) was probably limited to the passive kind of comprehension that any German might have of this heavily German-related language. However, in the 1930s he was clearly a kind of anti-Semitic Zionist, believing quite passionately that the Jews of Europe should be moved to a Jewish homeland, and becoming quite knowledgeable about the Zionist movement through his surveillance of its activities. His passion for extermination came later.

Page 136 The reference to the two trains diverted from Auschwitz may be based on a misunderstanding. In fact, Kastner struck a somewhat different deal with the Germans to move 18,000 Jews from Budapest to a labor camp in Vienna. Some 15,000 were still alive in 1945, but many perished in forced marches to Mauthausen in that year. See Yahil (1990: 634–5). Of course, even if the author is off on his numbers here, the basic argument that the SS, for a price, saved some Jews still holds. In fact, it later transpired that Eichmann had already received official instructions to send the

18,000 Jews to forced labor in Vienna rather than to Auschwitz, but he gave the impression that the matter was negotiable and set a price of $100 per passenger for this supposed favor.

Page 137   The Detective Center was the headquarters of the Political Police Department, which had been brought under the immediate control of Secretary of State Baky. As Braham (1981: 406) explains, 'Its name was changed to State Security Police, (*Állambiztonsági Rendészet*) – i.e. the Hungarian counterpart of the Gestapo – and its headquarters moved to the Svábhegy, where the Gestapo and the Eichmann-*Sonderkommando* were also located.' Svábhegy lay to the west of the city.

17   False Dawn

Page 139   King Michael's arrest of Marshal Antonescu, which moved Romania into the Allied camp, in fact took place on August 23. At ten o'clock that evening, a royal proclamation announced the change of regime and Romanian troops were ordered to cease hostilities against the Russians (see Georgescu 1983).

Béla Imrédy was Prime Minister from 1938 to 1939, when he was ousted by Horthy (see notes for page 2, above). Sztójay made him Minister without Portfolio in charge of economic affairs. Andor Jaross was Minister of Internal Affairs and Antal Kunder was Minister of Trade and Transport. Both Imrédy and Jaross were executed as war criminals in 1946.

Page 140   Géza Lakatos was regarded as a moderate and did much to ease the situation of the Jews. The change was made possible by Romania's switching sides and the increasing need to come to terms with Germany's ultimate defeat. Lakatos was able to purge the government of its strongest Nazi sympathizers.

The author's estimate of the number of Budapest Jews is, once again, on the low side. See the note for page 105, above.

Page 144   Ferenc Keresztes-Fischer, the Minister of Internal Affairs, was arrested immediately following the German seizure of power. Miklós Kállay, the Prime Minister, took refuge in the Turkish Legation, where he remained until Horthy's fall. He was subsequently sent to Mauthausen by the Germans. General Bakay was commander of the military forces responsible for the defense of the Budapest region. He was abducted on October 8.

Page 146 The Germans had had plans to arrest the young Horthy for some time. He was apparently involved in discussions with numbers of people, perhaps including leftist elements, to plan Hungary's extrication from the alliance with Germany. Horthy was on his way to a meeting at the office of the Csepel Free Port with people he believed to be agents of Marshal Tito. The abduction was planned by SS Major Otto Skorzeny, who had been responsible for the rescue of Mussolini. The building, which belonged to the Soros family and where Tivadar had his earliest hideout, was staked out and an exchange of gunfire ensued in which the head of the Budapest Security Office of the SS was killed (Szent-Miklosy 1988: 60). Regent Horthy himself (1957: 229), mentions two deaths, one German and one Hungarian. Horthy and Félix Bornemissza were captured, rolled inside carpets, and taken away by plane. The young Horthy ended up at Mauthausen concentration camp. He survived the war. (Fenyo 1972: 230–1; Braham 1981: 825–6; Macartney 1957: 399–401.)

Page 149 'Intoxicated by years of anti-Semitic propaganda and incited by their leaders, almost immediately after the coup frenzied gangs of Arrow-Cross youths, many in their early teens, began an anarchic spree of murder and looting . . . Armed with various types of weapons, including automatic rifles and grenades, the Nyilas [Arrow-Cross] gangs slaughtered several hundred Jews in the Yellow-Star houses and labor service units during the night of October 15–16. One of their excuses was that some labor servicemen in possession of arms had shown resistance a few hours earlier, at 31 Népszínház Street and 4 Teleki Square' (Braham 1981: 829–30).

18   Life under Szálasi

Page 151 In the days following October 16, 'Nyilas gangs seized a large number of Jewish forced labourers in the Óbuda suburb, drove them across the Margit and Chain bridges . . . and while they were still on the bridge, shot them and threw their bodies into the waters of the Danube' (Gilbert 1985: 752). This was evidently one of several such incidents. The Chain Bridge, Széchenyi Lánchíd, crosses the river in the center of town, right below the Castle.

Page 152   *'Fogózz, Malvin, jön a kanyar!'* ('Hang on, Malvina . . .'), from *Pesti Posta*, November 10, 1944, became a popular saying (Békés 1977: 365).

Page 155   The so-called Prónay Detachment, known as the 'black legion of death', was originally formed by Colonel Pál Prónay as a part of the White Terror following the collapse of the Béla Kun regime. At his trial after the war, Emil Kovarcz, minister of war-readiness under Szálasi and commander of the Arrow-Cross forces, testified that in October 1944 Pál Prónay, now seventy years old, proposed to him that the Prónay Detachment be reconstituted. Kovarcz, a notorious anti-Semite who had been a leader of the murderous Ostenburg Detachment after World War I, acted on this recommendation, but the new Prónay Detachment, perhaps 250 strong, seems not to have been very effective, primarily because of Prónay's inability to cooperate with others. See Ungváry (1998: 88–90), Braham (1981: 998–1011). In his history of the Zionist resistance in Hungary, Lambert (1974) gives several examples of similar infiltration by Jews.

At 5: 00 a.m. on October 20, the authorities began systematically emptying the Jewish Houses of all their male residents between the ages of sixteen and sixty. The plan was to send them to German factories as slave labor or to put them to work digging defensive trenches in the vicinity of Budapest. Among those captured was the poet Ernő Szép, who described his experiences in a book published soon after the war and later translated into English (Szép 1994). Szép was freed two weeks later, but many of those rounded up were marched westwards towards the Austrian border. Large numbers of women, rounded up in later raids, joined these forced marches (Braham 1981: 838–43). The forced marches, organized by Eichmann, began on November 8 and continued into December. Tens of thousands of people, maybe as many as 70,000, were involved (Yahil 1990: 518). With Auschwitz no longer in operation, the plan was to use these poor wretches as forced labor: 'Their task, they were told, would be to construct an "East Wall" for the defence of Vienna' (Gilbert

1985: 754). Raoul Wallenberg and other diplomats moved back and forth between Budapest and the border, doing what they could to rescue marchers and organizing aid. See Bierman (1995: 81–5). Valdemar Langlet, of the Swedish Red Cross, and Asta Nilsson, of the International Red Cross, were able to find a number of trucks to join in this humanitarian effort (Rosenfeld 1995: 62; Derogy 1994: 159–77). Presumably the author's truck (page 156) was one of these.

19   Further Horrors

'On November 15 . . . the Hungarian authorities agreed to the establishment of an "international ghetto" in the city, consisting of the seventy-two buildings assigned to house Jews under Swiss protection' (Gilbert 1985–761). This was the so-called 'Little Ghetto'. But at the same time, the authorities established a 'Big Ghetto', or 'General Ghetto', under their own jurisdiction. Ultimately, the Big Ghetto was closed off from the city. See Braham (1981: 852) for a plan of the Big Ghetto and for a detailed description of its operations. When the Russians arrived, they found in the Little Ghetto some 25,000 people and in the Big Ghetto 70,000 (Yahil 1990: 645–6). A further 25,000 Jews eventually came out of hiding once the Germans had left (Bierman 1990: 115). Attacks on the international safe houses were frequent; several were emptied on January 11 by Nyilas gangs and their residents thrown in the river (Gilbert 1985: 767). The Glass House had already been attacked on December 31 (see below). Plans for wiping out the Big Ghetto came perilously close to execution on December 22, the day before Eichmann fled the city. It is at least possible that only a misunderstanding by the porter at the Jewish Council headquarters (who took a telephone call in German that he did not fully comprehend) prevented the execution of Council members and the mass murder of the ghetto inmates. In January, with the advancing Russians only a couple of hundred yards from the edge of the ghetto, a second effort was also aborted, thanks in large measure to the intervention of Wallenberg. See Bierman (1995: 107–8, 114–16).

> *Page 164* *Budapesti Közlöny: Hivatalos Lap* (The Gazette of Budapest: Official Journal), was the place in which official decrees were published.
>
> *Page 165* The statement '*Wer Jude ist, bestimme ich*' was also attributed to Hermann Göring (Snyder 1976: 378).

20   Raid

Page 178 The Arrow-Cross building on Andrássy Street remained infamous: Suleiman (1996: 102) writes: 'I passed in front of number 60, a beautiful light green building, recently renovated – one would hardly know that for decades it was one of the most dreaded places in Budapest, the headquarters of the secret police, and before that (from 1939 to 1945) the headquarters of the Hungarian Nazi Party, the Arrow Cross.'

Page 179 Describing an event that took place in January, Gilbert (1985: 767) writes: '. . . many Jews, taken to the bank of the Danube, were tied together in threes. The middle one was then shot, and the three thrown into the Danube, so that the weight of the dead man would pull down the other two.' Bierman (1995: 109) and Braham (1981: 870) also describe this method. Evidently over time the executioners got better at their ghoulish task.

21   Passing the Time

Page 181 All the Budapest bridges were blown up by the retreating Nazis. By January 18, the Russians had gained complete control of the Pest side of the river.

Page 183 The Esperanto text (but not Bogyo's English translation) refers not only to the author's time in Russia as a prisoner-of-war, but also to his preventative arrest in Csót. See Afterword, page 217 and note.

Page 187 The decree, one of the last desperate efforts of the Szálasi regime, was announced on the radio on the same day as the Russians entered Budapest. By December 27 the city was surrounded (Macartney 1957: 463).

22   Siege

Page 192 'Even more damaging than Russian artillery were the thousands of small tactical bombs of Russian fighter-bombers, flying low over the rooftops, since anti-aircraft artillery had ceased to function. The Russian infantry would advance after these bombs seemed to have burned out or destroyed the lines of German trucks and tanks assembled in the narrow streets – burning out and destroying, as a matter of course, many of the surrounding houses in the process' (Lukacs 1988: 219–20).

Page 199 The raid on the Jewish Hospital at Bethlen Square occurred on December 28. The attack on the Jewish hospital at Maros Street took place rather later, on January 11. Some ninety-two patients, doctors and nurses were seized. All but one were shot (Braham 1981: 872). The January 14 raid on the Jewish Orthodox hospital in Városmajor Street resulted in the deaths of 150 people (Gilbert 1985: 767–8, Braham 1981: 872). Father András Kun was, or had been, a Minorite monk. He paraded the streets in the cassock of his order, with a rope and a gunbelt at his waist. He was credited personally with five hundred murders. See Bierman (1995: 109–10), Braham (1981: 1049).

Page 200 Both the Red Cross and the churches (despite the vacillation of some of their leaders) went to great lengths to protect Jewish children. Before the Nyilas regime began, the Red Cross established several houses for children, and these grew over time to accommodate several thousand. Efforts were made to arrange the evacuation of children to neutral countries, but these plans met with no success and had to be abandoned altogether when the Szálasi government came to power and priorities shifted simply to keeping the children alive. On life in these children's homes, see the memoir by Denes (1997: 100–16). The incident described by the author in fact involved children from the Jewish Orphanage, which was protected by the Red Cross. Frojimovics (1999: 419–20) explains how they were taken from the Orphanage, on December 24, lodged temporarily in two houses on Szív Street, and then marched to the Danube on December 25.

On the attacks on protected buildings see Braham (1981: 870–1), who cites Lévai (n.d. 129–30). On the afternoon of December 31, when some forty Nyilas thugs attacked the Swiss-protected Glass House (Vadász u. 29), killing three people, a detachment of Hungarian soldiers intervened to protect the 800 Jewish residents whom the gang had driven into the street, and the gang members were forced to retreat (Gilbert

1985: 762; Braham 1981: 870–1). The transfers to the ghetto took place over several days at the beginning of January (Braham 1981: 849–50). All told, some 5,000 people were moved from the Swedish houses and a similar number from those under the protection of the Swiss, Portuguese, and Spanish governments, and the Vatican. On the way to the ghetto, many Jews were robbed of all their possessions.

23   January 12, 1945

Page 206 Most of these statistics have been revised over time. Friesel (1990: 107), echoing the views of most scholars but with the benefit of more complete historical records than were available to our author, calculates that almost six million Jews lost their lives, of whom some four million died in the major extermination camps (1,800,000 in Auschwitz-Birkenau).

Five or six days after they reached Vásár utca, the Russians' possession of the Pest side of the city was complete. They took a further three weeks to seize control of Buda. It was not until April that they gained control of the entire country. As late as March 22–3, 1945, Germans were still massacring members of labor battalions in Hungary.

Tivadar writes of having come through 'the most difficult adventure of our lives'. The term 'adventure' turns up with surprising frequency in his description of his wartime experiences. Suleiman, in her *Budapest Diary* (1996: 77), writes of attending an 'Evening with Miklós Vajda', the editor and translator, in February 1993: 'Vajda . . . was a teenager during the war, son of a Greek Orthodox mother and converted Jewish father. He said he thought of the war, including the last terrible year, as an "adventure" (*kaland*). The 2000 editor who was doing the interviewing remarked that last month's guest, George Soros . . . had used the same word.' Earlier in the book (p. 36), she writes of 'the immense adventure that, with hindsight and retelling, the war became for me.' Suleiman reflects on her own use of the term: 'It must be due to our having been so privileged before, so loved and surrounded by adoring relatives, we thought we were invincible. That, at least, is how Vajda explained it. His parents had some powerful friends, including a famous actress who was his godmother. In my more modest way, I too was a totally spoiled and adored child who took all the adulation as her due. One more piece of luck, perhaps.' We might reflect on Tivadar Soros's opening phrases, in the present book, where adventure and luck are connected. Following the war, realizing how remarkable it was that her grandmother survived, Suleiman reflects: 'It was at that time, I believe, that I began to conceive of history as a form of luck' (p. 33).

Page 208 With his knowledge of Russian, the author was able to protect the ailing Jutka from the soldiers. Subsequently, Jutka returned to her father and brother, but she had contracted tuberculosis and, with medication unavailable, died soon afterwards. Tivadar's statement about having no trouble with the Russians, included in the Bogyo translation, is significantly missing in the Esperanto text. Paul's experiences were altogether less happy. On his first encounter with a Russian soldier he lost his Swiss watch. Later, he was harshly interrogated by the political police, and then he was caught in a round-up, from which he barely escaped.

Russian treatment of the civilian population was horrendous. In addition to rape and pillage on a massive scale, the Russians rounded up tens of thousands of people, more or less arbitrarily, and carried them off to the Soviet Union as 'prisoners-of-war'. They claimed to have captured 110,000 such German and Hungarian 'prisoners-of-war' during the fighting, but many were in fact civilians. With later round-ups, some 280,000 people were driven east; only 60,000 returned. Paul Soros, who quotes these statistics, was among those caught in the net. He escaped from a column marching eastwards out of Budapest by making a run for it and hiding in an abandoned farmhouse. Even after the fighting was over, random acts of violence against civilians were common. See Lukacs (1988: 220), Hoensch (1996: 163). As for material damage, Budapest was devastated: only around twenty-five per cent of the buildings survived intact. It was one of three major cities (the others were Stalingrad earlier and Berlin later) to be subjected to house-to-house fighting between Russian and German troops. One reason for the chaos following the fall of Budapest was the fact that the Russians had used almost two million men in the fighting, many of whom now had little to do.

Editor's Afterword

My sources on the Soros family include unpublished and informal memoirs by Paul Soros, transcripts of oral history interviews with Elizabeth Soros, conducted in 1985, some twenty items of correspondence between Juan Régulo and Tivadar Soros found among Régulo's papers in La Laguna (the earliest date from 1963, and the last is a note dated 17 February 1968, shortly before Soros's death), tapes of my own interviews with Kálmán Kalocsay, conducted in Budapest in 1963, and correspondence with Ervin Fenyvesi.

Page 211 For the quotation from George, in conversation with Byron Wien, see Soros (1995: 28–9).

Page 215 Although Tivadar's immediate family came through the war, many other family members perished, including (according to Elizabeth) Tivadar's three sisters, and Elizabeth's grandmother and two aunts.

Page 216 On the situation of Austro-Hungarian Jewish officers in captivity, see Deák (1990). Ervin Fenyvesi, who interviewed Soros for Radio Budapest in 1966, says that Pál Balkányi (1894–1977), active as a leader of the Hungarian Esperanto movement throughout his life, taught Esperanto to Tivadar when they served on the Eastern Front. When the Soviet Esperantist Union (*Sovetlanda Esperantista Unuiĝo*) was founded in Petrograd in 1921, among the members of the Central Committee was 'T. Shvarts', of Irkutsk (see page 220 above). He and Ernest Drezen signed the founding document as secretary and president respectively, though it is not clear whether Soros actually attended the Petrograd meeting (see *Esperanta Informilo: Monata Organo de Petrograda Societo Esperantista*, June-October 1921, p. 3, and *Agitanto: rusa-esperanta revuo de Kronstadta grupo de Sovjetlanda Esperantista Unuiĝo*, July 15, 1921).

Page 217 The town of Csót, north of Lake Balaton, was the site of a prisoner-of-war camp during World War I and then became a holding camp for returning Hungarian prisoners-of-war, both to prevent the spread of infectious diseases by holding them in temporary quarantine and also to check on their political affiliations: there was great anxiety about unwanted Bolshevik influences in Hungary and about communist agents, and numbers of the returnees had fought on the side of the Reds (*Révai Nagy Lexikona*, 1927; *Új Magyar Lexikon*, 1960). On the treatment of Jewish officers, see Deák.

Kalocsay published several influential volumes of poetry, original and translated, and numerous contributions to the stylistics and linguistics of Esperanto. Baghy, like Soros, was a recent returnee from military captivity in Siberia. A prolific writer of poetry, drama, and fiction, he wrote two fictionalized accounts of his Siberian captivity, *Viktimoj* (Victims, 1925) and *Sur sanga tero* (On Bloody Ground, 1933). According to Ervin Fenyvesi, 'Idea and practice, good luck and good intentions met in the moment of the birth of *Literatura Mondo*.' In these early days, Tivadar Soros 'financed everything out of his own pocket,' even paying Kalocsay and Baghy 'a modest honorarium'. 'After two years,' adds Fenyvesi, 'Tivadar had no wish to take on further losses.'

For editions of *Modernaj Robinzonoj*, see Schwartz 1924 and 1999 (in Esperanto *j* is pronounced as *y*). My introduction to the 1999 edition discusses the background to the work.

Page 218 Lupa Island, in the Danube some six or eight miles north of the city, consisted, according to Elizabeth Soros, of two rows of small summer houses, some twenty in all, on each side of a central path. The residents constructed two tennis courts on the island at Tivadar's suggestion. The Soros house, completed in 1935, was designed in Bauhaus style by György Farkas, whom Tivadar had met in Germany, where Farkas studied architecture and interior design and assisted Tivadar with his property in Berlin. Farkas married Elizabeth Soros's sister Klára.

Elizabeth Soros recalls trips to Davos and to Garmisch-Partenkirchen for skiing, frequent trips to Berlin because of the family's property there, and a visit to Paris and London. They were always, she says, simple trips – 'never with sleeping car and never with first-class compartments.' When Tivadar went to the World Congress of Esperanto in Geneva in 1925, he and Elizabeth took the train to Zurich and then walked much of the way to Geneva, taking ten days to do so. In addition to trips with the family, Tivadar often traveled on his own. He was twice in the United States – in 1928 and again shortly before the outbreak of the war – and twice in Russia.

Page 219 Elizabeth explains that later, after the Communists established themselves in Hungary and the private practice of law was abolished, Tivadar abandoned legal work and taught Russian to Hungarians and Hungarian to Russians at the Hungarian Soviet Institute, where he enjoyed considerable success.

Page 220 For details of the publishing agreement for *Maskerado*, my source is letters of March 2 and March 5, 1964, from Soros to Régulo, and November 12, 1964, from Régulo to Soros.

Page 221 The typewritten cover page of the Bogyo translation reads: 'Masquerade in the Shadow of Death by Theodore S. Svarc / Translated from Esperanto / by Sophie Bogyo.' Whether Sophie Bogyo understood much Esperanto is an open question: Paul Soros recalls that she did not. Very possibly she and Tivadar worked on the manuscript together. The title of the Esperanto edition was the subject of several exchanges between Régulo and Soros; Régulo seems to have been responsible for the choice of the main title, Soros for the subtitle.

Page 222 We should note that even the use of the term 'Holocaust' to describe the mass murder of Jews during the war did not become general usage until the mid-1970s, and the earliest examples of its use in English date only from the 1960s. As for early accounts of the Holocaust, there were a few in Hungarian, among the first being Ernő Szép's *Emberszag* (Szép, 1945). For other early Hungarian accounts see Handler (1982).

Page 223 J. Gifford Fowler remarks on the relative lack of introspection, in *Heroldo de Esperanto* (September 16, 1965), and Alec Venture on brazenness in *The British Esperantist* (November 1965). Lins's review appeared in *Germana Esperanto-Revuo* (December 1965). The fourth citation is from Ferenc Szilágyi's review in *Norda Prismo* (1965).

Acknowledgments

elp in preparing the translation and in gathering the notes came from numerous individuals and organizations. A year as a visiting scholar at the Whitney Humanities Center at Yale University gave me time to work on the project in addition to my other research and reading, and I am very grateful to the staff of the Sterling Library at Yale and the Mortensen Library at the University of Hartford for their many favors. Detlev Blanke, Ionel Onet, Pál Felsö, Ulrich Lins, Bernard Golden, Ervin Fenyvesi, Vilmos Benczik, Peter Breit, István Ertl Sr, Ferenc Kovács, György Nanovfszky, Julius Elias and others assisted me in tracking down specific information and in correcting errors. Antonio Ferrer hunted down correspondence in La Laguna. István Ertl Jr, my editor for the new Esperanto edition which I am currently completing, has answered numerous questions, productively raised others, and provided me with suggestions for reading – as well as the manuscript of the Esperanto translation of Nina Langlet's memoir which he is now preparing for publication. Paul Soros and Flora Fraser have patiently answered my questions and plied me with background information about the family. I am particularly grateful to Simo Milojević for suggesting that I take this project on in the first place. While many of the accuracies in this volume, to say nothing of the mistakes avoided, are due to people such as these, the errors are mine.

H. T.

Works Cited

Arendt, Hannah. 1994 [1963]. *Eichmann in Jerusalem: A Report on the Banality of Evil.* New York and London: Penguin.

Becker, Ulrich, and Fritz Wollenberg, ed. 1998. *Eine Sprache für Wissenschaft: Beiträge und Materialen.* Berlin: Gesellschaft für Interlinguistik.

Békés, István. 1997. *Napjaink szállóigéi* (Contemporary Quotations). Budapest: Gondolat.

Bierman, John. 1995. *Righteous Gentile: The Story of Raoul Wallenberg, Missing Hero of the Holocaust.* Revised edn. London and New York: Penguin.

Boulton, Marjorie. 1960. *Zamenhof Creator of Esperanto.* London: Routledge and Kegan Paul.

Braham, Randolph L. 1963. *The Destruction of Hungarian Jewry: A Documentary Account.* New York: Pro Arte, for the World Federation of Hungarian Jews.

—— 1977. *The Hungarian Labor Service System 1939–1945.* New York: East European Quarterly.

—— 1981. *The Politics of Genocide: The Holocaust in Hungary.* 2 vols. New York: Columbia University Press.

—— 1998. 'The Holocaust in Hungary: A Retrospective Analysis,' in Michael Berenbaum and Abraham J. Peck, eds, *The Holocaust and History.* Bloomington: Indiana University Press. 427–38.

—— ed. 1995. *The Wartime System of Labor Service in Hungary: Varieties of Experiences.* East European Monographs 170. New York: Columbia University Press.

Clendinnen, Inga. 1999. *Reading the Holocaust.* Cambridge: Cambridge University Press.

Deák, István. 1990. *Beyond Nationalism: A Social and Political History of the Habsburg Officer Corps 1848–1918*. New York: Oxford University Press.

Denes, Magda. 1997. *Castles Burning: A Child's Life in War*. New York: Norton.

Derogy, Jacques. 1994. *Raoul Wallenberg: Le juste de Budapest*. 2nd edn. Paris: Stock.

Dundes, Alan, ed. 1991. *The Blood Libel Legend: A Casebook in Anti-Semitic Folklore*. Madison: University of Wisconsin Press.

Fenyo, Mario D. 1972. *Hitler, Horthy, and Hungary: German-Hungarian Relations 1941–1944*. New Haven and London: Yale University Press.

Friesel, Evyatar. 1990. *Atlas of Modern Jewish History*. New York and Oxford: Oxford University Press.

Frojimovics, Kinga, Géza Komoróczy, Viktória Pusztai and Andrea Strbik. 1999. *Jewish Budapest: Monuments, Rites, History*. Budapest: Central European University Press. (Translation of *A zsidó Budapest*. Budapest: Városháza & MTA Judaisztikai Kutatócsoport, 1995.)

Georgescu, Vlad. 1983. *Istoria românilor*. Berkeley, CA: American-Romanian Academy.

Gilbert, Martin. 1985. *The Holocaust: A History of the Jews of Europe During the Second World War*. New York: Henry Holt.

—— 1993. *Atlas of the Holocaust*. New York: William Morrow.

Golden, Bernard. 1977. 'Teodoro Schwartz'. *Budapeŝta Informilo*, April. p 4.

Grossman, Alexander. 1986. *Nur das Gewissen: Carl Lutz und seine Budapester Aktion*. Wald, Switzerland: Im Waldgut.

Handler, Andrew. 1980. *Blood Libel at Tiszaeszlar*. East European Monographs 68. Boulder: University of Colorado Press.

—— 1985. *From the Ghetto to the Games: Jewish Athletes in Hungary*. East European Monographs 192. New York: Columbia University Press.

—— ed. 1982. *The Holocaust in Hungary: An Anthology of Jewish Response*. University, Alabama: University of Alabama Press.

Hoensch, Jörg K. 1996. *A History of Modern Hungary 1867–1994*. 2nd edn. London and New York: Longman.

Horthy, Nicholas. 1957. *Memoirs*. New York: Robert Speller.

Ignotus, Paul. 1972. *Hungary*. Nations of the Modern World. New York and Washington: Praeger.

Joseph, Gilbert. 1982. *Mission sans retour: L'affaire Wallenberg*. Paris: Albin Michel.

Kenez, Peter. 1995. *Varieties of Fear: Growing up Jewish under Nazism and Communism*. Washington, DC: American University Press.

Klemperer, Victor. 1998, 1999. *I Will Bear Witness: A Diary of the Nazi Years 1933–1941.* Tr. Martin Chalmers. 2 vols. New York: Random House. (Translation of *Ich will Zeugnis ablegen bis zum letzten: Tagebücher 1933–1945 von Victor Klemperer.* Berlin: Aufbau-Verlag, 1995.)

Lambert, Gilles. 1974. *Operation Hazalah.* Indianapolis and New York: Bobbs-Merrill.

Langlet, Nina. 1982, *Kaos i Budapest.* Vällingby: Harrier. (Translated into Esperanto by Kalle Kniivilä as *Kaoso en Budapeŝto,* Varna: Bambu, 2001.)

—— 1995. 'Esperantisto kontraŭ malhomeco'. *Esperanto,* 88: 82–4.

Langlet, Valdemar. 1946. *Verk och dagar i Budapest.* Stockholm: Wahlstrom & Widstrand.

Lázár, István. 1989. *Kis magyar történelem* (Hungarian History in a Nutshell). Budapest: Gondolat.

Lévai, Jenő. 1946. *Fekete könyv a magyar zsidóság szenvedéseiről* (Black Book on the Sufferings of Hungarian Jewry). Budapest: Officina.

—— 1948. *Zsidósors Magyarországon* (Jewish Fate in Hungary). Budapest: Magyar Téka.

—— n.d. *A pesti gettó.* Budapest: Officina.

Lins, Ulrich. 1988. *La danĝera lingvo: Studo pri la persekutoj kontraŭ Esperanto.* Gerlingen: Bleicher. (Published in German as *Die gefährliche Sprache. Die verfolgung der Esperantisten unter Hitler und Stalin.* Gerlingen: Bleicher, 1988.)

Lukacs, John. 1988. *Budapest 1900: A Historical Portrait of a City and its Culture.* New York: Grove Press.

—— 1997. *The Hitler of History.* New York: Random House.

Macartney, C.A. 1957. *A History of Hungary 1929–1945.* Vol. 2. New York: Praeger (Published in Britain by Edinburgh University Press as *October 15: A History of Hungary 1929–1945.*)

Maser, Werner. 1971. *Adolf Hitler: Legende, Mythos, Wirklichkeit.* München (2nd edn. München: Bechtle, 1989).

McCagg, William O., Jr. 1972. *Jewish Nobles and Geniuses in Modern Hungary.* Boulder, Colorado: East European Quarterly.

Mikes, George. 1957. *The Hungarian Revolution.* London: André Deutsch.

Pechan, Alfonso, ed. 1979. *Gvidlibro pri supera ekzameno.* 2nd edn. Budapest: Hungara Esperanto-Asocio.

Privat, Edmond. 1927. *Historio de la lingvo Esperanto: La movado 1900–1927.* Leipzig: Ferdinand Hirt.

Rosenfeld, Harvey. 1995. *Raoul Wallenberg.* 2nd edn. New York and London: Holmes and Meier.

Sakmyster, Thomas. 1994. *Hungary's Admiral on Horseback: Miklós Horthy, 1918–1944.* East European Monographs 396. New York: Columbia University Press.

Schlink, Bernhard. 1997. *The Reader.* New York: Vintage.

Schwartz, Teodoro. 1924. *Modernaj Robinzonoj.* Budapest: Literatura Mondo (2nd edn, with introduction by Humphrey Tonkin, Berkeley, Calif.: Bero, 1999).

Shirer, William L. 1960. *The Rise and Fall of the Third Reich.* New York: Simon & Schuster.

Sikosek, Marcus. 1999. *Esperanto sen mitoj.* Antwerp: Flandra Esperanto-Ligo.

Snyder, Louis L. 1976. *Encyclopedia of the Third Reich.* New York: McGraw-Hill.

Soros, George. 1995. *Soros on Soros: Staying Ahead of the Curve.* New York: Wiley.

Soros, Tivadar. 2001. *Maskerado ĉirkaŭ la morto.* 2nd edn. Ed. Humphrey Tonkin. Rotterdam: Universala Esperanto-Asocio.

Suleiman, Susan Rubin. 1996. *Budapest Diary: In Search of the Motherbook.* Lincoln and London: University of Nebraska Press.

Szent-Miklosy, Istvan. 1988. *With the Hungarian Independence Movement 1943–1947: An Eyewitness Account.* New York: Praeger.

Szép, Ernő. 1994. *The Smell of Humans: A Memoir of the Holocaust in Hungary.* Budapest, London, New York: Central European University Press. (Translation of *Emberszag.* Budapest: Keresztes. 1945.)

Szinai, Miklós. 1998. 'A magyar szélsőjobboldal történelmi helyéhez' (Historically Locating the Hungarian Extreme Right). In *Jobboldali radikalizmusok tegnap és ma* (Rightist Radicalisms Past and Present). Budapest: Napvilág.

Ungváry, Krisztián. 1998. *Budapest ostroma* (The Siege of Budapest). Budapest: Corvina.

Walters, E. Garrison. 1988. *The Other Europe: Eastern Europe to 1945.* Syracuse, NY: Syracuse University Press.

Waringhien, Gaston. 1983. *Kaj la ceter'* – *nur literaturo.* Antwerp and La Laguna: Stafeto.

Wieder, Ludvik. 1984. *I Promised My Mother.* New York: Shengold.

Yahil, Leni. 1990. *The Holocaust: The Fate of European Jewry.* New York and Oxford: Oxford University Press.

Zeke, Gyula. 1995. 'A nagyvárosi kultúra új formái és a zsidóság' (New Forms of Metropolitan Culture and the Jews). *Budapesti Negyed.* Summer. 90–106.

Index